■SCHOLASTIC

ALL NEW 100 LITERACY HOURS

- Differentiated lesson plans
- Photocopiable extracts
- Covers the Early Learning Goals and NLS objectives

YEAR R

Wendy Jolliffe

CREDITS

Author
Wendy Jolliffe

Illustrations
Cathy Hughes

Editor
Sally Gray

Series Designer
Joy Monkhouse

Assistant Editor
Victoria Lee

Designer
Anna Oliwa

Text © Wendy Jolliffe
© 2005 Scholastic Ltd

Designed using Adobe InDesign

Published by Scholastic Ltd
Villiers House
Clarendon Avenue
Leamington Spa
Warwickshire CV32 5PR

www.scholastic.co.uk

Printed by Bell and Bain Ltd.

23456789   5678901234

ACKNOWLEDGEMENTS

The publishers gratefully acknowledge permission to reproduce the following copyright material:
Nancy Chambers for the use of 'It's dark outside' by Nancy Chambers from Stickleback, Stickleback and other Minnow Rhymes by Nancy Chambers © 1997, Nancy Chambers (1997, Kestrel). **Tony Mitton** for the use of 'Frog Frolics' by Tony Mitton © 2005, Tony Mitton (2005, previously unpublished). **Marian Reiner Literary Agent** for the author for the use of 'Closet' by Judith Thurman from Flashlight and other poems by Judith Thurman © 1976, Judith Thurman (1976, Kestrel). **Joan Poulson** for the use of 'Like an animal' by Joan Poulson from Twinkle, Twinkle Chocolate Bar compiled by John Foster © 1991, Joan Poulson (1991, Oxford University Press). **Caroline Sheldon Literary Agency** for the use of an extract from 'Hopaloo Kangaroo' by John Agard © 1996, John Agard (1996, Bodley Head). **Celia Warren** for the use of 'Don't Tickle Tigers' by Celia Warren © 2005, Celia Warren, previously unpublished).
Qualifications and Curriculum Authority for the uses of extracts from the QCA/DfEE document Curriculum Guidance for the Foundation Stage © 2000 Qualifications and Curriculum Authority.

British Library Cataloguing-in-Publication Data
A catalogue record for this book is available from the British Library.

ISBN 0-439-97164-0
ISBN 978-0439-97164-5

The right of Wendy Jolliffe to be identified as the author of this work has been asserted by her in accordance with the Copyright, Designs and Patents Act 1988.

Extracts from The National Literacy Strategy © Crown copyright. Reproduced under the terms of HMSO Guidance Note 8.

Contents

ALL NEW 100 LITERACY HOURS: RECEPTION

About the series

The popular *100 Literacy Hours* series has been updated to reflect the new curriculum guidelines and to make links to the Foundation Stage curriculum. *All New 100 Literacy Hours* offers a set of new term-by-term lesson plans, complete with objectives and organisation grids and accompanied, where relevant, with photocopiable texts and activity sheets. The series offers a core of material for the teaching of the English curriculum within the structure of the Literacy Hour, perfectly matched to the recent National Literacy Strategy *Medium-term plans*, *Grammar for Writing* and *Speaking, Listening and Learning* guidelines.

Using this book

Although the book is entitled 'All New 100 Literacy Hours', in the Reception year it is not necessary to teach these lesson plans as discrete hours. All the activities covering text, word and sentence level can be taught as individual activities and the focused group work suggestions are intended to be effective alongside the independent-work or child-initiated activities. It may be appropriate, towards the end of the Reception year for teachers to use this material as discrete hours, but the key aspect is to ensure flexibility to fit in with the specific needs of the children being taught. It is not recommended to teach formal Literacy Hours with children at this age too soon, and instead the book provides fun and meaningful ways for young children to learn literacy skills with an appropriate balance of teacher-directed and child-initiated activities.

This book aims to ensure that literacy is taught holistically alongside the other areas of the curriculum with important links made. Guidance is therefore provided for all the six Areas of Learning, showing clear links. This will facilitate planning across the curriculum, and cross-curricular pages are provided for each unit as a valuable aid to teachers. It is intended that these activities, encompassing all six Areas of Learning, will be used in the indoor and outdoor classroom.

The importance of learning through play is emphasised throughout this book, with many links to role-play areas as a stimulus for literacy. Providing appropriate activities for this age, which enable learning through fun first-hand experiences, has been an essential ingredient of the material provided in this book.

Organisation of teaching units

The units are grouped into five or ten days' work to ensure sufficient opportunities to explore the literacy potential of each text, as is the common pattern in most Foundation Stage classrooms. The common pattern is for work on reading a text to be followed by writing activities, with speaking and listening activities underpinning both. The units are organised to include all the relavant information in an easy-to-follow format.

Unit overview

Introduction
A short introduction for each unit, explaining the key ideas covered.

Organisation grid
Outlines the key activities for each lesson and could form the basis of the teacher's weekly plans with additional specific information about the requirements of the class to be added by the teacher.

Key assessment opportunities
A bulleted list of key assessment opportunities is given. These notes will help you to plan assessment opportunities throughout each unit.

Cross-curricular activities
Ideas for independent work linked to the six Areas of Learning of the Foundation Stage curriculum.

Unit lesson plans
Each unit of lesson plans is written with the following headings:

Objectives
National Literacy Strategy objectives and Foundation Stage Early Learning Goals/Stepping Stones (the emphasis during Terms 1 and 2 is on working within the appropriate Stepping Stones, leading up to meeting the Early Learning Goals during Term 3).

What you need
Provides the list of resources required for each lesson.

Shared work
Sets out the shared text-, word- and sentence-level work in each lesson. Some of the text-, sentence- and word-level objectives are taught discretely, while others are integrated into the theme of the unit as the NLS recommends.

Focused group work
Sets out the guided writing or reading activities for each group.

Plenary
Sets out what to do in the whole-class plenary session. In planning sessions in which children present their work, it is important to ensure that every child will have an opportunity to participate every few weeks.

Differentiation
Ideas for supporting more or less able children, including ideas for peer and other adult support.

Links to the NLS Medium-term plans

The units in this book provide clear links to the requirements of the Primary National Strategy's Medium-term plans. Genres are matched exactly with appropriate texts for this age group and the range of objectives covered, as shown on the grid for each term, provides full coverage to meet the requirements of the *Curriculum Guidance for the Foundation Stage* (QCA) and the National Literacy Strategy objectives for Reception. Each lesson plan provides objectives to link with both documents.

Texts are all based on appropriate text types for young children, with an emphasis on print in the environment as a springboard to literacy. Developing knowledge of traditional stories from different cultures is also central, as is the importance of nursery rhymes as an aid to the ability to hear and generate rhymes. Some units (such as 'The snack shop' and 'The class art gallery') are all based on first hand experiences of visits to similar places, where possible. In addition, a developing understanding of the difference between fiction and non-fiction is provided with a wide variety of lists, captions, instructions and recounts, as well as looking at non-fiction texts.

Differentiation

In most lesson plans, suggestions for supporting the less able and stretching the more able are given. However, it is important to use these with care as a child may be 'less able' in some aspects of literacy but 'more able' in others (for example, the child who writes highly imaginative stories, but with many technical inaccuracies). Therefore, the suggestions for the more and less able should be applied only when they are appropriate for the individual child.

Assessment

Each unit includes a list of bullet points to help with ongoing assessment. These are not intended to replace National Curriculum Assessment, but represent the 'bottom line' that all children should have achieved by the end of the unit. If a number of children have failed to achieve satisfactory standards in any of the bulleted areas, then the unit may need to be revisited (with different resources). Strengths and weaknesses of individual children should be kept in mind when setting learning targets and planning future units.

Using the photocopiable resources

Photocopiable resources are provided at the end of each unit, including texts, teaching aids and activity sheets. These should provide a valuable resource in the classroom and many of them, such as the alphabet cards or writing frames can be used for a range of activities or adapted for further use.

Usually, the best way to share a resource with the class is to make a display version for an overhead projector or data projector. However, try to avoid this becoming an unvarying routine. An effective alternative is to sit with the children in a circle and to work with a hard copy of the text. Also, where possible, engage the children with actual books. Many editions of popular classics and selections of poetry are available for sale quite cheaply, so it is possible to buy small sets of books for group work, or even enough for a whole class if they share one between two.

Interactive whiteboard use

Permission is granted for those pages marked as photocopiable to be used in this way. Where third party material is used, permission for interactive whiteboard use must be obtained from the copyright holder or their licensor. This information can be found in the acknowledgements at the front of the book.

Speaking and listening

The crucial importance of children becoming proficient communicators is highlighted in this book. Links are made throughout to speaking and listening as the starting point for developing skills across the curriculum and in literacy in particular. Guidance is provided specifically on what to look for and how to encourage children in this, with particular emphasis given to children working with partners, or 'talk partners'. When a larger group is needed, 'talk partners' can join into fours. Groups of this size are ideal for discussion and collaborative work, as they provide a range of opinion and yet are not too large to make full participation difficult. It is important to vary group organisation so that children experience working with different partners who may have different approaches or different abilities.

Links are made in the grid on pages 8-11 to the Speaking and Listening guidance materials (DfES, 2003) which provide objectives and activities beginning in Year 1. It is, however, necessary to show how these can be facilitated with preliminary work in Reception.

Phonics

The value of phonics in the learning of reading and spelling is acknowledged throughout this book. It is also vital to provide many and varied opportunities for children to develop phonological awareness through activities involving rhythm, rhyme and alliteration. Many of the activities, particularly in Terms 1 and 2, concentrate on this, while also providing opportunities for children to become proficient with phonics as soon as they are able. Several activities enhance and cohere with those in the 'Playing with Sounds' materials from the Primary National Strategy (DfES, 2004). While references are made to the 'Progression in Phonics' (PiP) materials (DfES, 2001) and some of the well-known games and resources provided in this document are referred to in the grid on pages 8-11, further additions are made in this book. In particular, as recommended in the more recent 'Playing with Sounds' resources, the teaching of medial letter sounds is shown more quickly than originally suggested in the 'Progression in Phonics' guidance. The emphasis is given to the importance of children becoming proficient in blending sounds as soon as possible. The precise stage in teaching phonics, and the letters to be taught, are not specifically prescribed in this book, as this will depend on the needs of the children.

Developing early writing

The modelling of writing through the different forms of shared writing (teacher demonstration, teacher scribing and supported composition) is a powerful tool for young children in developing literacy. This is therefore fully explored throughout the units and links are made in the grid on pages 8-11 to specific units in the 'Developing Early Writing' materials (DfES, 2001). The focus in the activities in this book is on providing a meaningful context for the children, with a natural stimulus for writing – often through play-based activities.

Creativity

Recent reports such as 'Excellence and Enjoyment' (DfES, 2003) and 'Expecting the unexpected' (Ofsted, 2003) have emphasised the importance of creativity. It is not that the NLS *Framework* is lacking in creativity; indeed, it includes many creative approaches to texts, for example, rewriting a scene in a narrative from another point of view. The problem is that with so many objectives to cover, and an unvarying format for lessons, there just isn't the time to pursue opportunities for creativity as the children progress through the school system. So the first message is – *Find the time!* If a lesson or unit sparks off a creative process, follow it through, even if this means rewriting next week's plan. This is, of course, even more vital with Reception-age children and the emphasis in this book is on making links across the curriculum (provided particularly by the links made to all six Areas of Learning as well as Drama).

Medium-term plan	All New 100 Literacy Hours unit	Early Learning Goals	Text level	Sentence level	Word level	Number of days	Text(s)	Links with DEW, S&L, PIPs	Outcome
Print around us	Playing schools	Communication p54-55￼ Linking sounds and letters p60-61￼ Reading p62-63￼ Writing p64-65	T1￼ T11￼ T12￼ T15	W5￼ W6		5	Notices, labels and lists.	DEW: 1 'The Supermarket'￼ PIPs: steps 1, 2, 3	A role-play area resourced with lists, signs, notices which children create and use.
Alphabet books, chants, rhymes and songs	Alphabet Names	Communication p52-53￼ Linking sounds and letters p60-61￼ Reading p62-63	T1￼ T6￼ T11￼ T12	S4	W5￼ W8	5	Alphabet books, name cards and alliterative sentences.	PIPs: steps 1, 2, 3	Class alphabet book of names.
Nursery rhymes	Nursery-rhyme characters	Communication p54-55￼ Thinking p54-59￼ Linking sounds and letters p60-61￼ Reading p62-63￼ Writing p64-65	T6￼ T10￼ T12￼ T14	S4	W1￼ W2￼ W6￼ W10￼ W11￼ W14	10	Nursery rhymes and nursery-rhyme stories.	S&L: 4￼ PIPs: steps 1, 2, 3	Nursery rhymes with alternative endings; a performance of rhymes (whole class, group, individual); writing stimulated by a rhyme.
Print around us (2)	The snack shop	Communication p54-55￼ Linking sounds and letters p60-61￼ Reading p62-63￼ Writing p64-65	T1￼ T15		W2￼ W6￼ W10￼ W14	5	Lists, captions, signs, menus and recipes.	DEW: 1￼ S&L: 6￼ PIPs: steps 1, 2, 3	Menus and a class recipe book.
Narrative: predictable structures and patterned language through a traditional tale	The big pancake	Linking sounds and letters p60-61￼ Reading p62-63￼ Writing p64-65￼ Handwriting p64-65	T8￼ T10￼ T14	S1￼ S2	W1￼ W2￼ W4￼ W5￼ W14	10	Stories with predictable structures and patterned language.	S&L: 8￼ PIPs: steps 1, 2, 3	Retelling stories using a variety of props and artefacts.

TERM 2

Medium-term plan	All New 100 Literacy Hours unit	Early Learning Goals	Text level	Sentence level	Word level	Number of days	Text(s)	Links with DEW, S&L, PiPs	Outcome
All about me	My history	Communication p54-55 Thinking p56-59 Linking sounds and letters p60-61 Reading p62-63 Writing p64-65	T6 T13 T14	S1 S4	W2 W5	5	Recounts.	**DEW:** 'The Day the Fire Engine Came to School' **S&L:** 1 **PiPs:** steps 2, 3, 4	Children produce a book about themselves.
Narrative	The cave	Communication p50-51 Thinking p56-59 Linking sounds and letters p60-61 Reading p62-63 Writing p64-65 Handwriting p66-67	T6 T7 T8 T10 T11 T14 T17	S1	W2 W5 W11 W14	10	Simple repetitive text.	**DEW:** 'The Bear Hunt' **S&L:** 4 **PiPs:** steps 2, 3, 4	Story map and narrative retold in correct sequence.
Action verses and rhymes	Five counting rhymes	Communication p50-51, p54-55 Linking sounds and letters p60-61 Reading p62-63 Writing p64-65	T10 T11 T14		W1 W6 W7 W10	5	Action verses and counting rhymes.	**PiPs:** steps 2, 3, 4	Teacher scribed shared poem that differs from the original text; performance of action verses.
Labels and captions for information	The class art gallery	Communication p54-55 Thinking p56-59 Linking sounds and letters p60-61 Reading p62-63 Writing p64-65 Handwriting p66-67	T1 T11 T12 T14 T15	S1 S2	W2 W6	5	Labels and captions relating to a class visit.	**DEW:** 'The Exhibition' **PiPs:** steps 2, 3, 4	Written labels/ captions/ posters and invitations for an exhibition.
Traditional stories	What made Tiddalik laugh?	Communication p50-53 Linking sounds and letters p60-61 Reading p62-63 Handwriting p66-67	T2 T7 T8 T12	S2 S4	W2 W3 W10 W14	10	A traditional multi-cultural tale.	**S&L:** 4 **PiPs:** steps 2, 3, 4	Storyboards, sequencing boards and an alternative version of the story.

Medium-term plan	All New 100 Literacy Hours unit	Early Learning Goals	Text level	Sentence level	Word level	Number of days	Text(s)	Links with DEW, S&L, PIPs	Outcome
Narrative structure	The picnic	Reading p62-63 Writing p64-65	T3 T15	S1	W2 W5 W6 W14	5	Stories with predictable structures and patterned language.	DEW: 'The Bear Hunt' S&L: 5 PIPs: steps 3, 4, 5, 6	Story maps; re-enactment of story in correct sequence; writing based on familiar texts.
Recounts and shared experiences	The travelling theatre	Reading p62-63 Writing p64-65	T7	S1	W2 W6	5	Recounts.	PIPs: steps 3, 4, 5, 6	Individual recount of a shared experience; photographs and text to recount a shared experience.
Poems and chants	Playing with sounds and words	Communication p50-51, p54-55 Linking sounds and letters p60-61	T2 T14	S2 S4	W1 W2 W3 W4 W6 W14	10	Poems and chants.	PIPs: steps 3, 4, 5, 6	Writing nonsense poems; performance of favourite poems and chants
Narrative: language features	Rapunzel	Reading p62-63	T5 T14	S4	W2 W6 W10	5	Fairy story	PIPs: steps 3, 4, 5, 6	Writing and performing class fairy story.
Information texts (questions and answers)	Where do animals live?	Reading p62-63	T1 T6	S1 S2	W4 W5 W9	5	Information texts	S&L: 3 PIPs: steps 3, 4, 5, 6	Generating a series of questions and answers linked to aspects of work.

UNIT 1

Playing schools

This unit is based around playing schools and comprises five days' literacy activities. The work supports the National Literacy Strategy (Later Foundation Stage, Medium-term plan) focus on *Print around us*. The activities will help develop an awareness of a variety of print in a familiar context and will provide the children with a real purpose for writing. Linked activities are provided for all the six Areas of Learning with a strong emphasis on developing speaking and listening skills; co-operation in Personal, social and emotional development; and writing for a purpose in the form of lists, signs and notices. The activities build towards Year 1 Term 1, Objective 3 of the *Speaking, Listening, Learning* guidance: to ask and answer questions, make relevant contributions, offer suggestions and take turns.

Day	Shared text-level work	Shared word-/ sentence-level work	Focused group work	Independent work	Plenary
1 Notices in the classroom	Shared reading of a range of notices and labels in the classroom.	Matching high frequency words to notices.	Teacher as 'pupil' in role-play area – creating and writing rules.	**PSED:** Making rules for the role-play. **CLL:** Writing notices for the role-play area.	Sharing the rules. Reading the notices.
2 A hunt for print walk	Environmental print trail.	'Bingo' game of high frequency words.	Teacher in role-play area – developing rules.	**MD:** Doing the dinner register – how many school dinners today?	Writing a letter to the headteacher.
3 Writing notices	Shared writing of notices.	Help the puppet match the objects to the sound.	Teacher in role-play area – writing names.	**KUW:** Small-world play – making a map.	Talking to the puppet – what sound does this begin with?
4 Make a list	Shared writing of lists.	The phonic tray game.	Teacher in role-play area – writing lists.	**PD:** Obstacle course in the playground or hall.	Sharing lists and notices.
5 Ask a question	Hot-seating – questioning the headteacher or guest.	'Yes/No' phonic game.	Teacher in role-play area – appropriate questioning.	**CD:** Painting and representing the school.	Circle time – saying names.

Key assessment opportunities
When working with children during role-play determine if they are able to:
● match graphemes to phonemes
● form recognisable letters
● write for a real purpose
● ask questions coherently and in full sentences
● recognise high frequency words.
Record appropriately and ensure that this informs future planning.

Personal, social and emotional development

Making rules
Early Learning Goal
Work as part of a group or class, taking turns and sharing fairly, understanding that there needs to be agreed values and codes of behaviour for groups of people.
What you need
Role-play area - see Day 1 (page 13).
What to do
● Work with the children to create rules for the playing schools role-play area during focused group work.

Physical development

Over and under
Early Learning Goal
Travel around, under, over and through balancing and climbing equipment.
What you need
An obstacle course set up using a range of items.
What to do
● Ask an adult to supervise and encourage the children to find different ways of travelling around the course, providing support to the less confident.
● Next, ask them to help an adult to draw the course they took, annotating it with words such as *bridge*, *road* and so on.

Communication, language and literacy

Writing notices
Early Learning Goal
Attempt writing for different purposes, using features of different forms such as lists, stories and instructions.
What you need
A writing table; paper; card; pens; example notices (see photocopiable page 18); alphabet strips; high frequency words displayed: *come, play, go* etc.
What to do
● Tell the children that they will be making some notices for 'playing schools'. Read the sample notices.
● Discuss the notices and model writing one. Encourage the children to write their own notices to place around the classroom, using the alphabet strips and high frequency words to help them. Encourage more able children to write more complex notices.

Mathematical development

Counting dinners
Early Learning Goal
Say and use number names in order in familiar contexts.
What you need
A list of the children's names in large print on a clipboard (your 'Dinner register'); a notice board with three headings: School Dinners, Packed Lunches, Home (a fresh sheet for each day); money tin and pretend £1 coins; card numerals 1-30; Blu-Tack.
What to do
● Ask the children what they are doing for lunch. Mark D (for school dinner) P (for packed lunch) or H (for going home) on the prepared 'register'.
● Ask the children to make totals of each kind of dinner. Ask them to choose the correct number card to stick with Blu-Tack on to the prepared board.
● Now find out how many pounds they should have in total when each dinner costs £1 each. Suggest that they place a pound coin over each child's name in the register that is having a school dinner (to develop one-to-one correspondence).

Creative development

Painting school
Early Learning Goal
Explore colour, texture, shape, form and space in two or three dimensions.
What you need
Painting materials and easels; photographs of the school on display; junk modelling materials.
What to do
● Encourage the children to look carefully at the photographs and then to paint a picture of the school. Next, use junk materials to make models of the school.

Knowledge and understanding of the world

Make a model
Early Learning Goal
Observe, find out about and identify features in the place they live and the natural world.
What you need
Small-world play buildings and figures; clipboards; paper and pens.
What to do
● Ask the children to use the small-world play objects to represent the school. Why have they chosen to place the objects there?
● Encourage the children to draw their replica school. Explain that they have made a map.

Notices in the classroom

Objectives

Early Learning Goals
● Reading p62-63.

Stepping Stone
● Begin to recognise some familiar words.

NLS
T1: To recognise printed and handwritten words in a variety of settings.
T12: To experiment with writing in a variety of play, exploratory and role-play situations.
W6: To read on sight the 45 high frequency words to be taught by the end of YR.

What you need
● A selection of notices for the classroom (from photocopiable page 18 and your own classroom)
● props for a 'playing schools' role-play area including a teacher's chair and easel
● high frequency words on card.

Differentiation

Less able
● Support the children to speak clearly in sentences by elaborating their words or phrases and by modelling complete sentences.

More able
● Encourage the children to use a greater range of vocabulary.

Shared text-level work
● Show the children the different notices and explain that you need to put them in the correct places in the classroom.
● Read each notice carefully and choose a child to put it in the correct place, for example on the lunch-box crate.
● Discuss with the children that writing such as this has a real purpose and ask the children to think of some other examples of this kind of writing. Encourage them to notice other examples as they walk around school.

Shared word-level work
● Now explain that there are some words that we use frequently. Hold up some cards with high frequency words on them, such as *the, is, in, here.* Tell the children that it is important to know these words as it helps us to read quickly.
● Now ask the children to try and spot some of the words that you have just shown them. Place the words on display and ask different children to see if they can spot any of the words in the notices around the classroom. Consider one notice at a time to help the children to keep focused.

Focused group work
● Set up the role-play area for playing schools.
● Work with a group of four children in the role-play area to encourage meaningful interaction.
● Explain that you will be playing schools and that each pupil will take turns to be the teacher. Select the children in turn using the alphabetical order of their first names (explain this to the children, using an alphabet frieze or strip and the children's name cards).
● Before the first child assumes the role of teacher, discuss the importance of rules. Scribe some of them for the children.
● Talk about typical school-day activities together. How does the day begin?
● Invite the children to role-play the start of the school day. Ask the 'teacher' to take the register, and nominate someone to take the dinner register. Then encourage the 'teacher' to ask the children to select from a range of activities (which you have already organised) such as writing a list, reading a book, or listening to a tape of a familiar story.
● As time allows, ask the children to swap roles and start again.

Independent work
● See the activities for the six Areas of Learning on page 12.

Plenary
● With the children all on the carpet, ask them to share the notices that have been written during the independent activity (see page 12).
● Ask each child to read his or her notice to you all. Talk about the high frequency words that he or she used.

 13

A hunt for print walk

Objectives

Early Learning Goals
● Reading p62-63.

Stepping Stone
● Begin to recognise some familiar words.

NLS
T1: To recognise printed and handwritten words in a variety of settings.
W5: To read on sight a range of familiar words.
W6: To read on sight the 45 high frequency words to be taught by end of YR.

What you need

● A selection of notices for the classroom from photocopiable page 18
● your role-play area set up for playing schools (see Day 1, page 13)
● 'Bingo' cards for high frequency words (photocopiable page 19 copied and laminated, enough for one of the three cards per pair of children)
● a dry-wipe pen for each pair of children
● enlarged and cut up words for you to show and call out and for use on the walk around school.

Differentiation

Less able
● An adult should sit with less able children as they play 'Bingo', helping them to look for the initial sounds of words, for example.

Shared text-level work

● Before the lesson, spend some time planning a route around the school that will take the children past various interesting notices. You might want to put up some additional notices at child height.
● Explain to the children that you are going on a 'hunt for print' walk around the school.
● Read examples of notices from the previous day and then give out examples of some high frequency words enlarged and copied on card or laminated. Read the words together and ask the pupils who have been given cards to find them in the notices from the previous day.
● Explain that you are going to look for these words as you go on your school walk. Tell the children that perhaps by recognising some of these key words they will find it easier to read the whole notices. Provide different words to pairs of children and help them to read them first.
● Lead the children around your planned route and point out examples of print.
● Ask the children to work out what the print says and talk about the clues that they use (where the notice is positioned, words, letters and so on). Ask them to look for the high frequency words that they have been given.
● Back in the classroom, ask the children to tell their talk partner about a notice they saw. Share some of these and write a few on the flipchart with the children helping you to spell the words by sounding out.

Shared word-level work

● Next (or later on), explain that you are going to play 'Bingo'. Give each pair of children one of the 'Bingo' cards.
● Read the words carefully and explain that, as you call out the words, the children need to check their cards and then cross out a word if it matches. Tell them to shout 'Bingo' when all their words are crossed out.
● Play the game once or twice as time allows.

Focused group work

● Continue as the previous day asking different children to work with you in the role-play area. The support you provide will depend on the particular children and their developmental needs.

Independent work

● See the activities for the six Areas of Learning on page 12.

Plenary

● Explain that you would like to write a letter to the headteacher inviting him or her to come and visit the class 'school'.
● Model writing the letter using teacher demonstration and emphasising the use of spacing, capital letters, full stops and so on. Point out how you begin and end each letter.
● Choose a pair of children to deliver the letter to the Headteacher.

Objectives

Early Learning Goals
● Linking sounds and letters p60-61.
● Writing p64-65.

Stepping Stones
● Hear and say the initial sound in words and know which letters represent some of the sounds.
● Use writing as a means of recording and communicating.

NLS
T11: To understand that writing can be used for a range of purposes.
T15: To use writing to communicate in a variety of ways, incorporating it into play and everyday classroom life.

What you need

● A selection of notices for the classroom from photocopiable page 18
● your role-play area set up for playing schools (see Day 1, page 13)
● flipchart
● coloured paper and pens
● puppet
● objects in a bag all beginning with the current sound being taught.

Differentiation

Less able
● Provide additional adult support to help those children with less developed phonological awareness as they sound out the words.

Writing notices

Shared text-level work

● Say you are going to write a notice for the class 'school'. This is to advertise a forthcoming event (try and link this to something happening in school, such as the Harvest Festival).
● Orally rehearse a sentence such as *Please come to our Harvest Festival Service.* Then sound the words out together and ask the children to suggest letters to write this. Write the notice using teacher scribing.
● Read the completed notice when it is finished and emphasise that children who choose to work in the writing area can use the large coloured paper and pens to create their own notices. Provide a 'notice board' for this purpose within the role-play area.

Shared word-level work

● Show the children the puppet (it may be one that you use regularly). Explain that the puppet only understands individual sounds/phonemes, so the children have to talk to him in phonemes.
● Now present your bag of objects that all begin with the sound you are currently learning (if possible choose objects representing CVC words, such as pen). Take out one object at a time and ask the children to say what it is.
● Tell the children that they must tell the puppet what the object is, using phonemes. For example, *p/e/n, p/e/g, p/i/n.* To ensure all the children are involved in the activity, ask them to first say the phonemes to their talk partner before asking individuals to tell the puppet. Please note that, although this is quite an advanced concept for the children to master, it is important that children practise blending sounds as soon as possible.

Focused group work

● Continue as the previous day asking different children to work with you in the role-play area. This time focus on encouraging the children to write for a real purpose. For example, suggest that they write the children's names (in the group) to form a group register. Use the register for some further role-play.

Independent work

● See the activities for the six Areas of Learning on page 12.

Plenary

● With the children sitting in a circle on the carpet, pass an object around and ask the children to say what it is and then ask the puppet (you) to repeat it.
● Have fun by asking the children to correct the puppet's frequent mistakes!
● Finish by asking the puppet to read a word from one of the class notices by sounding out the letters – for example, *p/u/t.* Encourage the children to help him.

Make a list

Objectives

Early Learning Goals
● Writing p64-65.

Stepping Stone
● Use writing as a means of recording and communicating.

NLS
T11: To understand that writing can be used for a range of purposes.
T15: To use writing to communicate in a variety of ways, incorporating it into play and everyday classroom life.
W2: Hearing and identifying initial sounds in words.

What you need

● A selection of notices for the classroom from photocopiable page 18
● your role-play area set up for playing schools (see Day 1, page 13)
● a list you have written, such as a 'to do list'
● individual whiteboards and pens for half of the class
● a flipchart
● photocopiable page 20
● a tray
● a selection of objects in a box or bag (some beginning with your current sound).

Differentiation

Less able
● For those children whose phonological awareness is not well developed, use adult support where possible to repeat the sounds when playing the game with the box of objects.

More able
● Show the children photocopiable page 20 and read it to them. Explain that you will put copies of this sheet in the writing area for them to use for making further lists.

Shared text-level work

● Show the children a list you have written – where possible try and make this a list for a real purpose, for example a 'to do list'. Discuss why people make lists and ask the children if they have ever seen anyone writing lists at home or school.
● Explain that you are going to write a list of things that are needed in the class 'school'. Use the notices as a starting point.
● Ask the children to tell their talk partners at least five things that can be found in any classroom.
● Share a few examples and write one or two on the flipchart, such as: *register, pen, pencils*. Show that drawings of objects can also be helpful and that children can use both when compiling their own lists.
● Emphasise that lists often consist of single words and use your example list to demonstrate this.
● Now ask pairs of children to write their lists, using individual whiteboards and pens. Ask them to share their lists with you, and from a range of suggestions, compile a composite list on the flipchart.

Shared word-level work

● Take out the box or bag of objects and a tray and say that you would like the children's help to sort out the objects. Explain that you are going to put items on the tray that begin with (the current sound), and that other items must stay in the box or bag.
● Remove one item at a time from your selection in a box or bag and ask the children to help you to decide whether it should go on the tray. Pass the objects around for the children to hold as they make their decisions.
● Place each chosen item on the tray in front of the children.
● Finally, check through the items on the tray in front of the children to make sure no mistakes have been made.

Focused group work

● Continue as the previous day asking different children to work with you in the role-play area.
● Today, ask the children to bring in their lists to incorporate in the play. Encourage them to add to their lists when they have looked around the role-play area to see what is missing.

Independent work

● See the activities for the six Areas of Learning on page 12.

Plenary

● Gather the children together to share examples of the lists that have been written. Start by re-reading the list that you wrote together earlier.
● Now ask the children to read out what is on their lists.
● Finish by discussing how useful lists are to remind us of what is needed.

Ask a question

Objectives

Early Learning Goals
● Linking sounds and letters p60-61.
● Communication p54-55.

Stepping Stones
● Hear and say the initial sound in words and know which letters represent some of the sounds.
● Use a widening range of words to express or elaborate ideas.

NLS
T15: To use writing to communicate in a variety of ways.
W2: Knowledge of grapheme/phoneme correspondences.

What you need
● A selection of notices for the classroom from photocopiable page 18
● your role-play area set up for playing schools (see Day 1, page 13)
● the headteacher (if possible!) or another guest
● pictures of objects, some beginning with the current sound being taught
● large cards saying *Yes* and *No* (displayed on the wall at opposite sides of the classroom).

Differentiation

More able
● Encourage more able children to ask a range of questions, extending their vocabulary where appropriate.

Shared text-level work
● Tell the children that you have a visitor to the class today. Explain who it is and ask the children to think of questions to ask. Their questions could be about routines in school, for example why a register is needed and how often it should be taken.
● Suggest that they practise asking their questions with their talk partners.
● As soon as the children have prepared their questions (write some of these on the flipchart), send a messenger to fetch the guest. When the guest arrives, ask one or two children to show the guest the role-play area.
● Next, ask different children to share some of the notices and lists that the children have created.
● Now explain that the children have some questions to ask. With the headteacher or other guest in the hot seat, choose children to ask their questions with their partners prompting (and yourself where necessary).
● Conclude the session by emphasising the importance of children working together and sharing, and the need for rules in school.

Shared word-level work
● Play the 'Yes/No' game for words beginning with a specific sound – this will depend on the current sound you are teaching.
● Remind the children of the sound you are currently learning and show them your pile of pictures of objects. Write the letter on the flipchart. Explain that some of the objects begin with that letter sound and some do not.
● Now pick a card from the pile, saying the word clearly. Ask the children to say 'Yes' if it begins with the specific sound, pointing to the Yes card in the classroom. If it does not they must say 'No' and point to the No card.

Focused group work
● Continue as the previous day asking different children to work with you. This time focus on asking good questions and talking in complete sentences.

Independent work
● See the activities for the six Areas of Learning on page 12.

Plenary
● Finish with a circle-time activity. Warm up by asking the children to quickly say their names in turn around the circle, changing directions and gathering speed!
● Now provide a sentence starter, such as I like... at school, and explain that they have to say their favourite activity. Start off by giving an example and then ask each child in turn to contribute, allowing some to 'pass'.

Classroom notices

Writing area
Please put the pens and paper
in the right places.

Please put on a painting apron.
Only two people painting at a time.

Match the pictures and letters.
Which picture matches which letter?

How many school dinners today?
Write the number and match
the faces.

Bingo

in	the	is
at	here	school

look	play	school
is	are	here

going	is	am
school	in	they

TERM 1

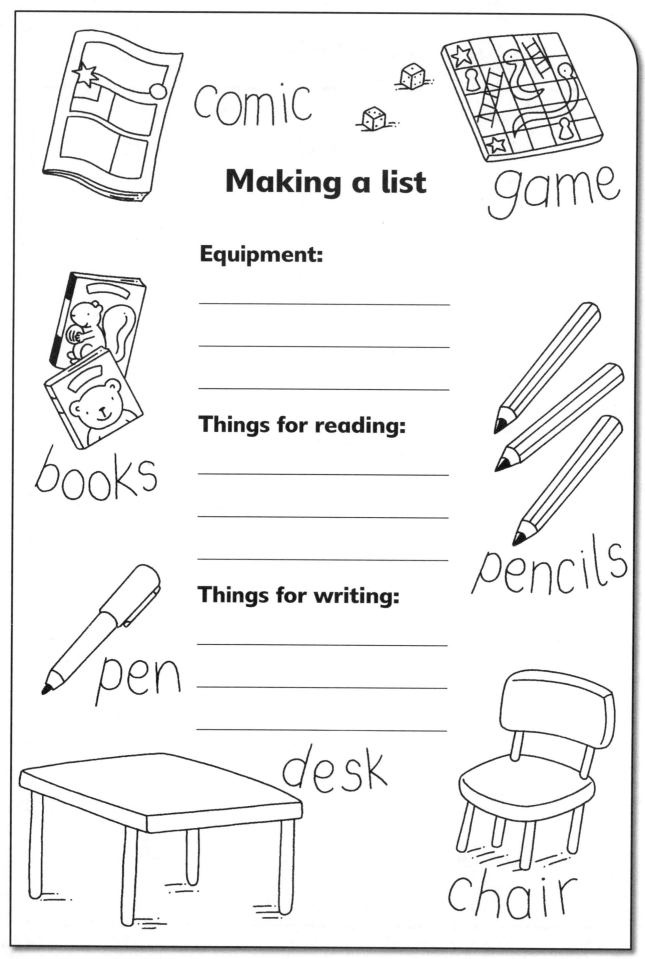

comic

Making a list

game

Equipment:

_____

_____

_____

Things for reading:

_____

_____

Things for writing:

_____

_____

books

pencils

pen

desk

chair

UNIT 2

Alphabet names

This unit comprises five days' literacy activities and supports the National Literacy Strategy (Later Foundation Stage, Medium-term plan) focus on *Alphabet books, chants, rhymes and songs.* It follows on from the previous unit on 'playing schools'. The activities will help to develop phonological awareness alongside improving the children's knowledge of the alphabet. The outcome of the unit will be a class alphabet book based on the children's names. Linked activities are provided for all the six Areas of Learning with a strong emphasis on developing speaking and listening skills, cooperation in Personal, social and emotional development and developing literacy skills based on the children's names. The activities build towards Year 1 Term 1, Objective 3 of the *Speaking, Listening, Learning* guidance: to ask and answer questions, make relevant contributions, offer suggestions and take turns.

Day	Shared text-level work	Shared word-/ sentence-level work	Focused group work	Independent work	Plenary
1 What's my job?	Read an alphabet book in shared reading.	Identify words beginning with given letters. Play 'Just like me' with name cards.	Teacher-directed activity – teacher scribing sentences for different children in the class.	**PSED, CLL:** Role-play area – 'a school'. Developing rules. Using a register of names and other props.	Singing name songs. Share one or two name sentences.
2 Alphabetical jobs	Reading alliterative name sentences.	Play 'Yes/No' game to identify words beginning with a given letter.	Continue teacher scribing sentences for the children's names.	**MD:** Sorting name cards.	'Guess whose name?' Sorting name collages into the correct corresponding letters.
3 Saying silly sentences	Shared writing of name sentences.	Spotting capital letters – interactive whiteboard.	Continue teacher scribing sentences for the children's names.	**KUW:** Learning about jobs.	Alphabet chant with actions.
4 Picture captions	Captions for digital photos of children working in class.	Individual practice of modelling letter formation.	Continue teacher scribing sentences for the children's names.	**PD:** Action alphabet rhymes.	Hot seating – as the teacher answering questions.
5 A class book of names	Creating the class book of names – reading together.	Identifying capital letters and correct spacing during shared writing.	Continue teacher scribing sentences for the children's names.	**CD:** Name collages.	Find your place in the class alphabet, emphasising phonological awareness.

Key assessment opportunities
When working with children on writing alliterative name sentences, look closely for:
- the ability to hear and discriminate individual sounds
- knowledge of print including spacing between words
- the use of capital letters for names
- the ability to write first names accurately
- knowledge of alphabetical order.

Personal, social and emotional development

Taking turns
Early Learning Goal
Have a developing awareness of their own needs, views and feelings and be sensitive to the needs, views and feelings of others.
What you need
'School' role-play area from Unit 1 (see page 13).
What to do
● Use the role-play area from the previous unit and ask the children to revisit the rules for their 'school', deciding who should be the 'teacher'.

Physical development

Move to the tune
Early Learning Goal
Move with confidence, imagination and in safety.
What you need
A tape of action rhymes and alphabet songs such as 'Round and Round the Garden' by Sarah Williams (OUP); tape recorder.
What to do
● Ensure that the children can switch on the tape recorder and then encourage them to jump, stamp, march and so on to the songs.

Communication, language and literacy

Alphabet sounds
Early Learning Goal
Link sounds to letters, naming and sounding the letters of the alphabet.
What you need
Role-play area from Unit 1 (see page 13); a range of realistic props such as a home-made register and dinner register; name cards for each child; coloured bands; a board or easel; signs with *What we are learning today...*, and *The teacher today is...* with space for the children to write on (or add their name cards to).
What to do
● Explain that the children will continue to play at 'schools' as per the previous week. Tell them that only five children may play at a time (issue coloured bands to indicate this).
● Ask them to take turns to be the teacher with up to four children 'in the class'.
● Encourage the children to change roles regularly and demonstrate how to use the various props and signs.

Mathematical development

Sorting names
Early Learning Goal
Count reliably up to 10 everyday objects.
What you need
Name cards for the children; a chart (see below) drawn on a large sheet of paper or easel; counters.

2	3	4	5	6	7
Jo	Ben	Anne	Karen	Simrat	Michael

What to do
● Give each child their name card.
● Tell the children to represent each letter of their name with a counter and then count the total number of counters in their name. Ask them to write their name under the corresponding number on the chart.

Creative development

Decorate your name
Early Learning Goal
Explore colour, texture, shape, form and space in two or three dimensions.
What you need
Salt dough (or similar); assorted buttons or collage materials; stiff card.
What to do
● Ask an adult to help the children to shape the letters of their name using salt dough.
● Let them decorate their names. Place them on card to dry.

Knowledge and understanding of the world

Choose a job
Early Learning Goal
Find out about past and present events in their own lives, and in those of their families and other people they know.
What you need
A range of dressing-up outfits and props for children to role-play different jobs (fire-fighter, nurse, builder and so on); digital camera.
What to do
● Encourage the children to select a dressing-up outfit and some props that might be useful for doing their chosen 'job'.
● Ask an adult to take digital pictures of the children for inclusion in a class book.
● Encourage discussion about the jobs people do and if they know anyone who does a similar job.

What's my job?

Objectives

Early Learning Goals
● Communication p50-51.
● Linking sounds and letters p60-61.
● Reading p62-63.

Stepping Stones
● Hear and say the initial sound in words and know which letters represent some of the sounds.
● Listen to others in one-to-one/small groups when conversation interests them.
● Know information can be relayed in the form of print.

NLS
T6: To re-read frequently a variety of familiar texts.
S4: To use a capital letter for the start of own name.
W8: To read and write own name and explore other words related to the spelling of own name.

What you need
● An alphabet book, such as *Alice is an Astronaut* by Michaela Morgan (Collins Pathways) or similar that uses names in alphabetical order
● a name card for each child
● photocopiable page 28 with pictures of occupations, enlarged, cut out into individual cards and laminated (you may need several cards of the most common letters).

Differentiation

Less able
● Provide access to name cards with a phonic representation of the first letter of the child's name, such as a dolphin for Daniel!

More able
● Challenge more able pupils to write their own name sentences.

Shared text-level work
● Show the alphabet book to the children. Talk about the cover (back and front) and read the title and the blurb to the children. Emphasise any alliteration in the words in the title or blurb.
● Now read the book with the children, encouraging them to join in where they can and using a pointer to emphasise one-to-one correspondence of spoken to written word and print conventions (such as that print in English runs from left to right and back to left).
● Explain the link between the letters of the alphabet and objects on each page.
● Tell the class that they will all be contributing to their own version of an alphabet book during the week.

Shared word-/sentence-level work
● Hand out the name cards to the children. Ask them to sit in a circle and explain that they will play a game, called 'Just like me'.
● Model the game. Stand up, hold up your name card, for example, Mrs Jones, and say your name. Invite everyone else with a name beginning with the same letter (as your last name) to say *just like me* and stand and hold up their name card.
● Read the name cards with the class joining in. For example, *James, Jennifer, Joanne, Joseph.*
● Choose other pupils to repeat the activity.

Focused group work
● Show the children the prepared occupation cards. Read some out and try and help the children to distinguish the initial sound such as *butcher, printer.* Explain what each job means.
● Now ask the children to choose a job to match the first letter of their name. Help them to do this.
● Ask the children to tell their partner what job they do (encourage interaction by using talk partners).
● Scribe simple sentences for children, such as '*James is a juggler*' – either on a blank Big Book you have prepared or on the computer (to print out). Make sure that you talk about the use of capital letters for names as you write the sentences.
● Explain that you will use these sentences to make into a class alphabet book, which will be added to during the week.

Independent work
See the activities for the six Areas of Learning on page 22.

Plenary
● Encourage the children to join you on the carpet for the plenary session as you sing a name song.
● Share one or two name sentences with the class. Ask individuals to hold up their sentences for you to read to the class. Then encourage the children to read it with you.

Early Learning Goals
● Linking sounds and letters p60-61.

Stepping Stone
● Hear and say the initial sound in words and know which letters represent some of the sounds.

NLS
T1: To recognise that words can be written down to be read again for a wide range of purposes; to track the text in the right order.
S4: To use a capital letter for the start of own name.
W8: To read and write own name and explore other words related to the spelling of own name.

What you need
● An alphabet book
● a name card for each child
● examples of alliterative name sentences such as those on photocopiable page 29 (written in large script or using a 48-point font on a computer)
● the book you began making on Day 1 (see page 23)
● *Yes* and *No* cards placed in opposite corners of the classroom
● A4-size upper-case letters pegged on to a washing line alphabet around the classroom.

Differentiation

More able
● Encourage more able children to 'have a go' at their own sentences.

Alphabetical jobs

Shared text-level work
● Remind the children of the alphabet book they looked at yesterday and the sentences that were written by some of the children.
● Focus on the alphabetical order of the book and relate it to an alphabet frieze if you have one in the classroom.
● Now look at the sentences written on Day 1 (see p23). Show the children the book that you have started to make together and explain that these sentences need to be put in alphabetical order on the correct pages of the book. Choose different children to help you put them in the right places.
● Now share some of the sentences you have written, read them to the children and then ask a child to point as the whole class reads them. (This will give you a valuable opportunity to assess the child's understanding of concepts of print, such as one-to-one correspondence of spoken to written words and directionality of print.)
● Ask different children to come and underline the words that begin with the same sound and then ask the whole class to join in by reading and emphasising the sounds as they read.
● If time allows, match your sentences to the correct pages in the class alphabet book, although do not stick them in at this stage as the book will just refer to children in the class. (You could add them later if you have any gaps to fill.)

Shared word level work
● Play the 'Yes/No' game for words beginning with the specific sound you are teaching (this game is outlined on page 17).

Focused group work
● Continue as the previous day, asking different children to work with you to write alliterative name sentences.

Independent work
● See the activities for the six Areas of Learning on page 22.

Plenary
● Play 'Guess whose name?' to refer to the sentences that the children have heard. For example, say *I am a name beginning with the letter C* (hold up the corresponding letter*) and the sound* /c/ (say the phoneme) *and I am a carpenter* (Catherine the carpenter). If the sentence refers to a child in the class, ask them to stand up, holding their name card. Then ask the child to peg his or her name card to the matching letter on the washing-line alphabet that is strung around the classroom (see 'What you need').
● Finish by choosing one or two completed name collages and asking the children to help you match them to the correct positions on the washing-line alphabet.
● Use the examples on page 29 a a starting point for any children who are finding it difficult to think of appropriate words.

Saying silly sentences

Objectives

Early Learning Goals
● Linking sounds and letters p60-61.
● Writing p64-65.

Stepping Stones
● Hear and say the initial sound in words and know which letters represent some of the sounds.
● Use writing as a means of recording and communicating.

NLS
T11: To apply knowledge of letter/sound correspondences in helping the teacher to scribe, and re-reading what the class has written.
S4: To use a capital letter for the start of own name.
W8: To read and write own name and explore other words related to the spelling of own name.

What you need
● An alphabet book
● a name card for each child
● the laminated cards from Day 1 (see page 23)
● the class home-made alphabet book (work in progress)
● examples of alliterative name sentences
● flipchart
● an enlarged extract of your own text (or text saved on the computer and shown with an interactive whiteboard)
● alphabet frieze
● the alphabet chant on on photocopiable page 29.

Differentiation
Less able
● Support less able children by suggesting a range of words beginning with the same phoneme as their name.

Shared text-level work
● Begin by referring to the alliterative name sentences read the previous day and re-read one or two together.
● Scribe some further alliterative sentences. Ask the children to suggest names from the class or other common names and occupations and descriptions to go with them, such as *Thomas is a train driver who travels tremendously fast.* Use the laminated occupation cards (see photocopiable page 28 for inspiration.
● As you scribe, make one or two deliberate mistakes for the children to spot (such as forgetting to use a capital letter or a full stop). Also, ask the children to help you spell words using the phonemes/graphemes they know.
● Read each sentence with the children and ask a child to underline the repeated letter in the alliterative phrase.

Shared word-/sentence-level work
● Play a 'Spot the capitals' game using an extract of text which includes some children's names (preferably a short extract you have written with names from children in the class). Ensure that the extract is large enough for the class to see.
● Read the text with the class, using a pointer. Every time you come to a word with a capital letter, the children should shout 'capital letter'! If you have an interactive whiteboard, this is particularly effective if you reveal one word or line at a time.

Focused group work
● Continue as the previous day asking different children to work with you.
● Read previous examples to the children and then encourage them to think of their own sentences which either you could scribe or they could try to write on their own.

Independent work
See the activities for the six Areas of Learning on page 22.

Plenary
● Introduce an alphabet chant to the class (such as the one on photocopiable page 29, or any other you choose). Link the chant to the alphabet frieze in the classroom and any other alphabet songs that you know. As you say the chant, invite individuals to point to the relevant letters and pictures on the alphabet frieze, using a long pointer.
● Now read the chant again and explain that you need to think of some actions to match the words. Take plenty of suggestions and ask the class to help choose one, (for example, the children may choose to point upwards to signify the 'astronaut who ascends into the sky').
● Now say the chant together and encourage the children to join in with the corresponding actions, providing a model for them to copy! This can then form part of a regular class activity.

UNIT 2 DAY 4 ▫ Alphabet names

Picture captions

Objectives

Early Learning Goals
● Linking sounds and letters p60-61.
● Writing p64-65.

Stepping Stones
● Hear and say the initial sound in words and know which letters represent some of the sounds.
● Use writing as a means of recording and communicating.

NLS
T12: Through guided and independent writing: to write sentences to match pictures or sequences of pictures.
W14: To write letters using the correct sequence of movements.

What you need

● A name card for each child
● the class home-made alphabet book (work in progress)
● examples of alliterative name sentences
● digital photos taken and printed out, or available to show on an interactive whiteboard
● individual whiteboards and pens for each child
● the role-play area set up as a school (see Unit 1, page 13).

Differentiation

Less able
● Provide access to the 'Alphabet jobs' cards to support children when matching names to occupations.

More able
● Encourage the children to write their alliterative name sentences independently.

Shared text-level work

● Show the children some photographs that have been taken of them in dressing-up clothes (see 'Choose a job' on page 22).
● Now explain that you are going to do some writing together to match the photographs.
● Show the children one of the photographs. Ensure that everyone knows who it is and then ask for suggestions of what to write. Stress that they should turn to their talk partner and help each other to say a sentence.
● Now take one or two suggestions and emphasise any examples of alliteration, such as *Peter is a policeman*, if appropriate.
● Write the sentence underneath the photograph. Together, find the appropriate page in the class alphabet book and fix the photograph and sentence in place.
● As you scribe the words of the sentences for the children, ensure that they are listening and encourage them to help you to sound out the words as you write.
● Read the sentences together.

Shared word-/sentence-level work

● Practise letter formation of the specific letter sounds that you are currently working on. Draw each letter in the air and then ask the children to write with their fingers on each other's backs.
● Give every child a whiteboard and pen and ask them to listen to your cues as they practise writing specific letters. Give your cues slowly so that the children can write the letters carefully.
● Now let the children continue the activity in pairs. Ask them to watch and help each other as they take turns to write the letter.

Focused group work

● Continue as the previous day, working with different children.
● Read through the book so far and comment on the photographs and sentences. Do some letter pages have more than one sentence?

Independent work

See the activities for the six Areas of Learning on page 22.

Plenary

● Talk about the role-play area together (a school within a school). Tell the children that you are going to choose someone who you have noticed has made a really good effort to be the teacher.
● Give the child your seat and explain that he or she is in the 'hot seat' and will be the teacher for a while.
● Invite the children to ask lots of questions about what rules are needed in the 'school'.
● Ask the children to work in pairs to decide on suitable questions. Provide support to ensure that all the children have a question to ask.
● Remind the class to keep these rules when they are playing schools.

A class book of names

Objectives

Early Learning Goals
● Linking sounds and letters p60-61.

Stepping Stone
● Hear and say the initial sound in words and know which letters represent some of the sounds.

NLS
T11: To apply knowledge of letter/sound correspondences in helping the teacher to scribe, and re-reading what the class has written.
S4: To use a capital letter for the start of own name.
W5: To read on sight a range of familiar words.

What you need

● A name card for each child
● examples of alliterative name sentences
● class alphabet book (see page 23) with added back cover blurb
● examples of alliterative sentences in large print (for 'unused' letters) with capital letters and full stops omitted
● the alphabet chant (photocopiable page 29).

Differentiation

Less able
● Support less able children to read unfamiliar words by emphasising use of initial letter cues.

Shared text-level work

● Share the almost complete class alphabet book with the children, praising the children for all their hard work. Comment on how it contains alliterative sentences that relate to the children's names.
● Say the title together and the blurb you have prepared (such as: *Read how everyone in this book has a job beginning with the same letter as their name.*)
● Read the book together, using a pointer and encouraging all the children to join in.
● Ask different children to come and read the sentence that relates to their name and support them where necessary. Do as many sentences in this way as time permits.
● Tell the children that you will leave the book out for everyone to share later.

Shared word-/sentence-level work

● Explain that you have written some further sentences for the book. Tell the children that these sentences are about letters for which no one in the class has a corresponding name.
● Display the sentences and read them to the children. Ask them if there is anything missing.
● Invite them to discuss the sentences with their talk partners. Can the children decide together what the mistakes are? Tell them that they have to find three mistakes, for example.
● Choose partners to help you correct the sentences (if you have an interactive whiteboard, it would be good to correct them by highlighting the mistakes first and then correcting them).
● Now write one or two sentences correctly and ask the children to help you put them in the correct place in the class alphabet book.

Focused group work

● Continue as the previous day asking different children to work with you.
● Ask the children to help you to check that the book is complete.

Independent work

See the activities for the six Areas of Learning on page 22.

Plenary

● Explain that you have muddled up all the name cards and that they need to be in alphabetical order.
● Give each pupil their name card and ask them to stand underneath the corresponding letter on the alphabet washing line.
● Finish by saying the alphabet chant from photocopiable page 29 with each child holding up their name card when it gets to their place in the alphabet.
● Collect up the name cards from the children and emphasise alphabetical order as you do so.

Alphabet jobs

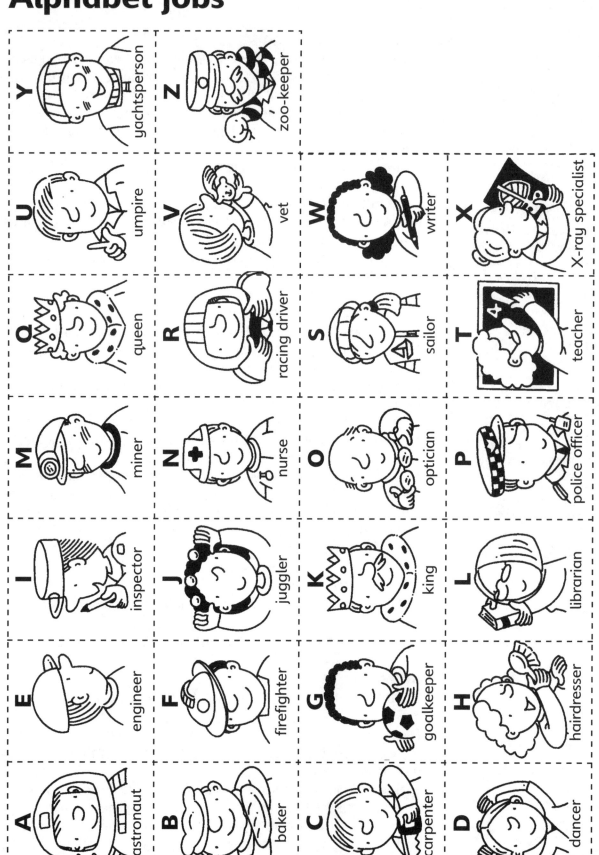

Y yachtsperson

Z zoo-keeper

U umpire

V vet

W writer

X X-ray specialist

Q queen

R racing driver

S sailor

T teacher

M miner

N nurse

O optician

P police officer

I inspector

J juggler

K king

L librarian

E engineer

F firefighter

G goalkeeper

H hairdresser

A astronaut

B baker

C carpenter

D dancer

Alphabet Chant

A is for astronaut who ascends into the sky

B is for baker who bakes a beautiful pie

C is for carpenter who carefully carves and chops

D is for dancer who dances with leaps and hops

E is for engineer whose engine echoes and shouts

F is for firefighter who fights to put the fire out

G is for goalkeeper who grips the golden ball

H is for hairdresser who heaps hair up so tall

I is for inspector who inspects tickets all

J is for juggler who juggles jumping balls

K is for king whose crooked crown falls

L is for librarian who looks at lots of books

M is for miner who mines with lamps and hooks

N is for nurse who tends to all our needs

O is for optician who observes all we read

P is for police officer who paces up the streets

Q is for queen who queues for all the seats

R is for racing driver who races round each bend

S is for sailor who sails the boat he lends

T is for teacher who talks to every single child

U is for umpire who utters the score like wild

V is for vet who treats various beasts

W is for writer who writes about great feasts

X is for x-ray specialist who keeps things in a jar

Y is for yachtsperson who sails a yacht so far

And Z is for zoo-keeper zooming up to Mars

Which one do you want to be, go on reach for the stars!

Nursery-rhyme characters

This unit is based on nursery rhymes and comprises ten days' literacy activities which support the National Literacy Strategy (Later Foundation Stage, Medium-term plan) focus on *Nursery rhymes*. It will help develop phonological awareness through rhyme and provide a focus for writing through stories based on familiar rhymes, character sketches and letter writing. Linked activities are provided for all the six Areas of Learning with a strong emphasis on developing speaking and listening skills through role-play; and forming good relationships in Personal, social and emotional development. The activities build towards Year 1 Term 1, Objective 5 of the *Speaking, Listening, Learning* guidance: to retell stories, ordering events using story language.

WEEK 1

Day	Shared text-level work	Shared word-/ sentence-level work	Focused group work	Independent work	Plenary
1 Reading rhymes	Reading different nursery rhymes.	Rhyming words – play the 'Pebble game'.	Completing rhymes.	**PSED:** Re-enacting nursery rhymes.	A performance of traditional rhymes.
2 Nursery-rhyme problems	Nursery-rhyme stories (1).	Missing capital letters and full stops.	Writing own stories.	**CLL:** Listening to rhymes. **MD**: Nursery-rhyme patterns.	Sharing stories.
3 More nursery-rhyme problems	Nursery-rhyme stories (2).	Match the words.	Writing own stories.	**KUW:** Making a sock puppet.	Hot-seating: nursery-rhyme characters.
4 Nursery-rhyme characters	Nursery-rhyme characters.	Extending vocabulary – word wall.	Writing own stories.	**PD:** Put it on – dressing up.	'Who am I?' Guess the character.
5 Wanted characters	A poster of 'Wanted characters'.	'Jump in the hoop' phonic game.	Writing own stories.	**CD:** Creating Nursery-rhyme land – painting characters.	Arrest that character! Role-play.

UNIT 3

WEEK 2

Day	Shared text-level work	Shared word-/ sentence-level work	Focused group work	Independent work	Plenary
6 Jack's journey	A journey through Nursery-rhyme land	Extending vocabulary – world wall.	Teacher in role-play area – re-enacting the journey.	**PSED:** Sharing. **CLL:** Write a letter.	Play memory game: 'I went to Nursery-rhyme land and I saw …'.
7 Jack's letter	Writing letters.	'Bingo' – high frequency words.	Guided writing of letters.	**MD:** 2–D shapes.	Reading letters from *The Jolly Pocket Postman*.
8 Jack's postcard	Writing postcards.	Letter formation.	Guided writing of postcards.	**KUW:** Map of a journey.	Sharing postcards.
9 Invitations	Writing invitations.	Match the name to the character.	Guided writing of invitations.	**PD:** Taking a journey using balancing and climbing equipment.	Playing 'Guess who?' is at the party.
10 Different rhymes	Alternative rhymes.	Out of order – re-ordering sentences.	Writing alternative rhymes.	**CD:** Creating a mural for nursery-rhyme land.	A party in Nursery-rhyme land.

WEEKS 1 AND 2

Key assessment opportunities
When working with children look closely for:
- ability to match graphemes to phonemes
- ability to generate rhyming words
- ability to read high frequency words
- beginning attempts at forming recognisable letters
- ability to write for a real purpose.

Record appropriately and ensure that this informs future planning.

Personal, social and emotional development

Act it out!
Early Learning Goal
Form good relationships with adults and peers.
What you need
Pictures of nursery-rhyme characters and nursery-rhyme books; assorted props associated with the characters, such as a crook and toy lamb, spider, bowl, large cushion.
What to do
● Arrange the props in your role-play area with the associated rhymes clearly displayed.
● Encourage the children to re-enact the rhymes using props.
● Emphasise the importance of sharing resources and taking turns. Praise the children accordingly.

Physical development

Put it on!
Early Learning Goal
Use a range of small and large equipment.
What you need
A range of dressing-up clothes, if possible including some that resemble the clothes characters wear in different nursery rhymes (such as dresses for Polly Flinders, a hat and coat for Doctor Foster and so on).
What to do
● Encourage the children to try and manage independently to dress up as different nursery-rhyme characters.
● Ask them to act out the rhymes, if possible sharing the props with the children in the 'Act it out' area (see PSED, above).

Communication, language and literacy

Listen to the rhyme
Early Learning Goal
Listen with enjoyment, and respond to stories, songs and other music, rhymes and poems and make up their own stories, songs, rhymes and poems.
What you need
Tape recorder; headphones; nursery-rhyme tapes; nursery-rhyme books.
What to do
● In a quiet area of the classroom, show the children how to work the tape recorder independently to listen to the various nursery-rhyme tapes.
● Provide copies of the rhymes for the children to match to the taped version.

Mathematical development

Make a pattern
Early Learning Goal
Talk about, recognise and recreate simple patterns.
What you need
Photocopied Humpty outline shapes (see below), or alternatively a set of 'Matheggs' (available from Asco Educational Supplies) and a photocopy of blank Matheggs per child.
What to do
● Ask the children to create different Humpties, varying the colours of waistcoats, shorts, shoes and hair. Model the activity first for the children.
● Encourage more able children to create a repeating pattern.

Creative development

Paint a character
Early Learning Goal
Explore colour, texture, shape, form and space in two or three dimensions.
What you need
Painting equipment; easels; large cartridge paper; pictures of nursery-rhyme characters.
What to do
● Ask the children to paint large versions of nursery rhyme characters, particularly Little Jack Horner, Humpty Dumpty, Little Bo Peep and Jack-a-Dandy, using your pictures as models.
● When outlining the task emphasise the use of bright colours and the shape of each character.
● Explain that the children's paintings will be used to create a 'Nursery-rhyme Land' mural.

Knowledge and understanding of the world

Make a puppet
Early Learning Goal
Select the tools and techniques they need to shape, assemble and join materials they are using.
What you need
A range of socks; gummed paper; card; felt; glue; scissors.
What to do
● Ask an adult to model making a sock puppet, creating eyes and a mouth using card, paper or felt glued to the sock.
● Encourage the children to design and make their own puppets and have fun playing with them.

Personal, social and emotional development

Take a turn
Early Learning Goal
Work as part of a group or class, taking turns and sharing fairly.
What you need
Pictures of nursery-rhyme characters; nursery-rhyme books; assorted props to support specific nursery rhymes in role-play area with associated rhymes clearly displayed as per previous week (see page 32); alphabet strips.
What to do
● Continue to extend role-play as per week 1 in this unit, see 'Act it out!' (page 32).
● Encourage interaction and acting out 'nursery-rhyme problems' from week 1 of this unit.

Mathematical development

Shape characters
Early Learning Goal
Use language such as 'circle' or 'bigger' to describe the shape and size of solids and flat shapes.
What you need
A range of 2-D shapes such as pattern blocks; prepared illustration of a shape character using 2D shapes (resembling a nursery-rhyme character such as Humpty Dumpty); paper; pencils/crayons.
What to do
● Show the children your shape character and ask the children to make one of their own using shapes such as pattern blocks (or similar).
● Encourage the use of a range of mathematical vocabulary with help from an adult if available.
● Provide paper for the children to draw round their shapes and then ask them to give their character a name.

Physical development

Over and under
Early Learning Goal
Travel around, under, over and through balancing and climbing equipment.
What you need
In the outdoor area set up mats, benches and boxes to create 'Nursery-rhyme Land' (see photocopiable page 47 for inspiration).
What to do
● Ask the children to take a journey around, under and over the various objects.

Creative development

Paint the scenery
Early Learning Goal
Explore colour, texture, shape, form and space in two or three dimensions.
What you need
Painting equipment; easels; sheets of sugar paper; a prepared outline of 'Nursery-rhyme Land' (see photocopiable page 47 for ideas – to include hills, roads, houses and so on).
What you do
● Ask the children to help you to paint the scenery for Nursery-rhyme Land.
● Talk about the possible features of the land (some of which you have pre-drawn) and ask the children to help you with more ideas.

Communication, language and literacy

Write a letter
Early Learning Goal
Attempt writing for different purposes, using features of different forms.
What you need
Range of letter-writing materials in writing area; prepared writing frames for letters with: *Dear...* and space to write, followed by: *Love from...*
What to do
● Encourage the children to experiment with writing letters to nursery-rhyme characters.
● Provide alphabet strips and display a range of useful words to help.

Knowledge and understanding of the world

Draw the journey
Early Learning Goal
Observe, find out about and identify features in the place they live and the natural world.
What you need
Large sheets of sugar paper stuck to a table; felt-tipped pens; crayons; small-world models of houses, cars and so on; photocopiable page 47.
What you do
● Encourage the children to draw roads and features on the paper and place the small-world models in appropriate places.
● Read the story on photocopiable page 47 and encourage the children to make links to the journey of the nursery-rhyme characters, imagining Jack's journey.

Reading rhymes

Objectives

Early Learning Goals
● Linking sounds and letters p60-61.

Stepping Stone
● Continue a rhyming string.

NLS
T6: To re-read frequently a variety of familiar texts.
T10: To re-read and recite stories and rhymes with predictable and repeated patterns and experiment with similar rhyming patterns.
W1: To understand and be able to rhyme through recognising, exploring and working with rhyming patterns, extending these patterns by analogy.

What you need

● Nursery rhymes from photocopiable page 44, photocopied and enlarged to A3 size
● a range of nursery books and posters
● *Progression in Phonics* materials (DfES)
● a pebble
● an enlarged copy of photocopiable page 44 with the rhyming words blanked out
● magnetic board and letters
● paper and pen.

Differentiation

Less able
● Provide some rhyming pictures to support the children (such as *moon, spoon*).

More able
● Challenge more able children to generate rhyming words by saying: *How many words can you think of that rhyme with cat?*

Shared text-level work

● Begin by showing the children pictures of nursery-rhyme characters (from nursery-rhyme books). Do they recognise any of the characters?
● Reinforce familiarity with the characters by playing a game where you describe a character for the children to guess. For example, say: *I am thinking of someone who is very round and shaped liked an egg and who liked to climb walls, but kept falling off.*
● Now read the rhymes on the enlarged version of photocopiable page 44 with the children. Use a pointer and encourage them to join in, especially by pausing before a rhyming word for the children to supply the appropriate word.
● Talk about the different rhymes and whether they are all familiar to the children. Discuss some of the unfamiliar words, such as *cinders,* and ensure that the children understand the meaning.
● Re-read the rhymes, encouraging plenty of participation.

Shared word-level work

● Play the 'Pebble game' from *Progression in Phonics* (DfES) page 18. It is a rhyming circle game.
● Read some nursery rhymes and ask the children to pick out any rhyming pairs that they notice (such as *wall* and *fall* in 'Humpty Dumpty').

Focused group work

● Work with a small group of children and show them the nursery rhymes you have prepared with the rhyming words missing.
● Read the rhymes together and pause while the children talk about words that might fit in the space.
● Encourage plenty of possibilities of different rhymes and either write these as a separate list, or use magnetic letters to make the words.
● Write in the missing words at the children's suggestion, asking them to help you with initial letters for the words.
● Re-read the rhymes together.

Independent work

● See the activities for the six Areas of Learning on page 32.

Plenary

● With the children gathered together on the carpet, invite individuals to help you act out one or two rhymes.
● Ask the children to mime the different characters, using props from the role-play area as you and the rest of the children recite the rhyme.
● Finish by singing a song such as 'Polly Put the Kettle On':

> Polly put the kettle on
> Polly put the kettle on
> Polly put the kettle on
> We'll all have tea.

Nursery-rhyme problems

Objectives

Early Learning Goals
● Thinking p56–59.
● Writing p64–65.

Stepping Stones
● Use talk to connect ideas, explain what is happening and anticipate what might happen next.
● Use writing as a means of recording and communicating.

NLS
T10: To re-read and recite stories and rhymes with predictable and repeated patterns and experiment with similar rhyming patterns.
S4: To use a capital letter for the start of own name.

What you need
● 'Little Jack Horner' and 'Dr. Foster' nursery-rhyme stories from photocopiable page 45, copied and enlarged on to A3 paper
● nursery-rhyme books or posters
● an enlarged version of a nursery rhyme from photocopiable page 44 with capital letters and full stops missing
● an easel
● an alphabet frieze showing upper and lower case letters
● interactive whiteboard or flipchart.

Differentiation

Less able
● Provide adult support to help children to make predictions of nursery-rhyme problems and to link events.

More able
● Challenge the children to describe the problem in each nursery rhyme.

Shared text level work
● Re-read the rhymes 'Little Jack Horner' and 'Doctor Foster' from photocopiable page 44. Talk about the characters in the rhymes.
● Talk about the problems that these characters had. Why do they think Jack was sitting in a corner? How did Dr Foster end up in a puddle?
● Now read the stories found on photocopiable page 45.
● Stop after each story and talk about the cause of the problem (such as Jack being very shy and afraid to join in with things). Have the children ever felt shy like Jack?
● Talk about Doctor Foster getting lost. Have the children ever been lost?

Shared sentence level work
● Explain that you have a nursery rhyme to share but someone has forgotten to put in the capital letters and full stops.
● Look at the alphabet frieze together and talk about the upper- and lower-case versions of each letter. Talk about when you use capital letters.
● Place the rhyme on an easel and read it out line by line, stopping to invite individual children to come and put in the missing capital letters and full stops.
● Invite the children to help you identify all the names and underline them. Ask them to make sure that each name starts with a capital letter.

Focused group work
● Work with a small group of children to write another 'nursery-rhyme problem' together. Take another familiar rhyme, such as 'Little Bo Peep', and read it together.
● Ask the children to talk with a partner about what Little Bo Peep's problem was (she kept losing her sheep). Can they think of a reason why this was – perhaps people walking through the countryside kept leaving the gates open.
● Share the suggestions and, as a group, choose one to write about.
● Write the story with the children's help. A computer and interactive whiteboard would be an ideal vehicle for sharing the story later with the class. Alternatively write on a flipchart.

Independent work
● See the activities for the six Areas of Learning on page 32.

Plenary
● In a plenary session, share the 'nursery-rhyme problem' created in group work with the rest of the class. Talk about the problem and what caused it as well as the other elements of the story.
● If time allows, quickly brainstorm another example, such as why Mary Mary is so contrary.
● Ask the children to follow these up in the role-play area later in the week and to think about how they could help these characters.

More nursery rhyme problems

Objectives

Early Learning Goals
● Communication p54–55.
● Thinking p56–59.
● Writing p64–65.

Stepping Stones
● Use a widening range of words to express or elaborate ideas.
● Use talk to connect ideas, explain what is happening and anticipate what might happen next.
● Use writing as a means of recording and communicating.

NLS
T10: To re-read and recite stories and rhymes with predictable and repeated patterns and experiment with similar rhyming patterns.
W6: To read on sight the 45 high frequency words to be taught by the end of the year.

What you need
● The rhymes on photocopiable page 44
● an enlarged version of photocopiable page 45
● an enlarged version of photocopiable page 46
● a selection of nursery-rhyme books or posters
● a range of high-frequency words printed on to cards.

Differentiation

Less able
● Help the children to describe problems in the stories by prompting with a range of additional questions.

More able
● Encourage the children to read nursery rhymes independently and talk about the problems in each one.

Shared text-level work
● Discuss the 'nursery-rhyme problems' read the previous day (see photocopiable page 45).
● Explain that you are going to read some more problems. Begin by reciting together the rhymes 'Jack Sprat' and 'Little Polly Flinders'.
● Talk about the problems that they had – why was Polly Flinders sitting in the cinders? Why were Jack Sprat and his wife so fussy about what they ate?
● Read the two stories from photocopiable page 46 to the children, using plenty of expression and pointing to pictures of the characters that you have from various books or posters.
● Talk about the problems and what caused them and ask the children if they have foods they do not like and what they are.
● Talk about Polly being naughty and ensure that you discuss safety and staying away from fire.

Shared word level work
● Display the nursery rhymes from photocopiable page 44, and hand out the high frequency word cards to individuals (choose words that can be found in the rhymes, such as *in, the, and, said, boy, of, up, to, went*).
● Now invite the class to read the rhymes with you, using a pointer. Ask the children with word cards to put up their hands when they have a corresponding word as it is read out. Repeat with different children if time permits.

Focused group work
● Continue as the previous day (page 35) writing stories of nursery rhymes (possible rhymes include 'Ladybird, Ladybird, Fly Away Home' – why was her house on fire? Or 'Hey Diddle Diddle, the Cat and the Fiddle' – why did the cow jump so high?). Ensure that you provide plenty of time to discuss the rhymes.
● Write the stories together, ready to share with the rest of the class.

Independent work
● See the activities for the six Areas of Learning on page 32.

Plenary
● Share the stories written in the focused group work and discuss the problems and causes.
● Now explain that you are going to be one of the characters in a story that you have read. Choose which character, such as Little Jack Horner and remind the class of the problems and what sort of person Jack was.
● Challenge the children to think of a good question to ask Jack (sharing ideas with a partner first). Provide time for discussion and prompt if necessary.
● Ask for different questions and answer them in role (ensuring that the children understand this).

Nursery-rhyme folk

Objectives

Early Learning Goals
- Communication p54-55.
- Thinking p56-59.
- Writing p64-65.

Stepping Stones
- Use a widening range of words to express or elaborate ideas.
- Use talk to connect ideas, explain what is happening and anticipate what might happen next.
- Use writing as a means of recording and communicating.

NLS
T6: To re-read frequently a variety of familiar texts.
T10: To re-read and recite stories and rhymes with predictable and repeated patterns and experiment with similar rhyming patterns.
W10: Pupils should be taught new words from their reading and shared experiences.

What you need
- Nursery rhymes from photocopiable page 44, photocopied and enlarged to A3 size
- nursery-rhyme books and posters
- words from the nursery rhymes, printed on card in a large font size (such *as corner, pie, boy, rain, mother, daughter, clothes, fat, wife, clean*)
- a flipchart.

Differentiation

Less able
- Encourage the children to suggest phonetically plausible spellings of nursery-rhyme characters.

More able
- During shared work encourage the children to describe different nursery-rhyme characters orally and in independent work to write words to fit.

Shared text level work
- Share a nursery-rhyme book with the children (preferably a Big Book version).
- Read some rhymes together using a pointer, pausing for the children to fill in the rhyming words.
- Now go through the book and write down the names of the main characters in each rhyme on the flipchart (such as the Grand Old Duke of York, the old woman who lived in a shoe and so on).
- Explain that you want to think about what sort of people the characters were. Ask the children for suggestions, ensuring that they have time to talk to a partner first.
- Brainstorm together and write the words to describe the characters on the flipchart.
- Encourage the children to help you to spell the words using their knowledge of initial letter sounds and so on.

Shared word-level work
- Build on the children's developing vocabulary by explaining that you have a collection of words related to the rhymes that you would like to help them to read.
- Show the children the words one at a time and talk about how to read them – initial letter cues, graphic cues (parts of words) and so on.
- As the children read the words with you, put them on display as a word wall or in a pocket chart.
- Re-read the words and put them into meaningful sentences, such as 'The shop is round the *corner.*' Do this orally and then write it on sentence strip card (with the specific word highlighted).
- Display a few sentences containing the words for later re-reading and spend a few minutes regularly reading the words.

Focused group work
- Continue as on previous days (see pages 35 and 36) to write 'nursery-rhyme problems', choosing a different rhyme to work with each time.
- Emphasise the use of complete sentences and model orally rehearsing sentences before you write them.

Independent work
- See the activities for the six Areas of Learning on page 32.

Plenary
- Share the stories you have written in focused group work.
- The children will now be familiar with many characters. Use this knowledge to play a game of 'Who am I?'
- Choose a nursery-rhyme character and then give the class clues to help them guess who it is.
- Encourage confident children to challenge the rest of the class to guess which character they are describing.

Wanted characters

Objectives

Early Learning Goals
● Communication p54-55.
● Writing p64-65.
● Linking sounds and letters p60-61.

Stepping Stones
● Use language for an increasing range of purposes.
● Use writing as a means of recording and communicating.
● Hear and say the initial sound in words and know which letters represent some of the sounds.

NLS
T14: To use experience of stories, poems and simple recounts as a basis for independent writing, eg re-telling, substitution, extension, and through shared composition with adults.
W2: Hearing and identifying initial sounds in words.

What you need
● A range of posters and pictures of nursery-rhyme characters (including some of the children's paintings)
● the 'Jump in the hoop' game from *Progression in Phonics*, page 21 (DfES).
● two hoops
● a range of objects for each child corresponding to the two chosen initial-letter sounds.

Differentiation

Less able
● Provide adult support to help the children to describe a character orally.

More able
● Encourage the children to use a range of descriptive words.

Shared text-level work
● Discuss with the children a range of nursery-rhyme characters, especially those you have come across who are 'naughty'.
● Explain that you are going to pretend that these people are wanted by the police and that you are going to create a poster together.
● Select one character (such as the Knave of Hearts) and create a poster with the children. Include a box for a picture and a short description of the character, plus why he or she is wanted.
● Before you begin, encourage the children to practise their description skills by first describing a friend to their talk partner.
● Now ask the children to look carefully at a picture of the chosen character and talk to their partner about distinguishing features. Model this first, saying for example: *The Knave of Hearts looks young, his hair is dark and his eyes are blue and he is wearing a suit with hearts on.* Next, ask for the children's contributions to write the description under the box.
● Finish by asking the children to provide the text for what the character is 'wanted' for.

WANTED
For stealing jam tarts on a summer's day

Man aged about 20, dark hair and blue eyes, dressed in a red and white suit with hearts pattern.

Shared word-level work
● Play the 'Jump in the hoop' game' from *Progression in Phonics* (page 21).
● Choose two letter sounds and think of some props that are linked to nursery rhymes. For example, duck, dish, dolly and diamond; teddy bear, teapot and tart. Write the letters onto large pieces of card and ask the children to sort the selection of objects into piles next to the appropriate letters.

Focused group work
● Continue as on previous days (pages 35-37), writing 'nursery-rhyme problems'.
● Continue the story of the poster you have just created and discuss, for example, why the Knave of Hearts stole the tarts.

Independent work
● See the activities for the six Areas of Learning on page 32.

Plenary
● Choose some children to play the parts of different characters using the dressing-up clothes and props in the role-play area.
● Ask one or two other children to be police officers who are looking for people who have done 'naughty' things.
● Ask the children to question all the characters to see what they know.
● Have fun with the children in role and finally decide on a character to be arrested!

Jack's journey

Objectives

Early Learning Goals
● Reading p62–63.

Stepping Stone
● Begin to recognise some familiar words.

NLS
T6: To re-read frequently a variety of familiar texts.
W11: To make collections of personal interest or significant words and words linked to particular topics.

What you need

● Photocopiable page 47 'The journey through nursery-rhyme land' copied and enlarged to A3 size
● words from the story (*journey, wall, help, sheep, woman, man, town, cake, friend, home*) written onto card and laminated
● role-play area as for Week 1 PSED (see page 32) which will be developed during the week in creative development work (see page 33)
● Labels with the names of characters from the story (*Jack Horner, Humpty Dumpty, little boy who lives down the lane, Old Mother Hubbard, Peter, Peter Pumpkin-eater, Little Bo Peep and Jack-a-dandy*).
● The pictures of nursery-rhyme characters created in week 1 by the children (see CD on page 32).
● a flipchart.

Differentiation

Less able
● Provide support to match the names of the characters to the correct nursery rhyme.

More able
● Encourage the children to use a range of reading strategies to read unfamiliar words.

Shared text-level work

● Remind the children of the story that you shared about Little Jack Horner (see photocopiable page 45).
● Ask them how Jack changed during the story. Invite them to discuss this with their talk partners.
● Now read the story on photocopiable page 47.
● Ask the children if they can recall who Jack met on his journey.
● Re-read the story with the children joining in as much as possible, as you point to the text.
● Stop at various points and ask questions to see if the children realise who all the characters are.
● Make a list of the characters on the flipchart. Later, read the original rhymes relating to the characters.

Shared word-level work

● Continue to build on the children's vocabulary from the previous week and read the word wall you produced together on Day 4 (see page 37).
● Now introduce some new words from the story, one at a time, and talk about how to read them (initial-letter cues, graphic cues and so on).
● As the children read the words with you, add them to the word wall.
● Ask the children to help you put the words into meaningful sentences, such as *Jack went on a long journey*. Do this orally and then write it on sentence strip card (with the specific word highlighted).
● Display a few sentences containing the words for later re-reading and spend a few minutes regularly reading the words.

Focused group work

● Work with the children in the role-play area used in Week 1(see PSED, page 32). Remind the children about the story and list the places that Jack went to and the characters that he saw.
● Now explain that the children will all take on different roles from the story. Give out labels to them.
● Re-enact the journey encouraging plenty of improvisation and dialogue. If time allows, swap roles around.

Independent work

● See the activities for the six Areas of Learning on page 33.

Plenary

● With the children sat in a circle, explain that you are going to play a memory game. Tell the children that each time you begin by saying *I went to nursery-rhyme land and I saw…* (going on to say one of the nursery-rhyme characters, for example, *Humpty Dumpty*). The next child then repeats the first phrase and character and then adds one.
● As you go round the circle, the children need to try and remember as many of the previous characters as possible and add one.
● Have fun seeing how many things each child can remember.

Jack's letter

Objectives

Early Learning Goals
- Thinking p56-59.
- Writing p64-65.

Stepping Stones
- Begin to use talk to pretend imaginary situations.
- Use writing as a means of recording and communicating.

NLS
T11: Through shared writing: b) to understand that writing remains constant.
W6: To read on sight the 45 high frequency words to be taught by the end of YR.

What you need
- A flipchart and paper
- 'Bingo' game cards from Unit 1, 'Playing schools' (on photocopiable page 19
- high-frequency words on card
- examples of letters (possibly one you have written on your school letterhead with simple text)
- letter-writing frames with an address and the word *Dear...* with a space for writing and *Love from...* indicated
- the book, *The Jolly Pocket Postman* by Janet and Allan Ahlberg (Viking Children's Books).

Differentiation

Less able
- Provide adult support for playing the 'Bingo' game.

More able
- Encourage the children to have a go at writing letters as nursery-rhyme characters in focused group work.

Shared text-level work
- Show the children one or two letters and talk about letters generally.
- Look at the layout of the letter and explain that we usually have the address and date in the top right-hand corner. Letters usually start with the word *Dear...* and finish with endings such as *Yours sincerely* or *Love from...*
- Now invite the children to help you write a letter as if it was from Jack to his mum.
- In a shared writing session, write an address, such as *The Cottage, Toy Town, Nursery-rhyme land* and begin with *Dear Mum*. Give the children the opportunity to talk to their partner about what Jack might write. Ask the pairs of children to share their ideas with the class.
- Discuss the most suitable sentence and write it together. Invite the children to suggest suitable letters to match the sounds. Finish with *Love from, Jack.*
- Read the letter through with the children and explain that they will have the chance to write their own letters in the writing corner (see CLL on page 33).

Shared word-level work
- Next, or at a later time in the day, explain you are going to play 'Bingo', with one card for each pair of children.
- Explain that you are going to call out some words. If they have the word that you call out on their card they may cross it out, shouting 'Bingo' when all their words are crossed out.
- Play the game once or twice as time allows.

Focused group work
- Working with a small group of children, look at the letter you have written together.
- Explain that they will be writing letters, either as Jack or another nursery-rhyme character of their choice.
- Help each child to talk through who their letter will be from and to. Discuss what the content will be (for example, Little Bo Peep is writing to the farmer to ask if he has seen her sheep).
- Give out writing frames and pencils and support the children as necessary.

Independent work
- See the activities for the six Areas of Learning on page 33.

Plenary
- Share examples of letters that the children have read.
- If you have a copy, finish by reading *The Jolly Pocket Postman* by Janet and Allan Ahlberg to the children and discuss all the familiar characters in it. Look at examples of the letters.
- Alternatively share some invitations and postcards with the class. Say that you will be writing some postcards tomorrow.

Jack's postcard

Objectives

Early Learning Goals
● Writing p64-65
● Handwriting p66-67.

Stepping Stones
● Use writing as a means of recording and communicating.
● Begin to form recognisable letters.

NLS
T12: Through guided and independent writing: to experiment with writing in a variety of play, exploratory and role-play situations.
W14: To write letters using the correct sequence of movements.

What you need
● Various postcards
● blank postcards (one large size, and a number of small ones)
● individual whiteboards and pens
● pencils
● *The Jolly Pocket Postman* by Janet and Allan Ahlberg (Viking Children's Books) if available.

Shared text-level work
● Remind the children of the letters written the day before (see page 40).
● Now explain that you are going to write a postcard from Jack to his friend Humpty Dumpty.
● Show the children your examples of postcards. Talk about how we do not write so much on a postcard - usually just a short message.
● Together, talk about what Jack might write to Humpty.
● Now write a short message on the large postcard, such as: *I hope you are feeling better. I went on a long journey and made a new friend. Love Jack.*
● Involve the children in the writing process, sometimes making deliberate mistakes for them to spot. Invite some individuals to write a letter or word for you.
● Read the postcard with the children and explain that some of them will be writing postcards with you later. Tell them that you will also be putting some blank postcards in the writing area for them to use.

Shared word-level work
● Give out individual whiteboards and pens to the children and say you are going to do some handwriting practice.
● Reinforce the sounds and letters currently being taught by giving letter-formation cues (for example, for the letter 'a', prompt with: *around, up, down and flick*).
● Ask the children to practise in the air, on other children's backs and then on their whiteboards.
● Look carefully to make sure that the children are starting letters in the correct place and following the correct direction. Ask any additional adults in the classroom to help with this, providing support where necessary.

Focused group work
● Working with a small group of children, look at the postcard you have written together and explain that they will write their own from Jack or another nursery-rhyme character of their choice.
● Help each child to talk through who their postcard will be from and to. Discuss what the content will be (for example, the Pussy cat to the Queen in London, thanking her for a nice time!).
● Give out postcards and pencils and support the children as necessary.

Independent work
● See the activities for the six Areas of Learning on page 33.

Plenary
● Share some of the postcards written and read them together. Discuss who each postcard is from and who it is being sent to. If you have a copy, finish by reading some of the letters and postcards in *The Jolly Pocket Postman* by Janet and Allan Ahlberg (Viking Children's Books).

Differentiation

Less able
● Encourage them to suggest phonetically plausible spellings when writing postcards.

More able
● Encourage the children to write a range of words independently.

Invitations

Objectives

Early Learning Goals
● Writing p64-65.

Stepping Stone
● Ascribe meanings to marks.

NLS
T12: Through guided and independent writing to experiment with writing in a variety of play, exploratory and role-play situations.
W11: To make collections of personal interest or significant words and words linked to particular topics.

What you need
● A home-made party invitation (enlarged and photocopied several times for focused group work)
● nursery-rhyme character names on card
● pictures of the characters put into an envelope.

Shared text-level work
● Refer to the examples of print such as letters, cards and invitations that you have shared with the children.
● Ask the children if they have ever received an invitation. Discuss the inevitable numerous party invitations they will have received.
● Now say that you are going to have a party tomorrow for all the nursery-rhyme characters and that you want to send out invitations.
● Show the children the blank enlarged invitation and talk about what needs to be on it (who it is from and to; where the party will be and what time).
● With the children's help, write an invitation to the class party for the following day. (This could be done earlier in the week if you want to make this a 'grand affair'! You might also like to ask parents to help their children dress up as nursery-rhyme characters for a fancy-dress parade.
● Read the invitation through together.

Shared word-level work
● Explain to the children that you have muddled up some pictures of nursery-rhyme characters and their names and that you need the children's help to match them.
● Give out pictures to different children and ask them to stand at the front of the class holding them.
● Now give out the corresponding character's names to other children. Ask the children with the names to find the correct picture and stand next to the appropriate child at the front.
● Once the names and pictures are matched, read the names with the class and check that they are correctly matched.
● Leave the pictures and names available for children to play with independently.

Focused group work
● Working with a small group of children, look at the invitation modelled earlier.
● Explain that they are going to write some more invitations for the party (to nursery-rhyme characters or to children in another class).
● Give out blank invitations and support the children to write their own.

Independent work
● See the activities for the six Areas of Learning on page 33.

Differentiation

Less able
● Provide rhyming pictures to support children when they are generating rhymes.

More able
● Encourage the children to write their own invitations, providing some key words on the flipchart.

Plenary
● Play a guessing game with the children. Ask them to sit in a circle and take turns to describe a well-known nursery-rhyme character for the others to guess. Model this first yourself (for example, *I am thinking of a very old woman who had lots of children and who lived in a very strange place*).
● Write a list of all the characters suggested in the game and read it together.

Different rhymes

Objectives

Early Learning Goals
● Linking sounds and letters p60-61.

Stepping Stone
● Continue a rhyming string.

NLS
T10: To re-read and recite stories and rhymes with predictable and repeated patterns and experiment with similar rhyming patterns.
W1: To understand and be able to rhyme through recognising, exploring and working with rhyming patterns and extending these patterns by analogy.

What you need
● a range of alternative versions of nursery rhymes on photocopiable page 48, enlarged to A3 size
● a simple rhyming dictionary
● a traditional nursery rhyme cut up into individual lines (such as the one from photocopiable page 44)
● party food (a drink and biscuit or cake for each child, or something more elaborate if you wish)
● party hats
● labels with names of nursery rhyme characters on.

Differentiation

Less able
● Provide rhyming pictures to support less able children generate rhymes.

More able
● Challenge more able children to find a wide range of rhyming words.

Shared text-level work
● Have fun reading some alternative versions of nursery rhymes with the children.
● Talk about how the rhymes are different to the traditional versions.
● Explain that you are going to write an alternative version of 'Little Jack Horner' together.
● Recite the traditional version together and start to write the rhyme on the flipchart.
● Begin by writing *Little Jack Horner sat in a corner*.
● Now change the next line to something like *Eating an Easter egg!*
● Continue with the next line – *He put it on his belly and got covered in jelly*.
● And conclude with a final line, such as *And wiped it all over his leg!*

Shared word-level work
● Explain that you have some lines from a nursery rhyme that need to be put in the right order.
● Give out the lines to different children, reading them as you do so.
● Now ask the children to stand at the front of the class holding their lines. Read the lines from left to right and have fun with them out of order.
● Challenge the children to get themselves into the order of the rhyme.
● Re-read the sequence after each move until it is correct.

Focused group work
● Have fun working with a small group of children to write some alternative versions of different rhymes.
● Start by looking carefully at a conventional rhyme, underlining all the rhyming words. Explain that the children now need to think of some alternatives. Use a simple rhyming dictionary if you have one available.
● Write the rhymes together, for sharing later with the class.

Independent work
● See the activities for the six Areas of Learning on page 33.

Plenary
● Prepare some party food as the finale to the work on nursery rhymes.
● Have each child wear a party hat with a label on showing the name of a nursery-rhyme character. If the children dress up, then provide hats and appropriate labels to go with their costumes.
● Challenge the children who do not know who they are to work with their partners to read their labels on their hats.
● Play a few party games, such as 'Nursery rhyme pass-the-parcel' – when the music stops, the child holding the parcel must say a nursery rhyme as they rip off one layer of paper.
● End the party by having fun reciting the alternative nursery rhymes that the children have written.

Nursery rhymes

Little Jack Horner

Little Jack Horner
Sat in the corner,
Eating a Christmas pie;
He put in this thumb, and pulled out a plum,
And said, 'What a good boy am I!'

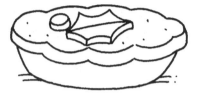

Little Polly Flinders

Little Polly Flinders
Sat among the cinders,
Warming her pretty little toes;
Her mother came and caught her,
And whipped her little daughter,
For spoiling her nice new clothes.

Doctor Foster

Doctor Foster
Went to Gloucester
In a shower of rain;
He stepped in a puddle
Right up to his middle,
And never went there again.

Jack Sprat

Jack Sprat
Could eat no fat,
His wife could eat no lean.
So between them both, you see,
They licked the platter clean!

Nursery-rhyme problems

Little Jack Horner

There was once a small boy who found it very difficult to make friends. He was very shy and never said much to anyone. He had seen a special doctor because he did not talk.

One Christmas, his family were all sitting down to Christmas dinner. They had some special Christmas pies and every year they hid plums in them for someone to find. Jack would not sit and eat with everyone else. Often he would not get much to eat if he did this. But today was Christmas, so his mother said he could take his pie and sit by himself.

Jack took his pie on a plate and off he went to be by himself. He huddled down in the corner of the sitting room, all cosy. Then he started to eat the pie. It was really delicious – juicy and sweet. It was so good that he decided to eat the pie with his fingers. All of a sudden he let out a cry, 'Wow!' Where he had put his thumb in the pie, he had found a great big plum. With a great 'Whoop' of delight he went running into the dinning room.

'Look, Mum! Look what I found!' he cried. 'What a good boy am I!'.

Mum was so pleased to see at last that Jack could talk. 'Yes, you are a good boy,' she said and hugged him hard. From that day on Jack always sat with his Mum and Dad at meal times and became quite a chatterbox.

Doctor Foster

Doctor Foster was a very good doctor but he had a bad memory. He once lost his coat after he had taken it off. He would also often get lost.

One day he was travelling home after visiting his friends and he completely forgot where he lived. Driving along the motorway he saw a sign to Gloucester and thought it was the right way. Then things got even worse and he kept driving around in circles. Finally he decided to park his car and walk to find someone to ask the way.

Just then there was a heavy clap of thunder and it started to pour with rain. Within minutes he was soaking wet and the rain was so heavy it was flooding the road.

Lost and wet, Dr Foster struggled to find his way, but it had got very dark and before he knew it he stepped in a puddle. Only this was no little puddle, it was hiding a big hole in the road. Splash! In he fell, right up to his middle. What a state he was in. Fortunately a kind passer-by pulled him out and asked him to come to his house to dry off and have a cup of tea.

Later, Dr Foster, helped by his new friend, found his way to his car and home. He decided that he was never going to Gloucester again and invited his friend to come and see him instead.

More nursery-rhyme problems

Jack Sprat

Jack Sprat was a very fussy eater. When he was a small child there were only one or two things he liked to eat. His mother used to say he lived on baked beans and chocolate cake. He did not get much better as he got older. The one thing he could not stand was fat on food, particularly meat, and he would cut every tiny bit off. This made it difficult when he went to a restaurant or to a friend's house for a meal and he got to the point when he would not eat out at all.

Fortunately he found a girlfriend who understood his problem and was also a very fussy eater. They got on really well and eventually got married. The great thing was that his wife loved fat. In fact she *only* liked the fat on meat. So their problems were solved. Jack and his wife between them ate everything up. He ate the lean part and she ate the fatty part and they could go out to eat without any problems.

Polly Flinders

Polly Flinders was a careless child. She never took care of her things and was always getting her clothes dirty.

One day she was wearing her best dress and went to see some friends. Before long she was running around the field with her friends, playing chase. It did not take long for her to fall down, right in a muddy ditch, and she was filthy. Her mother had to throw that dress away as she just could not get it clean.

Polly's mum bought her a nice new dress. It was pale blue with little flowers on and she had a ribbon to match for her hair. Polly looked splendid in it. Her mother told her sternly not to get it dirty and said she must stay in the house while she went to fetch Grandma for lunch.

Polly was bored and it was a cold day. Her mum had lit the fire and she sat in front of it warming her hands. She decided her feet were cold too, so she took off her shoes and stretched them out in front of the fire. She got closer and closer, not realising that not only was it dangerous and she could get burned, but also that the fireplace was sooty. Just then the door opened and in walked Mother and Grandma.

'What are you doing?' her mother shouted, 'You will get filthy!'.

And guess what, when Polly stood up, her lovely blue dress was covered in sooty marks! Her mum was really cross. Polly was very upset and told her mother how sorry she was. Polly's mother realised that Polly would never stay clean and decided that perhaps dresses were not practical. So from that day on, Polly always wore jeans and it did not matter if she got them dirty.

The journey through nursery-rhyme land

Little Jack Horner decided to go on a journey. He did not like sitting in a corner any more. So, off he went to see Humpty Dumpty. When he found him, Humpty was climbing a very high wall.

'Be careful!' Jack shouted, but it was too late – down fell Humpty. Jack tried to help, but the King's men and his horses were trying to put him back together again. Jack waved goodbye and kept on his travels.

Down the lane he went until he saw a little boy and a black sheep. He played with him for a while, but he started to feel hungry. Then he spied a little cottage and an old woman and a dog in the kitchen.

'Have you got anything to eat?' he asked.

She looked in the cupboard, but there was nothing in it. So Jack said, 'Thank you' and kept going down the road and over the hill until he saw a field of pumpkins. Inside a huge pumpkin was a woman, but just then a man said 'I'm Peter, leave my wife alone!'

Jack ran off and nearly bumped into a little girl with a crook.

'Can you help?' she said. 'I've lost my sheep and can't find them anywhere.'

But Jack couldn't see them either. He was getting very hungry now so he walked towards a town. Just as he was going past a shop, a boy came hopping out.

'Hello' said Jack. 'My name is Jack.'

'Hello' said the boy. 'My name is Jack too, but sometimes they call me Jack-a-dandy.'

Jack told him he had walked a long way and was very hungry. Jack-a-dandy said that he could go home with him. Off they went together and ate plum cake and sugar candy. Yum! Yum!

After that Jack and Jack became good friends and often shared their sweets. Jack found a short cut to the town from home and made sure he kept away from people who lived in pumpkins and girls with lost sheep.

Alternative nursery rhymes

Baa, Baa, Black Sheep

Baa, baa, black sheep
Have you any spots?
Yes, sir, yes, sir,
I've got lots.
Some on my tummy,
Some on my toes,
And one very big one
On the end of my nose.

Anon

Twinkle, Twinkle Little Bat!

Twinkle, Twinkle little bat!
How I wonder what you're at!
Up above the world you fly,
Like a tea-tray in the sky.
Twinkle, twinkle ...

Lewis Carroll

Mary Had a Little Lamb

Mary had a little lamb,
He had a sooty foot,
And into Mary's bread and jam
His sooty foot he put!

Anon

Little Miss Muffet Sat on a Tuffet

Little Miss Muffet sat on a tuffet,
Eating her curds and whey.
Along came a spider who sat down beside her
And said, 'Whatcha got in the bowl, sweetheart?'

Anon

■SCHOLASTIC

UNIT 4

The snack shop

This unit is based around developing a class snack shop and comprises five days' literacy activities and supports the National Literacy Strategy (Later Foundation Stage, Medium-term plan) focus on *Print around us (2)*. It also links with Developing Early Writing, Unit 1 *The supermarket*. It will help develop an awareness of a variety of print in a familiar context and provide a real purpose for writing. Linked activities are provided for all the six Areas of Learning with a strong emphasis on developing speaking and listening skills; cooperation in Personal, social and emotional development; and developing literacy skills in the form of notices, recipes, menus and posters. The activities build towards Year 1 Term 1, Objective 3 of the *Speaking, Listening, Learning* guidance: to ask and answer questions, make relevant contributions, offer suggestions and take turns.

Day	Shared text-level work	Shared word-/ sentence-level work	Focused group work	Independent work	Plenary
1 The visit	Visit to a fast food outlet.	Visit to a fast food outlet – finding words and signs.	Visit to a fast food outlet – focusing on foods and print.	**PSED:** Taking turns in role-play.	Making notes: what did we see?
2 Making signs	Making signs for the class snack shop.	Silly sentences using alliteration.	Role-play in the snack shop – writing orders.	**CLL:** Writing menus and orders for the role-play area.	'What's my role?' game.
3 Read the menu	Reading a menu.	Developing knowledge of new words from shared experiences.	Creating menus using ICT and writing frames.	**MD:** Counting stock. **KUW:** Making signs using ICT.	What's on the menu today? A game reading the menu.
4 Follow a recipe	Reading and following a recipe.	Phonic game – 'North, South, East and West'.	Cooking and following a recipe.	**PD:** Keeping healthy with exercise.	Taste test – using a range of vocabulary.
5 Make a poster	Healthy eating posters.	Write the corresponding letter.	Designing own posters.	**CD:** Model making – items for the snack shop.	Evaluating the snack shop – reading a range of print.

Key assessment opportunities
When working with children look closely for:
- ability to match graphemes to phonemes
- beginning to be able to form recognisable letters
- producing writing for a real purpose
- asking questions coherently and in full sentences
- being able to compose a meaningful sentence
- increasing vocabulary related to a topic.
Record appropriately and ensure that this informs future planning.

CROSS-CURRICULAR ⬛ UNIT 4 The snack shop

Personal, social and emotional development

Being fair
Early Learning Goal
Form good relationships with adults and peers.
What you need
Resources for class 'snack shop' to include cooking items, paper cups, plates, pretend foods and so on.
What to do
● Ask the children to help you set up the snack shop.
● What do the children think would be the fairest way to decide who will play the different roles (customers, cooks, shop assistants)?
● Discuss a turn-taking system, such as taking out labels from an envelope and at an agreed point, changing them for another.
● Leave the children to play in the shop. Listening out for fair turn-taking.

Mathematical development

Stock take!
Early Learning Goal
In practical activities and discussion begin to use the vocabulary involved in adding and subtracting.
What you need
Clipboards and pens/pencils; lists of food found in the 'Snack shop' with columns for the children to tick; store cupboard – with multiple copies of items for the snack shop (a range of empty cartons).
What to do
● Ask the children to count the number of each item and tick them as they count. Invite them to write the corresponding numerals.
● Explain that there should always be ten of each item stored to keep the shop well-stocked. How many more of each item will be needed?

Physical development

Keeping fit!
Early Learning Goal
Recognise the importance of keeping healthy and those things which contribute to this.
What you need
Skipping ropes; balls; small apparatus; egg timers.
What to do
● Explain that the children must see how many times they can perform certain actions (hops, jumps, catch a ball, skips) in the time shown by the egg timers.
● Count each other's actions.

Creative development

Make a sandwich!
Early Learning Goal
Explore colour, texture, shape, form and space in two or three dimensions.
What you need
Junk modelling materials; coloured card; tissue paper; glue; scissors; pictures of different foods.
What to do
● Explain that the children will make items for the Snack shop. Talk about what they will make such as different breads and fillings. Display the food pictures.
● Explain that they need to create a sandwich using boxes, card, tissue paper and so on!
● Encourage the children to be as creative as possible.

Communication, language and literacy

Write a menu
Early Learning Goal
Attempt writing for different purposes.
What you need
Snack shop role-play area; sample menus; assorted paper and card; writing materials; photocopiable page 56.
What to do
● Look at a range of sample menus together (see photocopiable page 56).
● Provide clearly labelled snack-shop items and encourage the children to use them as the basis for writing their own menus.

Knowledge and understanding of the world

Sign making
Early Learning Goal
Find out about and identify the uses of everyday technology and use information and communication technology and programmable toys to support their learning.
What you need
Computer – preferably more than one; the 'Clicker' programme (or similar) with a word bank and related pictures for the children to select; sample signs for the snack shop (such as *Order here*).
What to do
● Show the children the programme and the signs you have prepared. Explain that they are going to make some signs for the shop.
● Encourage the children to attempt their own signs. Show the children how to format, add Clip Art and print.

The visit

Objectives

Early Learning Goals
● Reading p62-63.

Stepping Stone
● Begin to recognise some familiar words.

NLS
T1: Through shared reading, to recognise printed and handwritten words in a variety of settings.
W6: To read on sight the 45 high frequency words to be taught by the end of YR.

What you need
● Arrange for parental consent to visit a local child-friendly café, restaurant, sandwich shop or fast food outlet (the healthier the better, but will depend on availability)
● adult helpers
● lists of things to look for (signs, notices, kinds of food on the menus, special offers, packaging and so on)
● a digital or ordinary camera (if you are unable to make a visit then bring in pictures to share with the children).

Differentiation

Less able
● Provide adult support to point out key words on signs in the environment.

More able
● Challenge the children to see how many words they can read from the list provided during the visit.

Shared text-level work
● Spend some time before the visit preparing the children by talking together about their experiences of buying snacks to eat, or eating out with their families. No doubt many of the children will have experienced fast food outlets. Use the opportunity to discuss healthy and non-healthy food.
● Before you leave the classroom, assign the children to groups and provide each accompanying adult with a list of things to look for - specifically a range of print.
● During the visit, stop and point out key features and take photographs, referring to the list (make it a game and see how many things each group finds).
● Encourage the children to discover what they will need to reproduce a 'snack shop' in the classroom and ask the adult to list these.
● If possible, collect items for use in the classroom later (such as unused wrapping, boxes, menus, and so on).

Shared word-level work
● If you have been able to arrange a visit then use the list and challenge the children to look for some of the words highlighted. Ask your adult helpers to scribe words for the children.
● Invite the children to point out any important signs, such as *outside*, *at the entrance, at the order point, till, at the tables* and so on. Ask the adults to copy examples.
● If you are not able to arrange a visit, ask the children to match some words that you have provided on card (such as *drinks, salad, chips* and so on).

Focused group work
● During the visit, as children work in small groups, focus on the types of food that are sold and in particular look for examples of environmental print and read them with the children.
● If you are unable to make a visit then in focused small groups summarise key features and types of signs using photographs and previous experiences.

Independent work
● See the activities for the six Areas of Learning on page 50.

Plenary
● With the children all together back in the classroom, discuss the important aspects of the food outlet that you visited and the types of food it provides.
● List these on the flipchart and explain that together you will use this information to plan your class 'snack shop'.
● Share some of the signs that adults have written. Discuss which signs they might have in their 'snack shop' and talk about healthy food they might include.

UNIT 4 DAY 2 ▢ The snack shop

Making signs

Objectives

Early Learning Goal
● Linking sounds and letters p60-61.
● Writing p64-65.

Stepping Stones
● Hear and say the initial sound in words and know which letters represent some of the sounds.
● Use writing as a means of recording and communicating.

NLS
T1: Through shared reading, to recognise printed and handwritten words in a variety of settings.
W2: Knowledge of grapheme/phoneme correspondences through: hearing and identifying initial sounds in words.

What you need

● Notes of signs and notices observed during your visit to a food outlet
● a flipchart and pens
● home-made order pads (make lists of different foods on separate A5 pieces of paper with corresponding Clip Art pictures next to each item; then make multiple photocopies of each page and compile pads by stapling the pages together)
● props and resources for role-play snack shop (see PSED page 50)
● photographs from the visit.

Differentiation

Less able
● Reinforce phonological awareness by repeating a range of words beginning with the same sound.

More able
● Ask the to suggest further words beginning with the same sound.

Shared text-level work
● Begin by reminding the children of the types of signs observed the previous day and show them some of the photographs taken.
● Explain that you need to make some signs for the class snack shop. Ask the children for suggestions of what will be needed.
● Start with a name for the shop. Suggest that you include the school name and encourage the children to use alliteration to help with phonological awareness. For example, *Bude's Brilliant Bites*. Brainstorm this together and then write, with the children helping you scribe.
● Finally create one or two other signs with the children, using similar signs observed on the visit. Keep the language simple and utilise some high frequency words such as: *Get your sandwiches here*.

Shared word-level work
● Write the name of the class snack shop on your flipchart and ask the children to identify all the matching letter sounds by highlighting them on the chart.
● Now say that you want to write some silly sentences using the same sounds. Give them an example, such as *Silly Susan spilt the sizzling sausages, soup and strawberries.*
● Have fun making up one or two examples and then write one on the flip chart. Invite individuals to come and underline the repeated letters (graphemes) representing the sounds (phonemes).
● Complete the activity by telling the children that they have to tell you a password to go to their next activity. Explain that this can be any word beginning with a specified letter of your choosing.

Focused group work
● Work with a group of children in the role-play area and ask them to help you to organise it as the 'snack shop' (see also PSED on page 50).
● Help the children to have specific roles and explain that you are going to be the Manager who makes sure everyone is doing their job.
● Encourage the children to improvise in their roles (supporting and extending where required).
● To encourage the children's writing, ask them to fill in the order pad for each order and then read it to the cook. Model this with them and praise all their efforts at mark making, including letters and pictures.

Independent work
● See the activities for the six Areas of Learning on page 50.

Plenary
● With the children on the carpet, explain to them that you are going to say something and they must try and guess which person from the snack shop you are pretending to be.
● Take on various roles and use body language and phrases to give clues. For example, you could say *Do you want your chicken well cooked?'* Ask the children to guess who you are.

Read the menu

Early Learning Goals
● Communication p54–55.
● Linking sounds and letters p60–61.
● Writing p64–65.

Stepping Stones
● Use language for an increasing range of purposes.
● Hear and say the initial sound in words and know which letters represent some of the sounds.
● Use writing as a means of recording and communicating.

NLS
T1: Through shared reading, to recognise printed and handwritten words in a variety of settings.
W10: New words from their reading and shared experiences.

What you need
● A range of menus
● copies of photocopiable page 56 (enough for one between two children, plus one enlarged to A3 size)
● small pictures of bananas copied onto card and cut up
● words from photocopiable page 57 copied onto card and cut up
● computer(s) with sample menu formats pre-prepared.

Differentiation

Less able
● If you have a programme such as 'Clicker' you can create a word bank for the children to click on to help them create their menus during focused group work.

More able
● Encourage the children to include a range of words in their menus and to add some pictures from Clip Art.

Shared text-level work
● Look at the range of menus and discuss these with the children. Talk about the differences and the types of food offered.
● Show the children the enlarged menu you have prepared. Read it together using the pictures as cues and decoding some words using phonic knowledge. Praise all good attempts.
● Now give out the smaller menus to pairs of children and explain you are going to play a game to see if each pair can order something from the menu. Give them a 'banana' for each one they can read correctly. You could also give an extra turn to a pair that ordered an item that had not been previously ordered.

Shared word-level work
● Show the children the word cards, one at a time, and talk about how to read them (initial-letter cues, graphic cues and so on).
● As the children read the words with you, put them on display as a word wall (or a pocket chart).
● Re-read the words and put them into meaningful sentences, such as: *Apples and bananas are types of fruit* (with the specific word highlighted).
● Display a few sentences containing the words for later re-reading and spend a few minutes each day over the week reading the words.

Focused group work
● Working with a group of children on the computer (or more than one if possible), explain that you are going to make some menus for the snack shop.
● Discuss what will go on the menu, referring to the word wall.
● Talk about how the menu is divided up into different sections.
● Make up a menu together, typing in the words for the children, but asking them for ideas of how to spell the words.
● If possible, provide the children with a computer between two, and with the menu formats already loaded, ask them to create their menus.
● Finally save and print the menus.

Independent work
● See the activities for the six Areas of Learning on page 50.

Plenary
● With the children gathered together, show them the menus you have created with one group.
● Ask the children you have worked with to explain that you have some 'Specials' on the menu today and ask them to read out some of the items on their menus (with your help as required).
● Invite the other children, in pairs, to choose and place an order. Go round the whole class in this way and finally write on the flipchart, *Our favourite today is…*
● Display the sign in the snack shop.

UNIT 4 DAY 4 ◻ The snack shop

Follow a recipe

Objectives

Early Learning Goal
● Linking sounds and letters p60-61.
● Reading p62-63.

Stepping Stones
● Hear and say the initial sound in words and know which letters represent some of the sounds.
● Know that information can be retrieved from books and computers.

NLS
T1: Through shared reading, to recognise printed and handwritten words in a variety of settings.
W2: Knowledge of grapheme/phoneme correspondences through: hearing and identifying initial sounds in words.

What you need

● Recipe for a healthy snack (photocopiable page 58) copied and enlarged
● ingredients as in recipe
● cooking utensils
● examples of recipe books
● pictures of healthy and unhealthy food cut out from magazines
● four A4 sized letters (from *Progression in Phonics* resources)
● objects beginning with the corresponding letters
● post-boxes with letters pasted to the front
● pictures of objects that correspond with the letters on the post-boxes.

Differentiation

Less able
● Support one-to-one correspondence of spoken to written words by asking the children to point as you read.

More able
● Encourage reading a range of words using different reading cues.

Shared text-level work

● Explain that you are going to make a healthy snack today, but before you do this you need to look at the recipe.
● Show the children some recipe books (preferably including a children's version with simple text and pictures) and talk about their experiences of recipes. Has anyone seen someone at home using them? Talk about why we need recipes.
● Discuss healthy eating and what foods the children think are good for you. Show the children the pictures you have cut out and ask them to decide with a partner whether to give each picture a 'thumbs up' or 'thumbs down' (signifying healthy or not healthy).
● Now read the recipe together (from photocopiable page 58) using a pointer. Discuss the layout of the recipe.

Shared word-level work

● Play 'North, South, East and West' from the *Progression in Phonics* materials page 24 (using step 2 (initial sounds) or 3 (final sounds) as appropriate). In the game the four chosen letters are placed in the four corners of the room. The children are given objects and they must find the corresponding letter.
● Provide some letter posting boxes (boxes with a slit cut out and a letter pasted to the front). Provide pictures of objects and ask the children to choose the corresponding post-box to post it into.

Focused group work

● Working with a group of children, follow the recipe to make the healthy snack.
● Go through all the ingredients together and match the words on the recipe with the actual item (it would be useful to label these, unless the names on the packets are clearly visible).
● Now provide the children with individual mixing bowls and spoons and, together, measure each ingredient and place it in their bowls, reading the recipe as you do this. Ask the children to mix it up.
● Put the mixture into small dishes and provide spoons to taste.

Independent work

● See the activities for the six Areas of Learning on page 50.

Plenary

● With the children gathered together in a circle, explain that they will have the chance to carry out a taste test of a healthy snack.
● Re-read the recipe and ask the children who worked with you to describe what they did.
● Pass around samples of the snack and ask for comments as the children try it. Write down the words that the children use on the flipchart.
● Provide the recipe, ingredients and finished product for the snack shop, together with a typed list of 'customer comments'.

UNIT 4 DAY 5 ☐ The snack shop

Make a poster

Objectives

Early Learning Goal
● Writing p64–65.

Stepping Stone
● Use writing as a means of recording and communicating.

NLS
T15: To use writing to communicate in a variety of ways, incorporating it into play and everyday classroom life.
W14: To write letters using the correct sequence of movements.

What you need

● Pictures of healthy and unhealthy foods from Day 4 (see page 54)
● large paper or card (A3 size)
● felt-tipped pens
● sample posters or magazine adverts for healthy eating
● individual whiteboards and pens.

Differentiation

Less able
● Encourage them to write words for posters by providing parts of the word for the children to add to.

More able
● Encourage independent writing of key words on posters.

Shared text-level work

● Explain that you are going to make some posters for the snack shop that will encourage people to eat the right kinds of food.
● Look at the pictures of healthy and unhealthy foods and draw up a list with a column for each type of food. Ask the children to suggest how to write the words.
● Look at some examples of posters and talk about the designs. Explain that it does not need to say much, just a few words.
● Brainstorm together some useful words to include and choose your prominent phrase or sentence (such as, *It tastes good and does you good*).
● Produce a draft poster with the children showing where words and pictures would go. Explain that some children will be helping you to complete this later.

Shared word-level work

● Now or later, give out whiteboards and pens and explain that you are going to say some sounds and that you want the children to write the corresponding letters (which letters will depend on the stage of the children's phonological development).
● Revisit a range of recently taught phonemes and ask the children to write the graphemes.
● Praise good attempts after you have seen each one, and then provide letter-formation cues (such as for the letter 't', *top to bottom, lift and across*) and ask everyone to practise.

Focused group work

● Working with a group of children, look at the poster begun in shared work and talk about how to complete it.
● Ask the children for a range of suitable words and then add pictures of healthy foods (either drawn or cut out from magazines).
● Once you have completed a version, provide A3 paper and pens and encourage the children to try and make their own.

Independent work

● See the activities for the six Areas of Learning on page 50.

Plenary

● With the children gathered together, discuss the snack shop. Look at what you have produced over the week (signs, menus, recipes and posters). Read a range of those produced together.
● Talk about the wide range of writing we do and how important it is to be a good reader and writer.
● Provide plenty of praise for all the children's efforts.
● For homework, ask the children to try and collect different types of writing, just as you have done this week (send home a note explaining what the children have been doing and what you would like them to do at home.

TERM 1

Menus

Quick snack shop

Main meals

Chicken pieces
Chicken wings
Drumsticks

Fish fingers
Fish fillets
Fish cakes

Meat balls
Ham
Sausages

Side orders

Tomato ketchup
Mayonnaise
Coleslaw
French bread
Chips
Green salad
Roast potatoes

Desserts

Ice-cream
   – chocolate
   – vanilla
   – strawberry
Banana split
Apple pie
Chocolate brownie
Fruit salad

Drinks

Orange juice
Mineral water
Lemonade
Coffee
Tea

Different kinds of food

apple	**banana**
carrot	**fish**
pasta	**cheese**
bread	**cake**
milk	**eggs**
salad	**nuts**
crisps	**melon**
peas	**ice-cream**
yoghurt	**biscuits**

A healthy snack

You will need:

1 cup of cereal *(any kind that is in small pieces and contains little or no sugar or nuts such as wheatflakes, branflakes, cornflakes and so on)*

1 large tablespoon of dried raisins

1 large tablespoon of dried apricots or bananas

1 teaspoon of dried cranberries

milk to taste

Equipment:

mixing bowl

large spoon

cup for measuring

tablespoon

teaspoon

small bowls

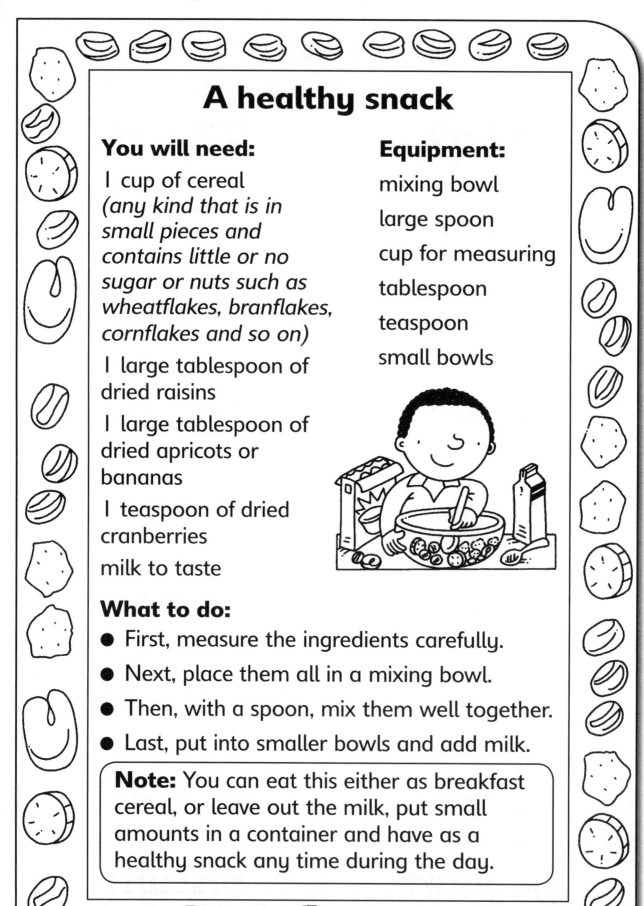

What to do:

- First, measure the ingredients carefully.
- Next, place them all in a mixing bowl.
- Then, with a spoon, mix them well together.
- Last, put into smaller bowls and add milk.

Note: You can eat this either as breakfast cereal, or leave out the milk, put small amounts in a container and have as a healthy snack any time during the day.

TERM 1

UNIT 5

The big pancake

This unit comprises ten days' literacy activities and supports the National Literacy Strategy (Later Foundation Stage, Medium-term plan) focus on *Narrative: predictable structures and patterned language through a traditional tale*. Linked activities are provided for all the six Areas of Learning with a strong emphasis on developing speaking and listening skills, through retelling the story using predictable and patterned story language, and developing literacy skills by making mini-books. The activities build towards Year 1 Term 1, Objective 4 of the *Speaking, Listening, Learning* guidance: to explore familiar themes and characters through improvisation and role-play.

WEEK 1

Day	Shared text-level work	Shared sentence level work	Focused group work	Independent work	Plenary
1 Read and retell the story	Shared reading of 'The Big Pancake' with props.	Creating a word bank of story vocabulary.	Teacher-directed activity – retelling the story with sequencing cards.	**PSED/CLL:** How did the characters feel? Puppet play.	A physical storyboard.
2 All join in	Shared reading of 'The Big Pancake' with choral reading of the refrains.	Matching high frequency words in refrains.	Teacher-directed activity – retelling the story with sequencing cards.	**MD:** Heavy and light; big and small.	Re-enacting the story.
3 Freeze it!	Retelling the story of 'The Big Pancake' with props.	Phonic game – 'Pebble game'.	Teacher-directed activity – retelling the story with sequencing cards.	**KUW:** Cooking pancakes.	Hot-seating – a busy mum.
4 Filming the story	Storyboard retelling of 'The Big Pancake'.	Letter formation.	Teacher-directed activity – retelling the story with sequencing cards.	**PD:** Rolling over and under objects.	Hot-seating – the pig's tale.
5 Finger puppets	Finger puppets to re-enact the story of 'The Big Pancake'.	Make a sentence.	As Day 1.	**CD:** Story collages.	Re-enacting the story using puppets.

Key assessment opportunities
When working with children look for:
● the ability to sequence a known story
● the ability to use story language
● the ability to speak in complete sentences
● the ability to match phonemes to graphemes
● the ability to speak clearly in character
● the ability to recall high frequency words.

UNIT 5

WEEK 2

Day	Shared text-level work	Shared sentence-level work	Focused group work	Independent work	Plenary
6 Write a story!	Shared planning for the alternative story of 'The Big Pancake'.	Write a sentence.	Guided writing – zig-zag books.	**PSED/CLL:** Tasting different foods and listening to stories.	Reading individual stories.
7 Once upon a time	Shared writing of the beginning of the story.	Reading and writing sentences.	Guided writing – zig-zag books.	**MD:** Ordering the characters (first, second and third).	Matching items to traditional stories.
8 You can't catch me!	Shared writing of the middle of the story.	Make a word – phoneme blending.	Guided writing – zig-zag books.	**KUW:** Maps of the journey of the pancake.	Listening to story tapes.
9 Happily ever after!	Shared writing of the ending.	Supported composition.	Guided writing – zig-zag books.	**PD:** Pancake races.	Reading individual stories.
10 Listen to our story	Shared reading of the alternative version of the story.	Silly sentences.	Guided writing – zig-zag books.	**CD:** Animal music.	Foods from around the world.

Key assessment opportunities

When working with children look for:
- the ability to sequence a known story
- the ability to use story language
- the ability to speak in complete sentences
- the ability to match phonemes to graphemes
- the ability to write recognisable letters
- the ability to write complete sentences.

Personal, social and emotional development

How does it feel?
Early Learning Goal
Have a developing awareness of their own needs, views and feelings and be sensitive to the needs, views and feelings of others.
What you need
Resources as for CLL below.
What to do
● This activity is linked to the CLL activity below. When the children are using the storyboard in CLL, encourage them to think about how the characters are feeling. If possible provide additional adult assistance to promote useful discussion.

Mathematical development

Sort and label
Early Learning Goal
Use language such as 'greater', 'smaller', 'heavier' or 'lighter' to compare quantities.
What you need
A selection of light, heavy, big and small objects (try to include some large objects which are light, and small ones which are heavy, to promote prediction and discussion). Labels saying: *heavy, light, big, small.*
What to do
● Ask the children to sort the range of objects into categories to match the four labels.
● Encourage the children to look first and predict, and then to pick up the objects to decide.

Physical development

Over and under
Early Learning Goal
Travel around, under, over and through balancing and climbing equipment.
What you need
A range of equipment to enable the children to roll over and under objects, such as mats, tunnels, benches and so on.
What to do
● Provide and set up the resources in a safe and spacious area and encourage the children to explore them.

Creative development

Create a collage
Early Learning Goal
Explore colour, texture, shape, form and space in two or three dimensions.
What you need
Easels and painting materials; a selection of fabric and types of paper.
What to do
● Use adult support if possible to assist the children to paint a background picture for the story of 'The Big Pancake'.
● Once their painting is dry, encourage the children to represent the pancake and other characters in the story, using a range of different materials. These should be stuck on with glue to create a collage picture.

Communication, language and literacy

Tell a story
Early Learning Goal
Listen with enjoyment, and respond to stories, songs and other music, rhymes and poems and make up their own stories, songs, rhymes and poems.
What you need
A range of cardboard/felt characters made from the patterns provided on photocopiable page 75; a large board approximately 1m x 60cm covered in felt (storyboard); an enlarged print-out of the repeated refrain from the story (found on photocopiable pages 73–74).
What to do
● Ask the children to retell the story of 'The Big Pancake' using the different characters.
● Remind the children of the repeated refrain and encourage them to use it as well as the correct story language.

Knowledge and understanding of the world

Make a pancake
Early Learning Goal
Look closely at similarities, differences, patterns and change.
What you need
Pancake recipe and cooking ingredients; cooking equipment.
What to do
● Using adult assistance, show the children the ingredients needed to make a pancake.
● Provide each child in the group with their own ingredients and utensils and let them make the mixture with adult help.
● With the children watching from a safe distance, cook the pancakes.
● Talk about the changes to the ingredients as they are cooked to form the finished pancake and encourage plenty of descriptive vocabulary.
● Eat the pancakes!

Personal, social and emotional development

Special foods
Early Learning Goal
Have a developing respect for their own cultures and beliefs and those of other people.
What you need
Foods and pictures of foods from a range of cultures, including pancakes (other foods could be chappatis, focaccia bread, matzos, and so on).
What to do
● With adult support, taste different foods and discuss who has eaten them at home.
● Talk about, and if possible show pictures of, different foods that are common to different cultures.
● Create a display to celebrate food from around the world.

Mathematical development

What's the order?
Early Learning Goal
Use developing mathematical ideas and methods to solve practical problems.
What you need
Storyboard characters from 'The Big Pancake' (made using photocopiable page 75); labels saying *1st, 2nd, 3rd, 4th, 5th*; a range of plastic animals that match the animals in the story.
What to do
● Provide the storyboard and characters and ask the children to match the appropriate labels to the animals or characters who were first/second and so on to run after the pancake.
● Encourage small-world play with the animals to show the order they were chasing after the pancake.

Physical development

Pancake races
Early Learning Goal
Travel around, under, over and through balancing and climbing equipment.
What you need
Paper, or card 'pancakes'; frying pans or pans; balancing and climbing equipment; marked start and finish points; an adult helper to ensure safety.
What to do
● Discuss pancake races with the children.
● Using paper or cardboard 'pancakes' and pans, have a clearly marked start and stop for the races. Talk about the ways to use the equipment. Encourage the children to play independently under the eye of an adult helper.
● Later in the week, ask for volunteers (including staff!) to run actual races.

Creative development

Follow me!
Early Learning Goal
Use their imagination in art and design, music, dance, imaginative and role play and stories.
What you need
Range of musical instruments.
What to do
● Ask the children to explore the different sounds they can make with the instruments.
● Challenge the children to try to produce the sounds that a cat, cockerel, duck, cow and pig would make.

Communication, language and literacy

Early Learning Goal
Listen with enjoyment, and respond to stories, songs and other music, rhymes and poems and make up their own stories, songs, rhymes and poems.
What you need
Traditional tales on tape; personal cassette recorders with headphones; finger puppets including those made in the activity on page 67 (using photocopiable page 75).
What to do
● Encourage the children to listen to traditional tales on tape using the headphones.
● Provide finger puppets that link to the tales to encourage interaction with the story.

Knowledge and understanding of the world

Create a map
Early Learning Goal
Observe, find out about and identify features in the place they live and the natural world.
What you need
Large sheets of flipchart paper; pens and pencils.
What to do
● Encourage the children to make visual representations of the journey of the pancake, with adult support, if possible.

Read and retell the story

Objectives

Early Learning Goals
● Reading p62–63.

Stepping Stone
● Begin to be aware of the way stories are structured.

NLS
T8: To locate and read significant parts of the text, eg picture captions, names of key characters, rhymes and chants.
T10: To re-read and recite stories and rhymes with predictable and repeated patterns and experiment with similar rhyming patterns.
S2: To use awareness of the grammar of a sentence to predict words during shared reading and when re-reading familiar stories.

What you need
● Cardboard/felt characters prepared using photocopiable page 75
● Velcro pieces for fixing the characters to the board
● a felt storyboard (a large board approximately 1m x 60cm).
● the story from photocopiable pages 73 and 74, enlarged, or scanned and displayed on an interactive whiteboard
● photocopiable page 76, enlarged and cut up
● phrases from the story in large font size, including *Once upon a time* and *they lived happily every after* and the repeated refrain from the story.

Differentiation

Less able
● Provide prompts for the children in the sequencing activity by making quick sketches of different incidents in order.

More able
● Encourage them to tell the story independently to a partner or the group.

Shared text-level work
● Introduce the story by telling the children the title. Talk about pancakes and the children's experiences of eating them. (If possible bring a pancake in to show them.)
● Now read the story (found on photocopiable pages 73 and 74) to the children using a pointer. Encourage them to join in with the repeated refrains.
● Show the children the characters from the story and place each one on the storyboard, asking the children who each character is in turn.
● Now remove the characters and re-read the story. Invite individual children to place each character on the board as you introduce them in the story.

Shared sentence-level work
● Talk about the words used in this story and explain that it is a 'traditional tale' which usually always starts and ends in the same way.
● Re-read the beginning and end of the story and talk about the words used. Ask the children if they know any similar stories, and later make a display of traditional tales.
● Show the children the phrases from the story you have prepared and read them together.
● Emphasise the use of grammar to predict appropriate words when reading. This can be done by substituting a grammatically implausible word such as a noun for a verb to show that this does not make sense. For example, *they **leaf** ever after*.
● Create a display of story language either separately or as part of a larger wall display of work on the story.

Focused group work
● Introduce the story-sequencing cards from photocopiable page 76 to the group of children and talk about each one.
● Give a different card to each child and ask them to try and put them in the order of the story.
● Next, ask the children to hold the cards and physically stand in the right order. Check to see if the order is correct by summarising what each card represents and then referring back to the text.
● Retell the story together using the cards as props and encouraging the correct story language.

Independent work
● See the activities for the six Areas of Learning on page 61.

Plenary
● Ask the children who have been working with you in a guided group to create a physical storyboard to show the rest of the children. They should do this by holding up cards to indicate the different parts of the story.
● Retell the story for the whole class in this way.

All join in

Objectives

Early Learning Goals
● Reading p62-63.

Stepping Stone
● Begin to be aware of the way stories are structured.

NLS
T10: To re-read and recite stories and rhymes with predictable and repeated patterns and experiment with similar rhyming patterns.
W5: To read on sight a range of familiar words.

What you need

● Cardboard/felt characters prepared using photocopiable page 75
● Velcro pieces for fixing the characters to the board
● a felt storyboard (a large board approximately 1m x 60cm).
● the story from photocopiable pages 73 and 74, enlarged, or scanned and displayed on an interactive whiteboard
● phrases from the story in large font size, including *Once upon a time* and *they lived happily every after* and the repeated refrain from the story
● story-sequencing cards from photocopiable page 76, enlarged and cut up
● high-frequency words on card in large point size (*I, me, to, and, a, you*).

Differentiation

Less able
● Encourage use of props to help sequence the story.

More able
● Encourage detailed descriptions of the different parts of the story in focused group work.

Shared text-level work

● Remind the children of the story from the previous day. What can the children remember about it?
● Ask the children to talk to their partners about the story. Can they tell each other who the characters in the story are?
● Hand out the cardboard/felt characters and ask the children to name them as they place them on the storyboard.
● Using the characters and the storyboard, revisit the correct sequence of the story.
● Now retell the story ensuring the correct story language, using the characters and asking the children to help.
● Encourage everyone to join in with the refrains with plenty of enthusiasm and noise!

Shared word-level work

● Show the children the sentences you have prepared from the story. Read them together using a pointer to reinforce one-to-one correspondence of spoken to written words.
● Next, read the high frequency words on card with the children.
● Hand out the words and as you re-read the refrains slowly, ask the child to shout 'Snap' if they are holding the same word.
● Repeat the game, giving out the cards to different children each time, as time allows.

Focused group work

● Continue as the previous day using the sequencing cards, asking different children to work with you.
● Ask the children to give you a complete sentence to describe a specific part of the story.
● Encourage the use of appropriate story language for a traditional tale. Remind the children of other favourite traditional tales and the language found in them.

Independent work

● See the activities for the six Areas of Learning on page 61.

Plenary

● Re-enact the story with the class, encouraging everyone to join in with the refrain.
● Choose different children to play the roles of the various characters and discuss how each one felt. Talk about appropriate body language, such as the pig being very pleased with himself and the mother being very cross. Encourage the children to incorporate these ideas into their role-play.
● Play a game of 'Press the pause button' (likening it to the video recorder). When you press the pause button the children must freeze to create a tableau. The children's expressions and body language should help to depict the specific moment in the story.

Freeze it!

Objectives

Early Learning Goals
● Linking sounds and letters p60-61.

Stepping Stone
● Continue a rhyming string.

NLS
T10: To re-read and recite stories and rhymes with predictable and repeated patterns and experiment with similar rhyming patterns.
W1: To understand and be able to rhyme through recognising, exploring and working with rhyming patterns.

What you need
● Cardboard/felt characters prepared using photocopiable page 75
● Velcro pieces for fixing the characters to the board
● a felt storyboard (a large board approximately 1m x 60cm)
● the story from photocopiable pages 73 and 74, enlarged, or scanned and displayed on an interactive whiteboard
● phrases from the story in large font size, including *Once upon a time* and *they lived happily every after* and the repeated refrain from the story
● story-sequencing cards from photocopiable page 76, enlarged and cut up
● digital camera and computer
● a pebble
● *Progression in phonics* materials (DfES, page 18).

Differentiation

More able
● Ask more confident children to think of a sentence to describe the scene on the sequencing card. Encourage them to share their sentences with the group, ensuring that it is a complete sentence.

Shared text-level work
● Explain that you are going to act out the story of 'The Big Pancake' in different parts.
● Using the story-sequencing cards from photocopiable page 76, shuffled and out of order, take one at random and say that you would like the help of the children in the class to create the scene.
● Choose individual children to take different parts and ask them to take up a position as if it was a video and you had pressed pause on the recorder (as used in the previous day, see page 64).
● Photograph the moments using the digital camera. Using a computer program, download and print the photographs to create your own sequencing cards.
● Continue to create a series of scenes in this way.

Shared word-level work
● Play the 'Pebble game' from the *Progression in Phonics* pack (page 18), where the children have to continue a rhyming string. Provide additional adult support for those children who find it difficult to generate rhymes.
● Write lists of the rhyming words that the children think of in the game. Read back through the lists, looking at any similarities in the spelling patterns of the words.

Focused group work
● Continue as the previous day asking different children to work with you.
● Make links to the photographs taken and, if these are available to share, use these as sequencing cards also.

Independent work
● See the activities for the six Areas of Learning on page 61.

Plenary
● Explain that you will be asking someone to be 'Mum' from the story.
● Discuss how Mum must feel at the different stages of the story. How might she feel at the beginning of the story when the children are pestering her and she is trying to do the cleaning? How might she feel later on when the pancake disappears out of the door?
● Now select someone to take the role of 'Mum' and explain that they are going to be in the 'hot seat' – answering questions as if they are 'Mum'.
● Invite the children to talk with a partner to think of some good questions (use adult support as necessary to help those who find this difficult).
● With a child in the hot seat and yourself supporting (you may need to model this briefly also), ask for questions such as *How did you feel when the children kept saying they were hungry and you were busy cleaning?*

Filming the story

Objectives

Early Learning Goals
● Handwriting p66-67.

Stepping Stone
● Begin to form recognisable letters.

NLS
T10: To re-read and recite stories and rhymes with predictable and repeated patterns and experiment with similar rhyming patterns.
W14: To write letters using the correct sequence of movements.

What you need

● The story from photocopiable pages 73 and 74, enlarged, or scanned and displayed on an interactive whiteboard
● a storyboard
● phrases from the story in large font size, including *Once upon a time* and *they lived happily every after* and the repeated refrain from the story
● story-sequencing cards from photocopiable page 76, enlarged and cut up
● video recorder
● print-outs of digital pictures from previous day
● individual whiteboards and pens.

Shared text-level work

● Explain that you are going to use the digital pictures of the tableaux you created yesterday (see page 64), to help create a video of the class version of 'The Big Pancake' story.
● Show the children the pictures and ask the children to help you to sequence them correctly.
● Display the pictures in the correct sequence on a storyboard. Retell the story using the pictures as prompts.
● Now ask individual children to play the different roles from the story. Tell the rest of the class that you need their support to tell the story and would like them to help by supplying some sound effects and joining in with the repeated refrain.
● When you are ready, re-enact the story with a member of staff operating the video camera as you direct events!
● Re-take scenes from the story as appropriate.

Shared word-level work

● Explain that you are all going to do some handwriting practice.
● Using the letters currently being learned, provide a prompt for letter formation, such as '*top to bottom, lift and across*' (for the letter 't').
● Ask the children to practise in the air, on each other's backs and finally on whiteboards.
● Monitor the children's attempts carefully with adult support. Emphasise the correct way to hold the pen or pencil.

Focused group work

● Continue as the previous day asking different children to work with you.
● Use the digital pictures, if possible, for further sequencing work.
● Ask the children to describe their roles in the tableaux from the previous day (see page 65).

Independent work

● See the activities for the six Areas of Learning on page 61.

Plenary

● Continue hot-seating (as in the plenary session the previous day – see page 64) but, this time, say you are going to choose someone to take the role of the pig.
● Discuss what part the pig plays and how he feels at the end of the story.
● Choose someone to take the part of the pig.
● Ask the other children to work with a partner to think of good questions to ask, such as *Why did you ask the pancake to sit on your nose?*
● Provide support to the 'pig' and ask for different questions.
● Finish by talking about the different types of characters in traditional tales and compare them.

Differentiation

More able
● Encourage more able children to have a go at writing appropriate captions underneath the pictures during focused group work.

Finger puppets

Objectives

Early Learning Goals
● Reading p62–63.

Stepping Stone
● Begin to be aware of the way stories are structured.

NLS
T10: To re-read and recite stories and rhymes with predictable and repeated patterns and experiment with similar rhyming patterns.
S1: To expect written text to make sense and to check for sense if it does not.

What you need
● The story from photocopiable pages 73 and 74, enlarged, or scanned and displayed on an interactive whiteboard
● photocopiable page 76, enlarged and cut up
● phrases from the story in large font size, including *Once upon a time* and *they lived happily every after* and the repeated refrain from the story
● photocopy the characters from photocopiable page 75 onto card and cut out, punch small holes and attach string or rubber bands to create finger puppets
● individual words (enlarged) from sentences from the story.

Differentiation

Less able
● Scribe sentences for the children for the different parts of the story.

More able
● Encourage writing in full sentences.

Shared text-level work
● Explain that today you are going to ask some children to help tell the story of 'The Big Pancake' using finger puppets.
● Show the children the prepared puppets and discuss who each character is.
● Now read the story (enlarged and displayed) using a pointer. Let individual children take it in turns to use the pointer to point to the words to reinforce phoneme/grapheme correspondences.
● Give out the finger puppets to volunteers and ask them to tell you something about their character if possible. Encourage them to use expression and body language as well as the repeated refrains to bring the story alive as you re-read it.
● If time permits, read the story again, encouraging other children to volunteer to take on a role.

Shared sentence-level work
● Explain that you need the children to help you to make a sentence from the story.
● Give out individual words from one of the prepared sentences (found in the story) to random children.
● Ask the children with words to come out to the front (with the other children sitting on the carpet).
● Now ask them to stand in a line in any order, holding up their words.
● Have fun reading the sentence with the words in the wrong order.
● Ask the children sitting on the carpet to help sort the sentence out. . Read the correct sentence together.
● Now ask the children if they can the children make any other sentences by substituting just one word.

Focused group work
● Continue as the previous day, asking different children to work with you.
● Ask the children to try to match your digital images with the original sequencing cards from photocopiable page 76.
● Once oral sentences have been produced to describe the specific section of the story, scribe some examples for the children.
● Play some games of mixing up sentences and pictures. Help the children to match the sentences to the appropriate images.

Independent work
● See the activities for the six Areas of Learning on page 61.

Plenary
● Re-enact the story for the final time using props. Invite some guests to come and watch!
● Place the finger puppets in a 'story sack' along with a copy of the story and any other props and invite the children to choose to act out the story at appropriate times.

Write a story!

Objectives

Early Learning Goals
● Writing p64–65.

Stepping Stone
● Use writing as a means of recording and communicating.

NLS
T14: To use experience of stories, poems and simple recounts as a basis for independent writing, eg re-telling, substitution, extension, and through shared composition with adults.
S1: To expect written text to make sense and to check for sense if it does not.

What you need

● Flipchart paper
● easel
● a range of sentences from traditional tales written or printed on large paper or sentence strip card (these need to be of varying lengths - some very short and some long and all printed in one continuous line to highlight that a sentence is not the same as a line of print)
● a Big Book - preferably of a traditional tale
● pre-prepared zig-zag books (these can be done using A3 paper cut in half lengthwise and folded four times concertina style).

Differentiation

Less able
● Encourage and value all attempts at mark making in the book-making activity. Ask the children to verbally rehearse their sentences.

More able
● Encourage the children to use a wider, more descriptive vocabulary, including common story language.

Shared text-level work

● Remind the children of the story of 'The Big Pancake'. Explain that they are going to help you to write a different version of the story.
● Brainstorm a range of ideas for the story. Begin with the characters. For example, ask: *What could be used instead of a pancake?* (For example a currant bun.)
● Write the children's suggestions on the board under the heading of *characters*.
● Now decide on the events of the story based on your chosen characters. For example, first Grandma bakes some currant buns; next a bun runs out of the door. Then have a range of characters chasing, followed by someone or something that eats the bun in the end.
● Ask the children to help you come up with a refrain, such as *Stop, stop you beautiful bun! - No, No you'll have to run!*
● Explain that this is the plan for the class story and you will continue with it tomorrow.

Shared sentence-level work

● Next or later, explain that you have some sentences from different traditional tales or well known stories and that you would like the children's help to work out which stories they are from.
● Put the pre-prepared sentences on the easel or board and, one at a time, read the sentences together, emphasising the capital letter and full stop. As you read each one, ask the children to identify the story.
● Talk about the differences in the sentence length and explain that sentences can be long and short. Show the children the Big Book to demonstrate this further.

Focused group work

● Explain that the children will each make their own book of their personal version of the story of 'The Big Pancake'.
● Brainstorm three or four events from each child's story.
● Ask the children to draw the characters and objects on separate sheets of their books.
● Model writing a sentence for the story and then encourage the children to 'have a go' at writing a sentence to correspond to one of their pictures. Ask the children to read their sentences out and if desired, scribe the sentence underneath. Encourage each child to complete their own zig-zag book in this way.

Independent work

● See the activities for the six Areas of Learning on page 62.

Plenary

● Ask the children who have been working with you to share their stories with the class.
● Read the stories together and discuss the similarities and differences.

Once upon a time

Objectives

Early Learning Goals
● Writing p64-65.

Stepping Stone
● Begin to break the flow of speech into words.

NLS
T14: To use experience of stories, poems and simple recounts as a basis for independent writing, eg re-telling, substitution, extension, and through shared composition with adults.
S1: To expect written text to make sense and to check for sense if it does not.

What you need
● Blank Big Book made by using large sugar paper folded for a cover with large A3 sized sheets of paper or card inside (fixed using treasury tags or ring fastenings)
● the refrain from 'The Big Pancake' story printed or written in large font size
● a range of texts and props for other traditional tales (such as a gingerbread man, red cloak, basket, bricks, straw, sticks and so on).

Differentiation

Less able
● Ask the children to orally rehearse sentences and support them with their writing.

More able
● Encourage a wider range of vocabulary and, in particular, the use of common story language.

Shared text-level work

● Remind the children of the plan of the class story from the previous day (see page 68). In particular talk about the characters, sequence of events and your chosen refrain.
● Now explain that you are going to write the beginning of the story.
● Remind the children of the sorts of ways traditional tales begin (*Once upon a time ...*).
● Ask the children to talk with a partner to suggest how the story should start.
● Use teacher scribing to write the opening sentence. Do this on the blank Big Book, leaving space for illustrations to be put in later. Write one sentence on each page.
● Devise and write one or two further sentences. Re-read them with the children. Emphasise that this is the beginning of the story.

Shared sentence-level work

● Now, or later, use the children's chosen refrain (from Day 6, page 68) and read it back together. Use a pointer to emphasise the direction of print and the one-to-one correspondence of spoken to written words.
● To emphasise that it is important to check for meaning as we read, make one or two deliberate mistakes. For example, substitute a word that does not make sense in the context - *Stop, stop you delicious* **bag!** *- No, No you'll have to run!*
● If you have time, cut up the words from the refrain and ask the children to help you to put them back in the right order.

Focused group work

● Continue as per the previous day, asking different children to work with you.
● Encourage the children to orally rehearse sentences for their books, discussing whether they make sense.
● Provide support and challenge as per Day 6 (page 68) where necessary. If the children finish their work early, encourage them to add extra details to their illustrations.

Independent work

● See the activities for the six Areas of Learning on page 62.

Plenary

● Explain that you have a bag of items that belong to other characters in stories and you need the children's help to decide who they belong to.
● Bring out an item at a time, such as a gingerbread man, and ask the children to help you identify the story. Match the item to a copy of the story and briefly summarise what happened.
● Leave the items and stories on display in the reading area in the classroom to encourage the children to interact with them during the week, as time allows.

You can't catch me!

Objectives

Early Learning Goal
● Writing p64–65.

Stepping Stone
● Begin to break the flow of speech into words.

NLS
T14: To use experience of stories, poems and simple recounts as a basis for independent writing, eg re-telling, substitution, extension, and through shared composition with adults.
W4: To link sound and spelling patterns.

What you need
● Blank Big Book begun the previous day.
● A4 sized letters (from *Progression in Phonics* resources (DfES)).
● Tape recorder and tapes of traditional tales.

Differentiation

Less able
● In focused group work, encourage the children to orally rehearse their sentences and elaborate for them where necessary.

More able
● In focused group work, encourage the children to write their own sentences, checking for sense as they do so, by rehearsing them orally.

Shared text-level work
● Explain that you are going to continue writing the story together of the agreed title, for example 'The Big Currant Bun'.
● Now re-read the opening part of the story from the previous day.
● Discuss what happens next, for example *The big currant bun jumped out of the oven and out of the kitchen door.*
● Write one or two further sentences for the middle of the story using teacher scribing, emphasising as you write the use of full stops and capital letters to demarcate sentences.
● Talk also about which letters you should write to represent different sounds.

Shared word-level work
● With the children sat on the carpet, distribute a range of large A4-sized letters.
● Explain that you want to see if you can make some words with these letters.
● Use the example of a phonetically regular word (preferably one used in the story, such as *bun*) and ask the children to see if they have any of the corresponding letters.
● Ask those children that have the letters to make the word to stand up. Sound out each letter with the children. Now blend the letters together to make the word.
● Repeat the activity with a variety of words that share the same rime with different onsets (such as *fun, run, gun, sun* and so on).
● Write the words that you make together on the flipchart each time. Invite confident children to write them up on the flipchart for you.

Focused group work
● Continue as the previous day, asking different children to work with you.
● Encourage the children to orally rehearse sentences for their books, discussing whether they make sense.
● Provide support and challenge where necessary.
● Invite the children to talk about their illustrations in detail.

Independent work
● See the activities for the six Areas of Learning on page 62.

Plenary
● Tell the children that you are going to play the beginning of a well-known story from a tape. Can they guess which story it is from? Does it start the same as any other stories that they know?
● Play the first few minutes of the tape and ask the children to tell their partners which story it is. Ask them to share this information with the class. Does everyone agree? What are the key words or phrases that give the story away?
● Repeat with another well-known story.

The big pancake

Happily ever after!

Objectives

Early Learning Goals
● Handwriting p66-67.

Stepping Stone
● Begin to form recognisable letters.

NLS
T14: To use experience of stories, poems and simple recounts as a basis for independent writing, eg re-telling, substitution, extension, and through shared composition with adults.
S1: To expect written text to make sense and to check for sense if it does not.
W2: Knowledge of grapheme/phoneme correspondences.

What you need
● Blank Big Book from the previous day (see page 70)
● whiteboards and pens (one between two children).

Differentiation

Less able
● Continue to support the children in focused group work by encouraging them to rehearse their sentences orally, checking for sense.

More able
● Challenge the children to write their sentences independently during focused group work.

Shared text-level work
● Show the children the Big Book that you have been writing and read the sentences written so far with the children joining in. Praise the children for the work to date.
● Ask the children if they think the story is finished. What is missing? (The ending!) Do the children have some ideas for the ending? Do they remember the plan that you made together at the beginning of the work (see Day 6, page 68)?
● Look at the plan together and ask the children to think silently for a minute.
● Now ask the children to work with their talk partners, telling each other, in turn, a sentence to complete the story. Invite the children to take turns to tell the rest of the class their ideas.
● Take the children's suggestions and write the final sentences, encouraging varied vocabulary and inclusion of a traditional ending, such as *and they lived happily every after*.

Shared word-level work
● Explain that you would like the children to practise writing a sentence for the ending with their partner's help. Give out a whiteboard and pen for each pair of children.
● Ask the children in pairs to write a suitable sentence using phonetically plausible spellings of words. Support the children as necessary and offer plenty of encouragement, praising the children's attempts.
● Read some of the examples of sentences to the class and pick out the particularly good attempts at spelling words.
● Use examples of common errors (sensitively, without referring to individual attempts) to reinforce spelling of particular words.

Focused group work
● Continue as the previous day, asking different children to work with you.
● Encourage the children to orally rehearse sentences for their books, discussing whether they make sense.
● Provide support and challenge where necessary.
● Let the children look at each other's books once they have completed them. Ask the children to say something nice to the person next to them about their work.

Independent work
● See the activities for the six Areas of Learning on page 62.

Plenary
● Ask the children who have been working with you to share their stories with the class, as on Day 6 (see page 68).
● Read the stories together and discuss the similarities and differences.

UNIT 5 DAY 10 ☐ The big pancake

Listen to our story

Objectives

Early Learning Goals
● Reading p62-63.

Stepping Stone
● Begin to recognise some familiar words.

NLS
T14: To use experience of stories, poems and simple recounts as a basis for independent writing, eg re-telling, substitution, extension, and through shared composition with adults.
S1: To expect written text to make sense and to check for sense if it does not.

What you need
● Big Book created during the week
● props to represent objects and characters from the class story
● silly questions, such as: *Can a pig talk?*; *Can a cat sing?*; or *Can a duck bark?* (see also *Progression in Phonics* resources (DfES) page 31)
● party hats
● different types of food from around the world (such as fruit).

Differentiation

Less able
● Encourage children to 'have a go' at writing sentences.

More able
● Challenge the children to write their sentences independently during focused group work.

Shared text-level work
● Proudly display the class book of the alternative version of the story of 'The Big Pancake'. Decide on a title and add it to the cover of the book in large print.
● Read the story together using a pointer and encourage all the children to join in, particularly with the repeated refrain.
● Now ask the children to help you to bring the story to life with the various props you have. Show the children the props and talk about which characters might use them or where they belong in the story.
● Invite volunteers to play the different characters and give them the corresponding props.
● Ask the rest of the class to help you read the story again with some of the children miming the actions, gestures and so on. Ensure that everyone joins in with the refrain.
● Explain that you hope to share the story at a later date, perhaps for parents or a class assembly.

Shared sentence-level work
● Now using some of the sentences from the *Progression in Phonics* resources (DfES) or questions you have prepared, explain that you have some rather silly questions.
● Hold up one question at a time and ask the children to read them, checking with a partner.
● After each sentence ask the children to give you 'thumbs up' if it makes sense, and 'thumbs down' if it does not!
● Choose a child to help you read each sentence and ask them to help you to check to see if it does make sense.

Focused group work
● Continue as the previous day asking other children to work with you.
● Encourage the children to orally rehearse sentences for their books.
● Provide support and challenge where necessary.
● Invite the children to add a title, picture and their own name to the 'cover' of their books.

Independent work
● See the activities for the six Areas of Learning on page 62.

Plenary
● To complete the unit, arrange a party of food from around the world.
● Ask the children to sit in a circle and pass round different tastes of foods, such as assorted fruits. Encourage a range of words to describe the smell, taste and texture of the foods.
● Discuss where each food comes from.
● Talk about what we eat for different celebrations, such as Easter eggs at Easter; pancakes on Pancake Day; Charoset at Hanukkah; special drinks such as Sharbat at Divali and so on. Ensure that you cover a range of foods, cultures and celebrations in your discussion.

The Big Pancake

A traditional folk tale

Once upon a time there was a mother who had seven little children who were always hungry.

One day the mother was busy cleaning the house, when the children appeared at the door and said: 'Mum, we are hungry!'

'Well, be good and when I have finished cleaning this room, I will make you something special to eat.'

The children waited patiently and finally Mum said, 'Right who would like a pancake?'

All the children said, 'ME!', so Mum started to mix eggs, flour and milk. The children helped mix and then sat ready with knives and forks. Mum got out the big saucepan and put some of the pancake mixture into the pan.

'Ready,' she said and tossed the pancake high in the air.

The pancake suddenly came to life as it leapt into the air, thinking, 'I don't want to be eaten!' Before anyone could stop it, it flipped a big somersault and landed on the kitchen floor and then rolled out of the door!

'Stop!' cried the seven hungry children and the mother. 'We want to eat you!'.

'Oh no!' said the pancake and rolled off down the garden with the mother and the children chasing after it.

'Stop!' cried the gardener who saw the pancake roll by. 'I'd like to eat you!'. But the pancake kept on rolling.

'I don't want to be eaten,' it said. 'Seven hungry children and a mother couldn't catch me, and I won't let you catch me!' But the man chased after the pancake.

Next the pancake passed a cat sitting on a wall. 'Stop!' miaowed the cat. 'I want to eat you!'. But the pancake kept on rolling.

'I don't want to be eaten,' it said. 'Seven hungry children, a mother and a man couldn't catch me, and I won't let you catch me!'. But the cat ran after the big pancake.

Further on, the pancake passed a cockerel sitting on a gate, 'Stop!' crowed the cockerel. 'I'd like to eat you!'

The Big Pancake

(continued)

But the pancake rolled faster. 'I don't want to be eaten,' it said. 'Seven hungry children, a mother, a man and a cat couldn't catch me, and I won't let you catch me!' But the cockerel jumped off the gate and flapped after the big pancake.

Round the corner the pancake passed a duck on a pond, 'Stop!' quacked the duck. 'I'd like to eat you!' But the pancake just rolled faster.

'I don't want to be eaten,' it said. 'Seven hungry children, a mother, a man, a cat and a cockerel couldn't catch me, and I won't let you catch me!'. But the duck waddled after the big pancake.

Soon the pancake passed a cow in a field. 'Stop!' mooed the cow, 'I'd like to eat you!' But the pancake rolled even faster.

'I don't want to be eaten,' it said. 'Seven hungry children, a mother, a man, a cat, a cockerel and a duck couldn't catch me, and I won't let you catch me!' But the cow charged after the pancake.

In the woods, near a river, the pancake passed a pig. 'Where are you going?' grunted the pig.

'I don't want to be eaten,' it said. 'Seven hungry children, a mother, a man, a cat, a cockerel, a duck and a cow couldn't catch me, and I won't let you catch me!'

'But I don't want to eat you,' said the pig, 'I'm on your side!'.

'Well,' said the pancake, 'Could you help me to cross the river? Pancakes can't swim you know.'

'No problem,' snorted the pig, 'Just climb onto my nose and I will carry you across.'

So the big pancake climbed on to the pig's nose and the pig made a strange noise. In a flash the pig tossed the pancake into the air.

Flip! Flop! There was no escape for the pancake and it fell right into the pig's open mouth and was gobbled up with one gulp.

Just then along came a cow, a duck, a cockerel, a cat, the man and the mother and seven hungry children.

'Have you seen a big pancake?' they panted.

'Was it very big and golden brown and did it roll along like a wheel?' asked the pig.

'Yes!' they all shouted.

'Yes, thank you,' said the pig. 'It was delicious,' and he licked his lips!

But the mother cheered the children up by saying they would make some more pancakes. They went home and lived happily ever after, remembering to always keep the door closed when they cooked pancakes.

The Big Pancake

(continued)

TERM 1

Sequencing cards

◀**SCHOLASTIC**

UNIT 1

My history

This unit is based on non-fiction recounts and comprises five days' literacy activities. It supports the National Literacy Strategy (Later Foundation Stage, Medium-term plan) focus on non-fiction *All about me*. The activities explore the features of non-fiction text (in particular recounts) and provide a natural starting point for the children to produce their own recounts. Linked activities are provided for all the six Areas of Learning with a strong emphasis on developing speaking and listening skills, promoting self-esteem in Personal, social and emotional development and developing literacy skills in the form of making books. The activities build towards Year 1 Term 1, Objective 1 of the *Speaking, Listening, Learning* guidance: to describe incidents or tell stories from their own experience.

Day	Shared text-level work	Shared word-/ sentence-level work	Focused group work	Independent work	Plenary
1 'My history' recount	Shared reading of the recount.	Nonsense sentences – correct word order.	Guided reading of recounts.	**PSED:** Children around the world – special but different.	Getting in order – sequencing.
2 First, next, finally	Re-reading of recount – annotating key features.	Sequencing recount with appropriate use of capital letters and full stops.	Guided reading – sequencing of recounts.	**CLL:** picture captions. **MD:** racing cars – ordinal numbers.	Pass it round – continuing a recount.
3 First memories	Shared writing of recount.	Using high-frequency words.	Guided writing of recounts.	**KUW:** Writing sentences using computer program.	Sentences – 'Thumbs up!' game.
4 Writing my history	Continued shared writing of recount.	Phonic – 'Yes/No' game.	Guided writing of recounts.	**PD:** Using hoops and beanbags.	Fiction or non-fiction? Looking at different books.
5 Reading 'My history'	Shared reading of class recount.	Phoneme talk – blending phonemes.	Guided writing of recounts.	**CD:** Portrait painting.	Sharing recounts.

Key assessment opportunities
When working with the children during focused group work look closely for:
- ability to match graphemes to phonemes
- ability to blend CVC words
- ability to speak in coherent sentences
- ability to sequence three events
- ability to recall and read on sight familiar words.

Personal, social and emotional development

We are all special
Early Learning Goal
Have a developing respect for their own cultures and beliefs and those of other people.
What you need
Pictures of children from different countries and cultures; role-play area with different props associated with different countries (such as a range of clothing).
What to do
● Ask an adult to work with the children to examine and talk about the pictures of children from around the world.
● Discuss similarities and differences between the children and those in the pictures.
● Encourage the children to dress up and imagine they are children from other parts of the world.

Mathematical development

Who won?
Early Learning Goal
Use developing mathematical ideas and methods to solve practical problems.
What you need
Toy cars; race track or road map; cards with 1st, 2nd, 3rd, 4th, 5th and so on.
What to do
● Encourage the children to make up a car race, deciding who has won and then labelling the cars 1st, 2nd and so on.
● Then use a wooden ramp and ask the children to explore the distance travelled by different cars.

Physical development

Hoopla!
Early Learning Goal
Use a range of small and large equipment.
What you need
Hoops and hoop board (with hooks) for the children to throw hoops on to; beanbags; large hoops.
What to do
● Encourage the children to throw hoops on to the board, counting the number of hoops (out of six) they manage to hook.
● Provide beanbags and large hoops and challenge the children to throw (from a set distance) the beanbags into the hoop. Ask them to see how many they get 'out of six' each turn. What was their best score?

Creative development

Painting faces
Early Learning Goal
Explore colour, texture, shape, form and space in two or three dimensions.
What you need
Painting equipment and easels; photographs of the children (faces only).
What to do
● Provide the children with photographs of themselves (either from home or ones you have taken).
● Encourage some careful observation of features, colours and textures (if possible with adult support). Invite them to paint their own faces matching their hair, skin and eye colour.

Communication, language and literacy

Put it in order!
Early Learning Goal
Speak clearly and audibly with confidence and control and show awareness of the listener, for example by their use of conventions such as greetings, 'please' and 'thank you'.
What you need
Pictures from photocopiable page 86; scissors; pencils; paper; glue sticks.
What to do
● Ask the children to work together to cut out and sequence the pictures in the correct order, sticking them on to a sheet of plain paper.
● Encourage the children to write a caption underneath each one.

Knowledge and understanding of the world

Make a sentence
Early Learning Goal
Find out about and identify the uses of everyday technology and use information and communication technology and programmable toys to support their learning.
What you need
Computer(s); program such as 'Clicker' with a word bank for the children to create sentences.
What to do
● Ensure that the children are familiar with the software and that they understand how to click and drag words to make sentences.
● Encourage the children to work with a partner to create some sentences.

'My history' recount

Objectives

Early Learning Goals
● Communication p54-55.
● Reading p62-63.

Stepping Stones
● Use a widening range of words to express or elaborate ideas.
● Begin to recognise some familiar words.

NLS
T6: To re-read frequently a variety of familiar texts.
S1: To expect written text to make sense and to check for sense if it does not.

What you need
● Photocopiable page 84 enlarged to A3 size
● the words *First, Next, Finally* on card
● the nonsense sentences from photocopiable page 85, enlarged to A3 size and cut into separate sentences
● a set of the individual words from each sentence cut up
● photocopiable page 86, enlarged to A3 size and cut into separate sequencing cards
● a flipchart.

Differentiation

Less able
● Help the children to speak in full sentences by gentle encouragement and by repeating and expanding upon their contributions.

More able
● Encourage the children to talk more extensively about their experiences using a range of vocabulary.

Shared text-level work
● Explain that you are going to read about how somebody learned to talk.
● Can the children remember learning to talk? Do they know what their first words were? (Ask the children to find out about their first words when they go home, to share with you the following day.)
● Read the recount on photocopiable page 84 with plenty of expression all the way through. Then re-read it slowly using a pointer and encouraging the children to join in with you.
● Stop at each section and ask the children to talk to their partner about any memories they have of learning to talk.

Shared sentence-level work
● Now show the children the nonsense sentences (on photocopiable page 85), one at a time. Put each sentence on the flipchart and read them together with the children.
● Ask the children to tell you what is wrong with the sentences. Can they help you to put the sentences in the right order?
● Give out the individual words to different children and ask them to make a line in the right order of the sentence.
● Read the sentence they make and have lots of fun with the class.
● Emphasise, when they do get it right, that they need a capital letter at the start and a full stop at the end.

Focused group work
● Working with a small group of children, explain that you are going to re-read the recount. Ask the children to join in.
● Now say you are going to *retell* the recount.
● Retell the recount, pointing to the words *first, next* and *finally* on cards to emphasise the structure of this type of writing.
● Ask the children to take turns to retell the recount encouraging the use of sequencing words.
● Finally, encourage the children to tell their own recount about how they began to talk.

Independent work
● See the activities for the six Areas of Learning on page 78.

Plenary
● Hand out the sequencing cards from photocopiable page 86 to different children and ask them to line up in the correct sequence. Ask the class to check if they are in the right order. Re-order if necessary.
● Use the cards to recount 'My history' encouraging sequencing words:

> When I was a tiny baby I could only cry. Then I learned to sit up and make lots of noises. Later I could stand up on my own and I could say, 'Dad'. Next I learned to walk and shout, 'Look!'. Later I could ride a bike and say, 'I'm clever'. Finally, now I can write my name and I talk all the time.

TERM 2

First, next, finally

Objectives

Early Learning Goals
● Communication p54-55.
● Reading p62-63.

Stepping Stones
● Use a widening range of words to express or elaborate ideas.
● Begin to recognise some familiar words.

NLS
T6: To re-read frequently a variety of familiar texts.
S4: To use a capital letter for the start of own name.

What you need

● Two copies of the recount from photocopiable page 84 (enlarged to A3 size) – one cut up and re-ordered to make a muddled sequence
● the words *First, Next, Finally* on card
● a flipchart
● sticky notes
● name cards.

Differentiation

Less able
● Help the children to speak in full sentences by elaborating the words and phrases that they use and by modelling complete sentences.

More able
● Encourage the children to talk more extensively using a rich and varied vocabulary.

Shared text-level work

● Remind the children of the recount that you shared the previous day (Day 1, page 79). Ask them if they have found out from home what their first words were.
● Now ask the children to talk to their partners about their first words. After a few moments invite individuals to share their experiences with the whole class.
● Write some examples of the children's first words on sticky notes.
● Now re-read the original recount (on photocopiable page 84), with the children joining in.
● Give out the cards with *First, Next* and *Finally* to three volunteers. Explain that you are going to re-read the recount again and that when they hear the word they are holding they should stand up showing the card to the rest of the class.
● After you have re-read the account again, highlight the three words on the text. Emphasise that these are important words to help get things in the right order.
● Finish by substituting some of the first words from the recount with the children's own first words from the sticky notes. Discuss the changes with the children.

Shared sentence-level work

● Now show the children the muddled recount and ask them to help you put it right.
● Read each section with the children and encourage them to talk to their partners to decide how to re-order the sequence.
● As you re-read and correct the recount, check with the children that each sentence has a capital letter to start and a full stop to finish.
● Discuss when else we use capital letters. Look at the children's name cards and talk about how we use capital letters for names.

Focused group work

● Continue as the previous day (Day 1, page 79), re-reading and retelling the recount.
● Encourage the children to retell their own recount. Emphasise the use of sequencing words to help.

Independent work

● See the activities for the six Areas of Learning on page 78.

Plenary

● In a circle, play a warm-up game such as: *I like... (name of an animal),* with each child taking a turn to speak.
● Now explain that you are going to retell someone's story (someone in the class or an imaginary person).
● Agree on the details and say it through once then pass the recount around the circle. Each child should add a line to retell the recount, as it reaches them around the circle.

UNIT 1 DAY 3 🔲 **My history**

First memories

Objectives

Early Learning Goals
● Thinking p56-59.
● Writing p64-65.

Stepping Stones
● Use talk to connect ideas, explain what is happening and anticipate what might happen next.
● Use writing as a means of recording and communicating.

NLS
T13: To think about and discuss what they intend to write, ahead of writing it.
T14: To use experience of stories, poems and simple recounts as a basis for independent writing eg retelling, substitution, extension, and through shared comparison with adults.
W5: To read on sight a range of familiar words.

What you need
● A flipchart
● the words, *First, Next, Finally, Then, When, Now, Last* and *Went* written on to cards in a large font size
● A3 paper
● two or three sentences you have prepared, (some of which are in the wrong order).

Differentiation

Less able
● Scribe words for the children in focused group work, if necessary.

More able
● Encourage the children to write more extensively.
● Suggest that they cut out their work and staple the pages together with a cover to make a little book.
● Challenge them to illustrate the cover and write their own title.

Shared text-level work
● Remind the children of the recount from the previous two days.
● Explain that this time you are going to write a recount based on your first memories.
● Model the brainstorming process and explain that you need to talk through ideas before you write and that you will just write a few words down to start.
● Show the children how you think aloud: *What's the first thing I can remember? Oh yes, my dad saying, 'Whee!' as he kept pushing my pram, letting it go and then catching it again!* Talk through a few more examples of your own memories and ask the children to help you choose and write down some key words.
● Once you have several incidents, talk through the order, then orally practise one or two sentences from the recount. Ask the children to remind you of things to keep them actively involved.
● Now ask the children to tell their partner a sentence that could be part of their own personal recount.

Shared word-level work
● Build on the children's developing vocabulary by showing them the words that you have prepared on cards. Show the words one at a time and talk about how to read them (initial-letter cues and so on).
● As the children read the words with you, put them on display as a word wall (or pocket chart).
● Re-read the words and put them into meaningful sentences, such as *The first word I said was 'more'.*
● Display a few sentences containing the words for later re-reading and spend a few minutes each day reading them.

Focused group work
● Working with a small group of children, help them to brainstorm their ideas for their first memories.
● Practise sentences orally and then provide the children with a sheet of A3 paper divided into three sections containing the words *First, Next* and *Finally.*
● Help the children to write their sentences, praising all attempts. Ask them to draw pictures in the boxes above to match their sentences.

Independent work
● See the activities for the six Areas of Learning on page 78.

Plenary
● Explain that you have written, but muddled up, some sentences. Put the sentences on a flipchart or interactive whiteboard.
● Read the sentences to the children and ask them to give you 'thumbs up' if they make sense and 'thumbs down' if they do not.
● Ask the children to help you reorder them. Tell them to talk to a partner first before telling you the correct sequence (this helps to involve all the children).

Writing 'My history'

Objectives

Early Learning Goals
● Thinking p56-59.
● Writing p64-65.

Stepping Stones
● Use talk to connect ideas, explain what is happening and anticipate what might happen next.
● Use writing as a means of recording and communicating.

NLS
T14: To use experience of stories, poems and simple recounts as a basis for independent writing
W2: Knowledge of grapheme/phoneme correspondences through hearing and identifying initial sounds in words.

What you need

● Notes from the previous day's shared writing session
● individual whiteboards and pens (enough for one between two)
● pictures of objects, some beginning with the current sound being taught
● 'Yes/No' cards (large and displayed on the wall at opposite sides of the classroom)
● A3 poster
● selection of books (fiction and non-fiction)
● folded cards with Fiction and Non-fiction written on.

Differentiation

Less able
● Emphasise speaking in coherent sentences and encourage the children to 'have a go' at writing, scribing for them if necessary.

More able
● Encourage the children to write independently using the word bank as a reference.

Shared text-level work

● Look through some of the notes and key words you wrote the previous day with the children.
● Now explain that you are going to write the recount. Again, orally rehearse a sentence before you write it. Write one or two sentences including plenty of examples of 'thinking aloud'(see page 81 for an example of how to do this).
● Re-read the sentences with the children and then ask them to tell their partner a sentence of their first memories. Provide a sentence starter such as My first memory is...
● Share some examples of sentences that the children have composed.
● Next, give out whiteboards and pens and ask the children to work in pairs to write a sentence together. Encourage all attempts at phonically plausible spelling and point out words on your wordbank.

Shared word-level work

● Play the 'Yes/No game' for words beginning with a specific sound – using a sound that you are currently teaching.
● Remind the children of the current sound you are learning and write it on the flipchart. Explain that you are going to hold up some pictures and you would like the children to say 'Yes' and point to the 'Yes' card if the sound begins with the sound you are learning and 'No', pointing to the 'No' card if it does not. This is a short, lively interactive game that should only take a few minutes.

Focused group work

● Work with a small group of children as per Day 3 (page 81), helping them to produce a three-stage sequence of first memories to form a simple recount.

Independent work

● See the activities for the six Areas of Learning on page 78.

Plenary

● Show the children a pile of books and explain that you need to put these in the book corner, but that they need to be sorted into two kinds of books – those that tell a story and are not about real events (we call fiction), and those that give information (we call non-fiction).
● Start with some obvious examples, such as 'The Three Little Pigs' or 'Sleeping Beauty' and show the children the covers. Look carefully at the pictures and read the blurb. Put the books in a pile with a folded card saying Fiction.
● Now show the children an obvious non-fiction text such as an information book about animals. Do the same process of looking at the cover and asking the children whether it is fiction (tells a story) or non-fiction (gives information and is true).
● Go through several books in this way, ensuring it remains interactive by involving the children in choosing which pile to place the books on.

UNIT 1 DAY 5 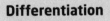 My history

Reading 'My history'

Objectives

Early Learning Goals
- Linking sounds and letters p60-61.
- Thinking p56-59.
- Reading p62-63.

Stepping Stones
- Hear and say the initial sound in words and know which letters represent some of the sounds.
- Use talk to connect ideas, explain what is happening and anticipate what might happen next.
- Begin to recognise some familiar words.

NLS
T6: To re-read frequently a variety of familiar texts.
W2: Knowledge of grapheme/phoneme correspondences through identifying and writing initial and final phonemes in CVC words.

What you need
- The recount written on Day 4 (page 82)
- a puppet.
- a list of suitable CVC words.

Differentiation

Less able
- Provide help by scribing words for the children if necessary. Give them ideas for the content of their recount by showing them examples of the other children's work.

Shared text-level work
- Show the children the recount from the previous day (Day 4, page 82).
- Discuss the main features of a recount – it tells real events in the order they happened; some words help to denote the order (such as *first, next* and *finally*).
- Display the text for the children to see and read it together using a pointer. Talk about any less familiar words as you read and strategies that the children can use to read them.
- Demonstrate strategies such as contextual cues by masking a word by putting your finger over it and reading on to the end of the sentence to see if the children can work out the missing word.
- Choose a child to point as you read (this involves greater participation, and also helps you to ascertain whether a child has fully grasped one-to-one correspondence of the spoken to written word).
- If time allows, share some of the children's own recounts with the class.

Shared word-/sentence-level work
- Show the children the puppet. Explain that the puppet can only speak in sounds (phonemes) and needs the children's help to say words. Ask if they will help the puppet.
- From the list of CVC words you have prepared, have the puppet say each word, saying each phoneme separately (p/i/n). Encourage the children to tell the puppet the whole word. If the children are not familiar with this activity, give quite clear examples to begin with and then proceed to a wider range of words once the children are confident with their responses.
- Make this a short, lively activity.

Focused group work
- Continue as the previous day, helping the children to produce a three-stage sequence of first memories to form a simple recount.

Independent work
- See the activities for the six Areas of Learning on page 78.

Plenary
- With the children gathered together, share and celebrate the recounts they have produced.
- Make a display of the children's work together with the class version and a reminder of the key features of a recount.
- Also revisit the key differences between fiction and non-fiction, using books as examples.
- Create a further display of the most common first words that the children said.
- Finish by modelling a retelling of a recent event in school with plenty of participation from the class.

TERM 2

Learning to talk

The first sounds I made were 'Ba, ba,' and 'Ga, ga.' My mum said I pointed to things when I said them.

Next I began to say my first words. My mum says my first word was 'More!' and I banged my spoon on my high chair.

Another word was 'Dog!'. We have a dog called Harry who likes to play with me.

Next I started to say lots of words but sometimes I didn't get it quite right and said things like 'Me go to park.'

Finally, now I am four my mum says I never stop talking and use lots of big words like 'enormous' and 'fascinating'. I am a real chatterbox now.

Nonsense sentences

word My dad. first was

said I dogs. all were animals

I say could Grandma so I said Ga Ga. not

My chatterbox. says now mum I am a

TERM 2

Put it in order

UNIT 2

The cave

This unit comprises ten days' literacy activities and is based on the book *Can't You Sleep, Little Bear?* by Martin Waddell (Walker Books). It supports the National Literacy Strategy (Medium-term plan) for *Narrative*. Linked activities are provided for all the six Areas of Learning with a strong emphasis on developing speaking and listening skills through the use of dialogue and role-play. The children will develop literacy skills by making their own cartoon books. The activities build towards Year 1 Term 1, Objective 4 of the *Speaking, Listening, Learning* guidance: to explore familiar themes and characters through improvisation and role-play.

WEEK 1

Day	Shared text-level work	Shared word-/ sentence-level work	Focused group work	Independent work	Plenary
1 Read all about it!	Shared reading of the story *Can't You Sleep, Little Bear?*	Creating a word bank of story vocabulary.	Writing questions and answers.	**PSED:** Creating a role-play area – The Cave.	My favourite part of the story is.
2 Talk, talk, talk!	A focus on dialogue.	Writing questions.	Writing questions and answers.	**CLL:** Writing notices for The Cave.	Sharing questions and answers.
3 How do you feel, Little Bear?	Hot-seating of Little Bear with questions.	Phonic game – circle swap shop.	Writing questions and answers.	**MD:** Ordering objects by size. **KUW:** Investigating light.	Describing feelings.
4 How do you feel, Big Bear?	Hot-seating of Big Bear with questions.	Letter formation.	Writing questions and answers.	**PD:** Bear gymnastics.	Writing captions for pictures.
5 Scary poems	Poems – being scared.	Make a sentence.	Writing questions and answers.	**CD:** Role-play activity in the Cave.	Circle time – helping others.

Key assessment opportunities
When working with children look for:
● the ability to sequence a known story
● the ability to work in role
● the ability to understand a character's role in a story
● the ability to match phonemes to graphemes
● the ability to formulate questions and answers.

UNIT 2

WEEK 2

Day	Shared text-level work	Shared word/ sentence-level work	Focused group work	Independent work	Plenary
6 Can't You Swim, Little Bear?	Shared planning for the alternative story, 'Can't You, Swim Little Bear?'.	Write a sentence.	Guided writing – cartoon books about Little Bear.	**PSED:** Role-play – caring for Little Bear.	Sharing alternative bear stories
7 The beginning	Shared writing of the beginning of the story.	Word wall.	Guided writing – cartoon books about Little Bear.	**CLL:** Role-play in The Cave – writing notes to Little Bear.	Advice to Little Bear – reading notes.
8 The middle	Shared writing of the middle of the story with 'thought bubbles'.	'Bingo' – high frequency words.	Guided writing – cartoon books about Little Bear.	**MD:** Using positional vocabulary to describe a model den.	Creating a story using story game cards.
9 The end	Shared writing of the ending.	Supported composition.	Guided writing – cartoon books about Little Bear.	**KUW:** Finding out about the Sun, moon and stars.	Making stories using *big* and *little*.
10 The final version	Shared reading of the alternative version of the story.	Phoneme blending.	Guided writing – cartoon books about Little Bear.	**PD:** Going on a bear hunt! **CD:** Modelling caves using malleable materials.	Reading other Little Bear stories.

Key assessment opportunities

When working with children look for:
- the ability to sequence a known story
- the ability to speak in complete sentences
- the ability to match phonemes to graphemes
- the ability to write recognisable letters
- the ability to write complete sentences.

Personal, social and emotional development

A dark, dark cave
Early Learning Goal
Form good relationships with adults and peers.
What you need
Range of props to create a dark cave such as large pieces of dark material or old curtains; cardboard; a supporting frame; teddy bears; bedding; cushions; chair; book; different-sized lanterns (paper or ready-made).
What to do
● Explain to the children that they are going to work with an adult helper to create a cave. Ask them to arrange the props and resources provided, with an adult fixing larger items in place.
● Encourage the children to co-operate with each other, sharing the resources and listening to each other's ideas.

Physical development

Bear gymnastics
Early Learning Goal
Travel around, under, over and through balancing and climbing equipment.
What you need
A range of equipment, including mats to encourage the children to roll and get into different positions; adult supervision and an open space.
What to do
● Encourage the children to pretend they are Little Bear as they explore different ways of rolling, jumping and turning using the equipment provided.

Communication, language and literacy

Notices in the cave
Early Learning Goal
Attempt writing for different purposes, using features of different forms such as lists, stories and instructions.
What you need
Different sized paper and assorted pens; one or two sample notices such as *Dark Cave, Be Careful*; the story *Can't You Sleep, Little Bear?* by Martin Waddell (Walker Books); the role-play area set up as a cave (see PSED, above).
What to do
● Provide a range of paper and sample notices to encourage the children to create their own to be displayed in the Cave.
● Encourage the children to use the word bank created on Day 1 (page 91).

Mathematical development

Different sizes
Early Learning Goal
Use language such as 'circle' or 'bigger' to describe the shape and size of solids and flat shapes.
What you need
Different-sized lanterns (either pictures or, if possible, real lanterns); a range of other objects to sort by size; labels with the words, *Large, Medium, Small*.
What to do
● Ask the children to sort the selection of objects by size and to label them appropriately.

Creative development

Playing in the cave
Early Learning Goal
Use their imagination in art and design, music, dance, imaginative and role-play and stories.
What you need
The role-play area set up as a cave (see PSED, above).
What to do
● Encourage the children to use the Cave and the props to role-play the story, extending it with further play and ideas.
● Suggest that they also use the Cave to act out their own bedtime stories – perhaps they are having a sleepover with a friend and they are missing their Mummy; or perhaps they are planning a midnight feast!

Knowledge and understanding of the world

Where does light come from?
Early Learning Goal
Find out about, and identify, some features of living things, objects and events they observe.
What you need
Range of objects that give out light such as torches, candles, night lights, lamps and so on.
What to do
● Using adult assistance, show the children the objects and talk about what they do. Where does the light come from? Ensure that correct safety procedures are adhered to when showing the children the equipment, keeping the children at a safe distance.
● Encourage discussion of other sources of light – such as the sun.

Personal, social and emotional development

Caring for Little Bear
Early Learning Goal
Consider the consequences of their words and actions for themselves and others.
What you need
Your role-play area set up as a cave; comfort objects for Little Bear such as a teddy bear, a cup of pretend milk, a blanket, story book and so on.
What to do
● Ask the children to take turns to act the roles of Little Bear and Big Bear. Remind them of how Big Bear looked after Little Bear in the story.
● Suggest that Big Bear provides Little Bear with lots of different comforters to help him relax and go to sleep.

Physical development

A bear hunt!
Early Learning Goal
Move with control and co-ordination.
What you need
A copy of the story *We're going on a Bear Hunt!* by Michael Rosen (Walker Books).
What to do
● With an adult reading the story, encourage the children to move accordingly (running through long grass, paddling through water, squelching through mud and so on).

Communication, language and literacy

Writing notes to Little Bear
Early Learning Goal
Attempt writing for different purposes using features of different forms such as lists, stories and instructions.
What you need
Example notes you have prepared to Little Bear (such as *Don't be scared Little Bear, I will look after you*); a range of different-sized and coloured paper; sticky notes; pencils; pens.
What to do
● Encourage the children to look carefully at the example notes and at the word wall produced in week 1 (see page 79).
● Ask the children to write to Little Bear encouraging all attempts at writing and drawing.

Mathematical development

Put it in position
Early Learning Goal
Use developing mathematical ideas and methods to solve practical problems.
What you need
Wooden blocks; paper; pens.
What to do
● Encourage the children to construct a cave from the wooden blocks.
● Next, ask them to draw the position of the blocks, encouraging the use of positional vocabulary such as *next, behind* and so on.

Creative development

Modelling caves
Early Learning Goal
Explore colour, texture, shape, form and space in two or three dimensions.
What you need
Mod-Roc or other modelling material; scissors; plastic carton (such as one for holding fruit), thick cardboard pieces for bases.
What to do
● Ask an adult to help the children to make a mould for their cave by cutting a plastic carton to shape. Put this on to a cardboard base.
● Then help the children to use the modelling material to form a cover to make the outside of the cave.
● Encourage plenty of talk about caves and their shapes.
● Let the children paint their caves when dry. Use them for small-world play with plastic animals.

Knowledge and understanding of the world

Sun, moon and stars
Early Learning Goal
Observe, find out about and identify features in the place they live and the natural world.
What you need
Range of texts or information downloaded from the internet showing pictures of the sun, moon and stars; paper, pens and pencils.
What to do
● Ask the children to look at the pictures and books.
● Provide paper and pens for them to draw 'Starry night' pictures.
● During a whole-class session, help the children to understand that the moon is not a source of light but that it reflects light from the sun.

Read all about it!

Shared text-level work
● Introduce the story by telling the children the title of the book. Have any of the children read the book before? If so, ask them what they remember about it.
● Look closely at the picture on the cover with the children and ask them to describe what they see. Ensure that the children talk to their partner before they respond to you.
● Now read the story to the children with plenty of expression and enjoyment. Encourage them to join in with the repeated phrase *Can't You Sleep, Little Bear?*
● Talk about the story - in particular about what sort of a person Big Bear is and how he tries to help Little Bear. Ask them what Little Bear is frightened of.
● Re-read the story, this time using a pointer to encourage the children to join in, and for them to see the correspondence between the written and spoken word.

Shared word-level work
● Now or later, show the children the key words from the story that you have printed or written out. Read them one by one with the children and display them in a pocket chart or on the wall.
● Ensure that the children understand the meaning of each word by reading the word individually and then saying the word in a sentence such as: *A lantern is a kind of lamp that gives out light.*
● Ask for a volunteer to point to a word as you say it. Say one of the words and ask the child to find it, assisted by the rest of the class.
● Repeat with further volunteers. This will help the children to recognise the words and will extend their vocabulary.
● Revisit these words regularly during the week for a few minutes.

Focused group work
● Tell the children that there are lots of questions in the story and that you are going to read through the story again, stopping every time you get to a question. Talk about the questions and the answers together.
● Now explain that the children need to think of a different question for you to write. Encourage them to work in pairs to think of questions.
● Write one or two on the flipchart and ask the children to think of the answers that Little or Big Bear might give. Scribe the children's ideas underneath the questions.

Independent work
● See the activities for the six Areas of Learning on page 89.

Plenary
● With the children gathered together, talk about the story, looking at the pictures to remind them.
● Now ask the children to talk to a partner about what they like about the story. Take a class vote on the favourite part.

Objectives

Early Learning Goals
● Reading p62-63.
● Writing p64-65.

Stepping Stones
● Begin to be aware of the way stories are structured.
● Begin to break the flow of speech into words.

NLS
T6: To re-read frequently a variety of familiar texts.
T11: Through shared writing, to apply knowledge of letter/sound correspondences in helping the teacher to scribe, and re-reading what the class has written.
S1: To expect written text to make sense and to check for sense if it does not.

What you need

● The story, *Can't you Sleep Little Bear?* by Martin Waddell (Walker Books)
● the speech bubbles from photocopiable page 101 enlarged to at least A3 size and cut into separate bubbles
● blank speech bubbles cut out of card.

Differentiation

Less able
● Help the children to speak in complete sentences by elaborating on their ideas and modelling examples for them.

More able
● Encourage the children to work with a partner in focused group work to think of some questions and answers.

Talk, talk, talk!

Shared text-level work

● Remind the children of the story from the previous day. Explain that the story consists of Big Bear and Little Bear talking to each other about going to bed and the fear of the dark. Ask the children to share their own experiences of night-time fears.
● Show the children the speech bubbles from photocopiable page 101 and read each one in turn. Explain that the bubbles refer to a mum and her little boy who is worried about going to bed in case there is a monster in his cupboard.
● Ask two children to take the parts of Mummy and the little boy and encourage them to read the words.
● Explain that you would like the children's help to put the speech bubbles into a sensible order.
● Give out the speech bubbles to different children and ask them to stand at the front holding their speech bubble. Ask the class to join in and help them to read the words. Try to order the speech into a sensible sequence together. Have fun reading the bubbles.
● Read your chosen sequence.

Shared word-/sentence-level work

● Remind the children of the original story and make some comparisons between Little Bear and Joseph.
● Show the children how the speech in both the book and in the speech bubbles contains lots of questions.
● Ask the children to think of some more questions for the mum in the speech bubble extract to ask (such as *Are you ready for bed?*). Write the question on to the flipchart with the children suggesting phonetically plausible spellings. Ensure that you discuss the use of a capital letter to start and how you put a question mark on the end of a question.
● If time allows, write a further question and ask a child to write in the question mark.

Focused group work

● Continue as the previous day (Day 1, page 91), asking different children to work with you.
● Refer to the speech bubbles used during shared work and explain to the children that they may think of questions for the mum to ask Joseph or for Big Bear to ask Little Bear.
● Scribe the children's questions onto blank speech bubbles.

Independent work

● See the activities for the six Areas of Learning on page 89.

Plenary

● Share some of the children's questions and answers with the whole class. Encourage the children who have devised the questions to ask the class and then invite the other children to think of a possible answer, before sharing the answers that the children have written.

How do you feel, Little Bear?

Objectives

Early Learning Goals
● Linking sounds and letters p60-61.
● Thinking p56-59.

Stepping Stones
● Hear and say the initial sound in words and know which letters represent some of the sounds.
● Begin to use talk to pretend imaginary situations.

NLS
T7: To use knowledge of familiar texts to re-enact or re-tell to others, recounting the main points in correct sequence.
W2: Knowledge of grapheme/phoneme correspondences.

What you need

● The book *Can't You Sleep, Little Bear?* by Martin Waddell (Walker Books).
● pictures of sad, scared, happy and silly faces
● 'Circle swap shop' instructions from *Progression in Phonics* (DfES, page 20) - choose initial, medial or final phoneme as appropriate, with a list of possible words
● a set of objects representing your chosen phonemes (see *Progression in Phonics* materials page 20 for a list of ideas)
● photocopiable page 101
● blank speech bubbles
● writing materials
● a furry coat or similar prop.

Differentiation

Less able
● Use adult support during shared work to encourage the children to frame suitable questions.

More able
● Encourage the children to use the word wall.

Shared text-level work
● Tell the children that you are going to take the part of Little Bear and that you would like them to ask you some questions. Put on a furry coat or other suitable prop to indicate you are in role!
● Ask the children to think about how Little Bear felt in the Bear Cave and then to talk to their partner about it. Ask different pairs to share their thoughts with the rest of the class.
● Now can they think (in their pairs) of a good question to ask Little Bear. Provide time for discussion and prompt them if necessary.
● Ask for different questions and answer them in role (ensuring that the children understand this).
● Summarise the way that Little Bear felt, writing a few words on the flipchart to reinforce the ideas. Encourage the children to use these ideas in their role-play (see Creative development, page 89).

Shared word-level work
● Explain that you are going to play a sounds game called 'Circle swap shop' (see *Progression in Phonics*, page 20) where the children sit in a circle and swap places with others who have objects representing the same phoneme. Repeat the game several times.
● Finish by playing a game of 'Odd one out'. Gather all the objects together and present the children with three or four objects, one of which is different phonically. Can the children identify the odd one out?

Focused group work
● Continue as the previous day (Day 2, page 91), asking different children to work with you, providing support and extension as appropriate.
● Build on the shared work completed earlier about how Little Bear felt, to help the children to think of questions to ask.
● Scribe these questions together and write them on blank speech bubbles.

Independent work
● See the activities for the six Areas of Learning on page 89.

Plenary
● Ask the children to sit in a circle and show them the different pictures of faces.
● Give a sentence starter to correspond to a face - *I feel sad when...* Provide an example of the rest of the sentence: *I feel sad when I don't have anyone to play with.*
● Go around the circle with each child taking a turn to complete the sentence, *I feel sad when...* and encourage everyone to take part and think of different reasons. As with all circle-time activities, allow children to say 'pass' if they are unable to think of a response.
● If time allows, finish with a fun game, such as quickly saying the person's name to their left or right.

UNIT 2 DAY 4 🔲 The cave

How do you feel Big Bear?

Objectives

Early Learning Goals
● Thinking p56-59.
● Handwriting p66-67.

Stepping Stones
● Begin to use talk to pretend imaginary situations.
● Begin to form recognisable letters.

NLS
T17: To use knowledge of familiar texts to re-enact or re-tell to others, recounting the main points in correct sequence.
W14: To write letters using the correct sequence of movements.

What you need
● Pictures of dark or scary places such as forests, spooky castles, cellars and cupboards (these could be from other children's books such as *The Park in the Dark* by Martin Waddell (Walker Books), *Funnybones* by Allan Ahlberg (Picture Puffin) or *We're going on a Bear Hunt* by Michael Rosen (Walker Books)
● individual whiteboards and pens for each child
● blank speech bubbles.

Shared text-level work
● Remind the children about how they asked you questions in the role of Little Bear (see Day 3, page 92). Now explain that you are going to take the part of Big Bear and that you would like them to think of some good questions.
● How do the children think Big Bear felt in the cave? Remind them of the constant interruptions made by Little Bear while Big Bear was trying to read his book. Discuss Big Bear's unfailing patience and concern for Little Bear.
● Now can the children think of a good question to ask Big Bear? Tell them to share ideas with their partner first. Provide time for discussion and prompt them if necessary.
● Answer the children's questions in role.
● Finish by reminding the children to think about how Big Bear felt when they are playing in the role-play area and taking his part. Make links to PSED (see page 89) and ask the children if they are being kind 'Big Bears'?

Shared word-level work
● Explain that you are going to practise handwriting. Link the work to the current phonemes or words being taught.
● Using the letters currently being learned, provide a prompt for the letter formation, such as *top to bottom, lift and across* (for the letter 't').
● Ask the children to practise in the air (have fun with telling them to rub it out and start again); on each other's backs and finally on whiteboards.
● Monitor the children's work carefully, emphasising the correct pencil grip.

Focused group work
● Continue as the previous day asking different children to work with you, providing support and extension as appropriate.
● Focus on Big Bear and ask the children to think of different questions for you to write to ask Big Bear.
● Scribe these on to blank speech bubbles to add to the class collection.
● Read together those you have written and encourage the children to use plenty of expression when reading.

Independent work
● See the activities for the six Areas of Learning on page 89.

Plenary
● Look at a range of pictures of dark or scary places. Look in detail and talk about what makes the picture scary.
● Explain that you are going to write a caption showing what is scary about it, for example:*The forest is dark and scary*.
● Now ask the children to help you to write some others, suggesting phonetically plausible spellings.

Differentiation

Less able
● Support the children to orally devise questions for you to scribe during focused group work.

More able
● Challenge the children to devise a range of appropriate questions during shared and group work.

Scary poems

Objectives

Early Learning Goal
● Communication p50-51.

Stepping Stone
● Listen to stories with increasing attention and recall.

NLS
T10: To re-read and recite stories and rhymes with predictable and repeated patterns and experiment with similar rhyming patterns.
W5: To read on sight a range of familiar words.

What you need
● The scary poems on photocopiable page 102, copied and enlarged to at least A3 size
● individual words from a sentence from the story, *Can't You Sleep, Little Bear?* by Martin Waddell (Walker Books) printed in large font, or written on to card
● blank speech bubbles.

Shared text-level work
● Introduce the poem 'It's Dark Outside' by Nancy Chambers (on photocopiable page 102). Talk about the title and ask the children what sort of poem they think it will be – funny or scary or sad?
● Read the poem to the children with plenty of expression.
● Then re-read the poem, encouraging the children to join in.
● Discuss different dark places in the children's homes and substitute 'behind the door' for other places, such as: *It's dark inside the cupboard.* Make up some alternative lines for the poem together.

Shared word-level work
● Explain that you would like the children to help you to make a sentence from the story, *Can't You Sleep, Little Bear?*
● Give out individual words from the prepared sentence at random to individual children.
● Ask the children with the words to come out to the front and ask them to try and stand in the right order to make a complete sentence.
● Have fun reading the sentence with the words in the wrong order and ask the children to help sort the sentence out.
● Read the correct sentence together, emphasising clues such as capital letters and full stops.

Focused group work
● Continue as for the previous day, asking different children to work with you, providing support and extension as appropriate.
● Refer to the work on sentences and talk about the punctuation you need. Discuss the use of question marks.
● Scribe the children's questions on to blank speech bubbles to add to the class display.
● Together, read the new sentences that have been written.

Independent work
● See the activities for the six Areas of Learning on page 89.

Plenary
● Ask the children to sit in a circle and begin with a fun warm-up game, such as swapping places with someone wearing the same item. For example, you could say, *Everyone wearing white socks swap places with each other!* Continue the game for a few minutes.
● Now talk about helping others and ask them who they think is kind and helpful in the story.
● Tell the children an example of helping you have seen in school, perhaps in the playground.
● Now go round the circle with a sentence prompt: *I am helpful when I...* Encourage all the children to contribute, but allow some to pass if they lack confidence.
● Finish by passing a squeeze round the circle by squeezing hands in turn!

Differentiation

Less able
● Support some less able children to use the pointer when you read the poem in shared text-level work.

More able
● Encourage the children to read some words from the poem independently.

UNIT 2 DAY 6 📖 The cave

Can't you swim, Little Bear?

Objectives

Early Learning Goal
● Writing p64-65.

Stepping Stone
● Begin to break the flow of speech into words.

NLS
T14: To use experience of stories, poems and simple recounts as a basis for independent writing, eg re-telling, substitution, extension, and through shared composition with adults.
S1: To expect written text to make sense and to check for sense if it does not.
W5: To read on sight a range of familiar words.

What you need

● A flipchart.
● mini books (made from folding several sheets of A5 paper in half and stapling down the side)
● individual whiteboards and pens, sufficient for one between two
● examples of cartoons
● white paper cut into speech bubbles
● glue sticks
● writing materials.

Differentiation

Less able
● Encourage and value all attempts at mark making in focused group work.
● Help the children as required and ask them to verbally rehearse their speech bubbles.

More able
● Encourage the children to use a wide and descriptive vocabulary.

Shared text-level work

● Remind the children of the story *Can't You Sleep, Little Bear?* and talk about the main events.
● Explain that the children are going to help you write a different version of the story and this time you will call it 'Can't you *Swim*, Little Bear?'.
● Now brainstorm all the things that Little Bear might be frightened of (to do with swimming) and write them on the flipchart.
● Ask, *Where might the story be set?*
● Talk about how Big Bear could help and what could happen in the end. Explain that this is the plan for the class story and you will continue with it tomorrow.

Shared word-/sentence-level work

● Give out the whiteboards and pens to pairs of children.
● Explain that you want the children to try and write a sentence together relating to the idea for the class story. Give them an example, such as: *I am scared*.
● Ask the children to help each other to write the sentence. Invite them to show you their writing and praise all phonetically plausible attempts.
● Use the children's mistakes (sensitively) as teaching points for the whole class.

Focused group work

● Tell the children that they will be writing their own versions of the story, (*Can't You Sleep, Little Bear?*). Explain that they will be cartoon stories and will be made into little books.
● Show the children some examples of cartoons and discuss the features, such as the use of pictures and speech bubbles.
● Now brainstorm together the main events in the original story.
● Challenge the children to draw four different pictures in their books to tell the story. Talk this through with each child before they begin, to ensure that they have a picture to represent the beginning and end of the story with two pictures for the middle.
● Model writing a speech bubble for the story and then encourage the children to 'have a go' at writing their own on the blank speech bubble.
● Let the children stick their speech bubbles with the relevant pictures in their books. Continue the process until all four pages are finished.

Independent work

● See the activities for the six Areas of Learning on page 90.

Plenary

● Ask the children who have been working with you to share their stories with the class.
● Read the stories together and discuss the similarities and differences.

Objectives

Early Learning Goals
● Linking sounds and letters p60-61.
● Writing p64-65.

Stepping Stone
● Begin to break the flow of speech into words.

NLS
T14: To use experience of stories, poems and simple recounts as a basis for independent writing, eg re-telling, substitution, extension, and through shared composition with adults.
S1: To expect written text to make sense and to check for sense if it does not.
W5: To read on sight a range of familiar words.
W11: To make collections of personal interest or significant words and words linked to particular topics.

What you need

● Prepared mini books
● the word wall from Week 1 (see Day 1, page 79)
● examples of cartoons
● white paper cut into speech bubbles
● glue sticks
● writing materials
● a flipchart and large paper
● card for writing words.

Differentiation

Less able
● Encourage all attempts at writing in focused group work.
● Ensure that the children verbally rehearse their speech bubbles.

More able
● Encourage the children to use a range of descriptive vocabulary.

The beginning

Shared text-level work

● Remind the children of the plan of the class story from the previous day. *What was Little Bear afraid of? How might Big Bear help?*
● Ensure that you have fully discussed all the essential elements of the alternative story (the setting, the problem, and the solution - reinforcing the features of the two characters). Also talk about the cartoon stories that some of the children made the previous day.
● Now explain that you are going to write the beginning of the story as a cartoon and ensure that the children understand what is different about a cartoon story.
● Ask them to talk with a partner to suggest how the story should begin.
● Draw a simple outline (or have a ready-prepared one, possibly using Clip Art, depending on your drawing skills!). Use teacher-scribing to write the first speech bubble for the beginning of the story.
● Write one or two further speech bubbles with the children's help and then re-read the story so far with the children.
● Emphasise that this is the beginning of the story and call it 'Part 1'.

Shared word-/sentence-level work

● Refer to the word wall made in Week 1 (see page 79). Read the words through with the class, choosing one child to be the 'teacher' who needs to point to different words.
● Add one or two further words that have occurred during the writing of the alternative story (such as *swim*). Write the new words on large pieces of card for the children to see.
● Put any new words into meaningful sentences, such as *I learned to* **swim** *in the sea with my dad.*
● Ask another child to take a turn to be the teacher to point to different words. Read them as a whole class.

Focused group work

● Continue as the previous day, asking different children to work with you.
● Encourage the children to orally rehearse the speech bubbles for their books, discussing whether they make sense.

Independent work

● See the activities for the six Areas of Learning on page 90.

Plenary

● With the children gathered together talk about the role-play area – The Cave. Ask them to show and tell you about any notes that they have been writing to Little Bear (see CLL, page 90).
● Read a range of the children's notes as well as the example ones that you prepared.
● Talk about further notes and ask the children for suggestions. Write a new note by scribing the children's ideas.

The middle

Objectives

Early Learning Goals
● Writing p64-65.

Stepping Stone
● Use writing as a means of recording and communicating.

NLS
T14: To use experience of stories, poems and simple recounts as a basis for independent writing, eg re-telling, substitution, extension, and through shared composition with adults.
S1: To expect written text to make sense and to check for sense if it does not.
W5: To read on sight a range of familiar words.

What you need

● Prepared mini books
● the word wall from Week 1 (see Day 1, page 79)
● examples of cartoons or picture books showing thought bubbles
● white paper cut into speech bubbles
● glue sticks
● writing materials
● a flip chart and large paper
● card for writing words on to
● 'Bingo' game cards (see photocopiable page 19, Term 1)
● the story game cards on photocopiable page 103, enlarged if possible and cut out.

Differentiation

Less able
● Help the children to attempt writing some words during group work, ensuring that they verbally rehearse their speech bubbles first.

More able
● Encourage the children to write independently.

Shared text-level work

● Look at the story you began the previous day (page 97) with the children and read through some of the speech bubbles.
● Explain that you are going to write the middle part of the story together and talk about what happens next.
● Draw pictures for the next part (or use some Clip Art if you wish!).
● This time say that instead of speech bubbles you are going to add thought bubbles showing what Little Bear and Big Bear are thinking.
● Ask the children to consider what the characters might be thinking and brainstorm some ideas together. Encourage the children to talk with their partner about their suggestions.
● Listen to the children's ideas and write one or two thought bubbles together, using teacher scribing. Read them through and each time emphasise the skill of reading for sense.

Shared word-/sentence-level work

● Next, or at a later time in the day, explain that you are going to play 'Bingo' (using the cards from photocopiable page 19, Term 1), with one 'Bingo' card for each pair of children (provide adult support for less able children).
● You will need a set of all the individual words from the cards to read out. Explain that the children must cross out the words on their card as they hear them. They should shout, 'Bingo' when all their words are crossed out.

Focused group work

● Continue as the previous day, asking different children to work with you.
● Ensure that the children orally rehearse speech bubbles for their books, discussing whether they make sense.

Independent work

● See the activities for the six Areas of Learning on page 90.

Plenary

● Ask the children to sit in a circle and explain that you are going to make up a story about being scared. Show the children the cards that give pictures of places, people and objects and explain that you are going to use these to help the class make up a story.
● Put the cards in separate piles in the middle of the circle. Begin the story, saying, for example: *I was very scared when one night...* (pick up a card from the 'places' pile and use this to continue) *I was in my bedroom when...* (now a child volunteers to pick up a card and carries on the story).
● Support the children to use the cards to make a story and encourage as many children to take part as possible.
● Finish by retelling the story that you have made together.
● Place the cards in the Cave to help the children create good stories.

The end

Objectives

Early Learning Goals
● Linking sounds and letters p60-61.

Stepping Stone
● Hear and say the initial sound in words and know which letters represent some of the sounds.

NLS
T14: To use experience of stories, poems and simple recounts as a basis for independent writing, eg re-telling, substitution, extension, and through shared composition with adults.
S1: To expect written text to make sense and to check for sense if it does not.
W5: To read on sight a range of familiar words.
W11: To make collections of personal interest or significant words.

What you need
● Prepared mini books
● examples of cartoons
● white paper cut into speech bubbles.
● glue sticks
● writing materials
● a flipchart and large paper
● whiteboards and pens (one between two children).

Differentiation

Less able
● Ensure that the children verbally rehearse sentences in group work and encourage all attempts at mark making.

More able
● Encourage the children to write independently.

Shared text-level work
● Show the children the parts of the cartoon story that you have been writing together and read the speech and thought bubbles written so far. Encourage the children to join in where possible.
● Now explain that you want to write the ending of the story and remind the children of the plan created previously.
● Ask the children to tell their partner what could happen in the end and then ask different children to share their possible endings.
● Draw the final part of the story (or have this ready prepared) and add one or two speech bubbles to complete the story using teacher scribing.
● Read the speech bubbles together.
● Now read the whole story you have created together and display it in the classroom for the children to re-read at a later time.

Shared word-/sentence-level work
● Explain that you would like the children to practise writing a speech bubble for the end of the story. Tell them that they may work with a partner and give out whiteboards to pairs of children.
● Ask the children to work with their partner to write a suitable speech bubble using phonetically plausible spellings of words. Provide support where necessary.
● Read some of the examples to the class and praise good attempts at spelling words.
● Pick up on common errors (sensitively) to provide teaching points and reinforce the spelling of common words.

Focused group work
● Continue as the previous day asking different children to work with you.
● Ensure the children orally rehearse speech bubbles for their books, and help them to create a sequence.

Independent work
● See the activities for the six Areas of Learning on page 90.

Plenary
● With the children on the carpet, explain that they are going to help you write some sentences using the words *big* and *little*.
● Brainstorm one or two sentences using these words. For example: *Big Bear was kind to Little Bear.* Write the sentences on to the flipchart with the children helping.
● Now ask the children to think of some other big and little animals. Challenge them to tell their partner a sentence using the words *big* and *little*.
● Write another sentence on the flipchart, asking different children to contribute to the spellings of the words.
● Read the sentences carefully together to check that they make sense.

UNIT 2 DAY 10 📖 The cave

Objectives

Early Learning Goal
● Linking sounds and letters p60-61.

Stepping Stone
● Hear and say the initial sound in words and know which letters represent some of the sounds.

NLS
T14: To use experience of stories, poems and simple recounts as a basis for independent writing.
S1: To expect written text to make sense and to check for sense if it does not.
W2: Knowledge of grapheme/phoneme correspondences.

What you need

● A flipchart with the class story on it
● dressing-up clothes
● 'The Closet' poem from photocopiable page 102, enlarged to at least A3 size
● prepared mini books
● blank speech bubbles
● glue sticks
● writing materials
● a puppet
● a list of words for blending (CVC words such as *tap* or CCVC words, such as *clap* – appropriate to the current phonics being taught)
● a bear story such as *You and Me, Little Bear* by Martin Waddell (Walker Books).

Differentiation

Less able
● Help the children to attempt writing some words during focused group work.

More able
● Encourage the children to write independently.

The final version

Shared text-level work

● Read the story that you have created – 'Can't You Swim, Little Bear?', talking about how we read pictures as well as words. Model how to carefully describe what is happening in each picture and then read the speech bubbles and thought bubbles together.
● Follow on by reading the poem, 'The Closet' together with the class. Begin by introducing it and ensuring that the children know what a *closet* is. Ask: *Have you ever hidden or played in cupboard?*
● Now read the poem to the children and discuss what is happening. Make sure that all the vocabulary is familiar (particularly the word *lair*).
● Talk to the children about games of 'pretending'. Can they think of any examples to tell you about?
● If you have any suitable dressing-up clothes, use these and ask a child to put on a large hat or a coat. Describe who they could pretend to be in these clothes. Ask the children what you could pretend a fur coat could be and make links to a bear.
● Finish by talking to the children about the role-play area (see PSED and CD, page 89).

Shared word-/sentence-level work

● Show the children your chosen puppet (it may be a special class one) and explain that the puppet can only speak in sounds (phonemes). Tell the children that the puppet needs their help to say words (see also Day 5 of 'My history', page 83).
● Have the puppet say each word from the list of CVC or CCVC words you have prepared, saying each phoneme separately (t/i/n) and so on.
● The children have to tell the puppet what the word is each time.
● If time allows, the children could also say words in phonemes for the puppet to copy.

Focused group work

● Continue as the previous day, asking different children to work with you.
● Ensure children orally rehearse speech bubbles for their books. Check the order of the children's sequences with them before they stick their speech bubbles into their books.

Independent work

● See the activities for the six Areas of Learning on page 90.

Plenary

● Complete the unit by reading a further bear story, such as *You and Me, Little Bear* by Martin Waddell (Walker Books).
● Ensure that you make links to the story read previously and spend some time introducing the story, encouraging predictions as to the content of the book before you read it.
● Discuss the similarities and differences with *Can't You Sleep, Little Bear?*

There's a monster in my cupboard

No, I'm not frightened of the dark!

Well, I'll check for you when you're asleep.

Yes, now go to sleep.

See, there's no monster in there.

I'm frightened.

You can check, but let me hide my eyes first.

Oh thanks, will you?

What are you afraid of then?

I think there might be a monster in the cupboard!

But a monster might come in the middle of the night.

Shall I put a night light on in your room?

I don't want to go to bed.

Why don't you want to go to bed, Joseph?

Would you like me to check for you?

TERM 2

It's dark outside

It's dark outside.
It's dark inside.
It's dark behind the door.

I wonder
if I'm brave enough
to walk across the floor.

I am –
at least I think I am.
I'll try it once and see

if Mum comes up
or stays downstairs
with Dad and cups of tea.

Nancy Chambers

Closet

I like to
pretend

the raincoat
sleeves
are the leaves.

I like to
pretend

the slippery
boots
are the roots

I like
to pretend

The old fur coat
is my friend
the brown bear,

who lets me
hide
in her lair.

Judith Thurman

Story game cards

UNIT 3

Five counting rhymes

This unit is based on a range of rhymes, comprises five days' literacy activities and supports the National Literacy Strategy (Later Foundation Stage, Medium-term plan) focus on *Action rhymes and verses*. It will help develop phonological awareness through rhyme and provide a focus for writing. Linked activities are provided for all the six Areas of Learning with a strong emphasis on developing speaking and listening skills, making links to Mathematical development and developing literacy skills through generating rhymes.

Day	Shared text-level work	Shared word-/ sentence level work	Focused group work	Independent work	Plenary
1 Fox in a box	Shared reading of rhyme.	Generating rhyming words.	Guided reading of rhymes.	**PSED:** Concentrating – listening to tapes.	Reading action rhymes.
2 How many kittens?	Shared reading of counting rhyme with actions.	Word wall – vocabulary extension.	Guided reading of rhymes.	**CLL:** Taped poems and rhymes.	Where do different animals live?
3 Make up a rhyme	Shared drafting of alternative counting rhyme.	Onset and rime wheels and dice.	Guided reading of rhymes.	**MD:** Counting, and sorting animals.	How many animals altogether?
4 Write a poem	Shared writing of alternative counting rhyme.	Rhyming word wall.	Guided reading of rhymes.	**KUW:** Small world play – zoos.	Moving like an animal.
5 Perform a rhyme	Performing own counting rhyme with sounds.	Spot the mistakes – missing full stops.	Guided reading of rhymes.	**PD:** Animal movements. **CD:** Musical animals.	Performing action rhymes.

Key assessment opportunities
When working with children during role-play look closely for:
● ability to generate rhyming words
● ability to read a growing range of words
● ability to produce writing for a real purpose
● ability to respond to a range of stimulus appropriately.

Personal, social and emotional development

Keep listening!
Early Learning Goal
Maintain attention, concentrate, and sit quietly when appropriate.
What you need
A cosy listening area; tape recorder(s) with headphones; poem tapes; corresponding books or poems.
What to do
● Show the children the cosy listening area that you have prepared and explain that it is a quiet area where they can choose to go to listen carefully to a poem or story on tape. Explain that you would like them to concentrate hard and sit quietly in this area.
● Provide adult help to operate the tape recorders. Ask the adult to note the children's response to the tapes and their ability to maintain concentration.

Knowledge and understanding of the world

Where do animals live?
Early Learning Goal
Find out about, and identify, some features of living things, objects and events they observe.
What you need
A toy farm with a range of different animals.
What to do
● Encourage the children to work together to organise the farm and put the animals in the correct places - the pigs in the sty; horses in the stable; and so on.
● If possible take some digital photos of the work to discuss in a plenary session.

Communication, language and literacy

Come and listen!
Early Learning Goal
Listen with enjoyment, and respond to stories, songs and other music, rhymes and poems and make up their own stories, songs, rhymes and poems.
What you need
Tape recorder(s) with headphones; poem tapes; corresponding books or poems.
What to do
● Ensure that the children know how to work the tape recorder and tapes and change the tape if necessary.
● Encourage the children to listen attentively and follow the printed versions of the poems to the best of their ability.

Physical development

Animal movements
Early Learning Goal
Move with control and coordination.
What you need
Large open space; signs with a different animal indicated on each one and a matching picture on card; the poem 'Like an Animal' by Joan Poulson, on photocopiable page 111.
What to do
● Set up your large space by placing the animal signs in different areas.
● Read the rhyme to the children and encourage them to develop some actions to go with each animal mentioned. Can they slither like a snake? Snap like a shark? And so on.
● Now hold up the pictures. The children should move in the manner of the animal to the area of the room designated by the matching sign.

Mathematical development

How many animals?
Early Learning Goal
Count reliably up to 10 everyday objects.
What you need
Range of plastic animals; number cards (1-20); sorting hoops.
What to do
● Ask the children to sort the different types of animals into sorting hoops, count them and then find the matching number cards to put in the hoops.
● Ask more able children to combine two groups of animals to find a total.

Creative development

Musical animals
Early Learning Goal
Recognise and explore how sounds can be changed, sing simple songs from memory, recognise repeated sounds and sound patterns and match movements to music.
What you need
Range of musical instruments; pictures of different animals.
What to do
● Ask the children to explore the different sounds they can make with the instruments.
● Provide pictures of animals and ask the children to try and make the noises that the animals make, using the instruments.

Fox in a Box

Objectives

Early Learning Goals
● Linking sounds and letters p60-61.
● Reading p62-63.

Stepping Stones
● Continue a rhyming string.
● Begin to recognise some familiar words.

NLS
T10: To re-read and recite stories and rhymes with predictable and repeated patterns and experiment with similar rhyming patterns.
W1: To understand and be able to rhyme through recognising, exploring and working with rhyming patterns.

What you need
● An enlarged copy of the poem 'Fox in a Box'
● pictures of animals and corresponding rhyming objects (laminated on card) such as a frog and a log, a snake and a cake, a cat and a hat, a mouse and a house and so on
● a Big Book of action verses
● any text of action rhymes or poems you have available, such as *All Join In* by Quentin Blake (Red Fox).

Differentiation

Less able
● Provide support to read less familiar words. Focus on reading and generating rhyming words.

More able
● Encourage the children to read rhymes, or parts of rhymes without assistance.

Shared text-level work
● Display an enlarged copy of the rhyme 'Fox in a Box'.

> **Fox in a Box**
> There's a fox in a box in my little bed, my little bed,
> My little bed.
> There's a fox in a box in my little bed
> And there isn't much room for me.
>
> There's a snake in a cake in my little bed, my little bed,
> My little bed.
> There's a snake in a cake in my little bed
> And there isn't much room for me.

● Read or sing the rhyme to the children with expression and enjoyment.
● Ask the children to read (or sing) the rhyme with you. Use a pointer to enable the children to follow the words. Invite the children to share any experiences they may have had of seeing foxes (in the garden, perhaps) or snakes (at the zoo).

Shared word-level work
● Start by saying or singing the rhyme 'Fox in a box' below.
● Explain that you have some pictures that are muddled up and you need to put them together into rhyming pairs.
● Give a card to each pupil (or as many pupils as you have cards) and ask a child to start by holding up their card and saying what is on it (for example, *cat*).
● The pupil with a rhyming picture (for example, *hat*) should hold up their picture and stand next to the person with the picture of the cat. Continue in this way until you have all the cards paired.
● Now say the rhyme 'Fox in a box' again, using the rhyming pairs to generate more verses.

Focused group work
● Use a Big Book of poems or action verses and carry out a guided reading session.
● Talk about the book and each poem before reading, demonstrating strategies to read less well-known words.
● Read the poems together with actions as appropriate. Talk about the poems and any similarities or differences with the one read earlier.

Independent work
● See the activities for the six Areas of Learning on page 105.

Plenary
● With the children gathered together, finish by reading further action rhymes.

How many kittens?

Objectives

Early Learning Goals
● Communication p50-51.
● Reading p62-63.

Stepping Stones
● Listen to favourite nursery rhymes, stories and songs. Join in with repeated refrains, anticipating key events and important phrases.
● Begin to recognise some familiar words.

NLS
T10: To re-read and recite stories and rhymes with predictable and repeated patterns and experiment with similar rhyming patterns.
W10: New words from their reading and shared experiences.

What you need

● Copy of 'Five Little Kittens' from photocopiable page 111, enlarged to at least A3 size
● digital photos of small-world play of farm (optional, see page 105)
● key vocabulary from the poem, printed in minimum 48 point font or handwritten on to card: *kittens, chair, mouse, wall, ball, silk, milk, tree, bird, nest, dish.*
● a flipchart.

Differentiation

Less able
● Provide plenty of support to read and generate rhyming words.

More able
● Encourage more able children to think of additional words that rhyme with the words in the poems.

Shared text-level work

● Begin by talking about kittens and ask if anyone has one at home, or has seen one. Talk about the typical things they do and what they eat and drink.
● Now display the poem 'Five Little Kittens' and read it together with plenty of expression and enjoyment, encouraging the children to join in wherever possible.
● Ensure that the children are familiar with the meaning of all the terms such as *nest*.
● Ask the children what they notice about the poem (that it is a counting poem). Can they think of any other counting poems or rhymes?
● Invite five children to take the parts of the kittens and re-read the poem together, with the children doing the appropriate actions.
● As time allows, repeat the activity allowing different children to take the part of the five kittens.

Shared word-level work

● Now or later, show the children some words from the poems you have printed or written out. Read them one by one with the children and display them in a pocket chart, or on the wall.
● Ensure that the children understand the meaning of each word by reading the word individually and then saying the word in a sentence. For example, *It was a nice chair to sit on*.
● Ask for a volunteer to help point to the words displayed. Say a word such as *mouse* for the child to point to, assisted by the rest of the class.
● Continue in this way to help word recognition and to widen vocabulary.

Focused group work

● Continue as Day 1 (page 106), ensuring that you provide opportunities to put actions to the poems.
● Discuss any similarities or differences with the rhymes read during shared reading.

Independent work

● See the activities for the six Areas of Learning on page 105.

Plenary

● With the children sat on the carpet, talk about the farm activity that some children have been involved with during independent work (see KUW, page 105).
● If you have managed to take some digital photos, show these to the class, possibly on an interactive whiteboard.
● Ask the children who worked on the farm activity to explain their choice of animal homes.
● Now write a list of animals and their homes on the flip chart with the children helping, such as dog and basket; bird and nest; pig and sty; horse and stable.

Make up a rhyme

Objectives

Early Learning Goals
● Linking sounds and letters p60-61.
● Communication p50-51.
● Reading p62-63.

Stepping Stones
● Continue a rhyming string.
● Listen to favourite nursery rhymes, stories and songs. Join in with repeated refrains, anticipating key events and important phrases.
● Begin to recognise some familiar words.

NLS
T10: To re-read and recite stories and rhymes with predictable and repeated patterns and experiment with rhyming patterns.
W1: To understand and be able to rhyme through extending these patterns by analogy, generating new and invented words in speech and spelling.

What you need
● A flipchart and pens
● the poem 'Five Little Kittens' on photocopiable page 111
● rhyming cards from Day 1 (see page 106)
● two blank dice with onset stickers (f, b, h, c, s, r) on one and rime stickers (at, it, in, og, an, ar) on the other.

Differentiation

Less able
● Say two or three rhyming words together plus one that doesn't rhyme. Encourage the children to spot the odd one out. Write the words down to show how the non-rhyming word looks different.

More able
● Encourage the children to read rhymes without assistance.

Shared text-level work
● Explain that the class is going to make up their own counting rhyme. Talk about 'Five Little Kittens' and re-read it quickly. Remind the children of any counting rhymes that you have read in the previous two days. Look at any similar features.
● Together, choose an animal to write a poem about. Once you have decided on an animal, talk about what could happen to them.
● Write a few words on the flipchart, but concentrate on working orally.
● Talk about the pattern of the poem and what is the same and what part changes. Underline or highlight particular words in 'Five Little Kittens' to show the repeated lines.
● Say you will continue with the poem the next day.

Shared word-level work
● Talk about how we often use rhyming words to make up poems. Discuss how the final part of a word can be the same in many words – such as *hat, cat* and *pat.*
● Point out that these words have the same sound and spelling (the rime). Show this by writing the words on the flipchart using two colours, with one colour for the onset (*h*) and another colour for the rime (*at*). Draw up a list of words that share the same rime.
● Now, using onset and rime dice you have made up, throw both dice and blend the onset with the rime to see if it makes a word. Write a list of words on the flipchart and talk about those that are 'real' words and those that are nonsense words.
● Encourage the children to generate a range of real and nonsense words as practice for blending phonemes.

Focused group work
● Continue as the previous day, ensuring that you provide opportunities to put actions to the poems.
● Discuss any similarities or differences with the rhymes read during shared reading and look at any with similar patterns (such as a number of animals or objects which decrease each verse).

Independent work
● See the activities for the six Areas of Learning on page 105.

Plenary
● Ask the children that have been working on the activity for mathematical development (see page 106) to share what they have been doing with the class.
● Using a pile of mixed animals, sorting hoops and number cards, carry out the activity with the class.
● Extend by adding two groups of animals together to make a total. Encourage vocabulary such as which hoop contains the most animals and so on.
● Make links to the counting rhymes and finish by reciting one.

Write a poem

Shared text-level work

● Remind the children of the poem you began yesterday and the animal you decided to write about.
● Now provide a poem format (see below) and ask the children to continue writing the poem with you, using the format as a guide. Pay particular attention to the final line and how to make a happy ending – for example:

Five little elephants went walking one day bumped into a mongoose And ran far away. (And so on, until): One lonely elephant went walking one day Bumped into his friends And never went far away.	Five little … went … … into a … And … Four little … went … … into a … And … (And so on until One …)

Shared word-level work

● Revisit the word wall created on Day 2 (see page 107) and explain that you are going to add some rhyming words.
● Ask the children to tell you some of the rhyming words in the poems you have read together during the week. Do this by re-reading the poems and writing and underlining all the rhyming words on the flipchart.
● Write some of the rhyming words on to card and display on a 'rhyming wall'.
● Read one word and then invite a child to point to a corresponding rhyming word.

Focused group work

● Continue as the previous day, ensuring that you provide opportunities to put actions to the poems.
● Discuss any similarities or differences with the rhymes read during shared reading and look at any with similar patterns (such as counting down from five to one, and any surprises at the end).

Independent work

● See the activities for the six Areas of Learning on page 105.

Plenary

● With the children on the carpet, read the poem 'Like an Animal' from photocopiable page 111. (Some of them will have been making movements to this poem during independent work (see PD, page 105).
● Choose some pupils to take the parts in the poem and read the poem with the children making the appropriate actions and noises.
● If time and space allows, perhaps in the school hall, encourage the whole class to move to the poem.
● Select other children to take the parts and read the poem once more.

Perform a rhyme

Objectives

Early Learning Goals
● Communication p54-55.
● Reading p62-63.

Stepping Stones
● Use a widening range of words to express or elaborate ideas.
● Begin to recognise some familiar words.

NLS
T10: To re-read and recite stories and rhymes with predictable and repeated patterns and experiment with similar rhyming patterns.
W1: To understand and be able to rhyme through recognising, exploring and working with rhyming patterns.

What you need
● Poem from photocopiable page 111 and any others read together during the week.
● the poem created by the class
● the class poem written out in big text with the full stops deleted
● a selection of musical instruments
● a long and short sentence from a familiar text
● pens.

Differentiation

Less able
● Let the children be first to choose and demonstrate their instruments for making animal sounds.

More able
● Invite one or two more confident children to read the class poem out loud for everyone to enjoy.

Shared text-level work
● Review some of the different poems read during the week and then re-read the class poem written the previous day, encouraging everyone to join in.
● Talk about what kinds of sounds and actions could be added to indicate the different animals and their actions (as described in the poem).
● Introduce some musical instruments and hand them out to individual pupils.
● Re-read the poem and invite the children to help you to annotate the poem with symbols to show the different sounds that will be included. Encourage plenty of expression and movement.
● Practise several times, keeping a careful eye on the volume of noise!

Shared word-level work
● Look at the class poem together again. Now show the children the version you have prepared without the full stops.
● Ask the children what is missing and then discuss the purpose of full stops.
● Read the poem together and ask the children to find the missing full stops, choosing children to come and add the full stops in the correct places.
● Make clear that they do not always go at the end of every line - only at the end of every sentence.
● For added emphasis, provide two different sentences from familiar stories or poems - one which is very short, and one long; or use an enlarged class text which demonstrates this.
● Praise all the children's attempts to add in full stops. Use any mistakes made (sensitively) to teach correct punctuation.

Focused group work
● Continue as the previous day, ensuring that you provide opportunities to put actions to the poems.
● Discuss any similarities or differences with the rhymes read during shared reading. Do any of them have matching rhymes or similar patterns?

Independent work
● See the activities for the six Areas of Learning on page 105.

Plenary
● Explain to the children that, together, you are going to re-read some of the poems you have read during the week.
● Ask the children to provide the actions.
● Read each poem with plenty of expression and enjoyment, choosing different children to take the parts.
● Finish by reading the class poem and if time allows, brainstorm another version.

Animal rhymes

Five Little Kittens

Five little kittens
Sleeping on a chair.
One rolled off,
Leaving four there.

Four little kittens,
One climbed a tree
To look in a bird's nest.
Then there were three.

Three little kittens
Wondered what to do.
One saw a mouse.
Then there were two.

Two little kittens
Playing near a wall.
One little kitten
Chased a red ball.

One little kitten
With fur soft as silk,
Left all alone
To drink a dish of milk.

Traditional

Like an Animal

I snarl and snap
around the park
pretend that I'm a
strong fierce shark

I jump and hop
off a fallen log
pretend that I'm a
bright-eyed frog

I slide zig-zag
beside the lake
pretend that I'm a
patterned snake

I leap and spring
bound
everywhere
pretend that I'm a
long-legged hare.

Joan Poulson

UNIT 4

The class art gallery

This unit comprises five days' literacy activities and supports the National Literacy Strategy (Later Foundation Stage, Medium-term plan) focus on *Non-fiction: labels and captions for information*. The activities in this unit provide a real purpose for writing through creating labels and captions. Linked activities are provided for all the six Areas of Learning with a strong emphasis on developing speaking and listening skillsand Creative development. The activities in this unit will encourage the children to listen carefully and ask relevant questions and will develop skills of speaking clearly in complete sentences.

Day	Shared text-level work	Shared word-/ sentence-level work	Focused group work	Independent work	Plenary
1 Visiting an art gallery	Visit to art gallery/class exhibition – devising questions.	Visit to art gallery/class exhibition – looking at captions.	Visit to art gallery/class exhibition – answering questions.	**PSED:** Valuing different cultures.	Discussing the visit and photos taken.
2 Caption it!	Shared writing of captions to photos and postcards.	High frequency word game.	Writing captions.	**CLL:** Writing captions.	Matching captions game.
3 Make a poster	Shared writing of posters.	Individual whiteboard practice – correct letter formation.	Writing posters.	**MD:** Adding and subtracting faces game.	Parts of the body – singing.
4 Invitations to the gallery	Shared writing of invitations.	Silly sentences.	Writing invitations.	**KUW:** Making a frame.	Looking at faces: art from around the world.
5 Listen	Creating a commentary for a class gallery.	Phonic game – blending.	Making an audio tape.	**PD:** Body songs. **CD:** Painting portraits.	Opening of class exhibition.

Key assessment opportunities
When working with children look closely for:
● ability to form recognisable letters
● ability to produce writing for a real purpose
● ability to speak clearly
● ability to recognise high frequency words.
Record appropriately and ensure that this informs future planning.

Personal, social and emotional development

Different faces
Early Learning Goal
Understand that people have different needs, views, cultures and beliefs, that need to be treated with respect.
What you need
A range of pictures showing faces from different times and cultures; drawing materials and paper.
What to do
● Encourage the children to look carefully at the range of paintings and observe differences. Use simple terms to describe the faces (such as *magical face*, *sad face* and so on).
● Provide drawing materials to encourage the children to draw their own different types of faces.
● Later in a plenary session, sensitively discuss cultural similarities and differences (see Day 4, page 117).

Communication, language and literacy

Make a caption
Early Learning Goal
Write their own names and other things such as labels and captions and begin to form simple sentences, sometimes using punctuation.
What you need
Computer; software such as 'Clicker' (a word bank with suitable words installed); a range of photographs and art postcards.
What to do
● Ensure that the children are familiar with using the software program, or provide adult support.
● Encourage the children to work in pairs to write their own captions for the photographs and postcards by clicking on the appropriate words.

Mathematical development

Counting faces
Early Learning Goal
In practical activities and discussion, begin to use the vocabulary involved in adding and subtracting.
What you need
Printed out Clip Art faces - with a different number of faces on different sheets; 1-20 number cards; pieces of card; pens.
What to do
● Provide a range of sheets showing different numbers of faces.
● Ask the children to work with a partner to take a sheet each and then see how many faces they have altogether. Ask them to record the number of faces, using the number cards to help them.
● Challenge more able children to write examples of addition and subtraction sums for others to use.

Knowledge and understanding of the world

Frame it!
Early Learning Goal
Select the tools and techniques they need to shape, assemble and join materials they are using.
What you need
Cutting and measuring tools; card strips; glue or sticky tape; picture frames and mounts.
What to do
● Ask an adult to show the children examples of picture frames and mounts.
● Encourage the children to make their own mount - for their portrait, or for another picture they have created.

Physical development

Name it!
Early Learning Goal
Show awareness of space, of themselves and of others.
What you need
Tape recorder; a tape of action songs, such as *Okki Tokki Unga* (A&C Black).
What to do
● Provide a tape recorder and tape with songs that relate to parts of the body, such as 'Heads, Shoulders, Knees and Toes' or 'Tommy Thumb'.
● Encourage the children to accompany the songs with actions, pointing to the relevant body parts.
● Follow up in a plenary session (see Day 3, page 116).

Creative development

Portraits
Early Learning Goal
Explore colour, texture, shape, form and space in two or three dimensions.
What you need
Unbreakable mirrors; a range of flesh-coloured paints; painting equipment.
What to do
● Give the children mirrors for them to closely observe their face and features. If possible, provide adult support.
● Ask the children to select appropriate colours for their skin tone. Encourage and support the children to paint their portraits, reminding them of portraits they have seen at the art gallery or elsewhere.

Visiting an art gallery

Objectives

Early Learning Goals
- Communication p54-55.
- Reading p62-63.

Stepping Stones
- Use language for an increasing range of purposes.
- Begin to recognise some familiar words.

NLS
T1: Through shared reading to recognise printed and handwritten words in a variety of settings.
T11: Through shared writing, to apply knowledge of letter/sound correspondences in helping the teacher to scribe, and re-reading what the class has written.
W6: To read on sight the 45 high frequency words to be taught by the end of YR.

What you need
- Plan a visit to a local art gallery to coincide with the unit. If this is not possible, download a range of copyright free pictures from the internet or use a range of art posters and pictures to create a class art gallery display.
- digital camera
- clipboards
- paper and pencils for each child
- a flipchart
- copies of the list of questions.

Differentiation

Less able
- Encourage all attempts at answering the list of questions in focused group work.

More able
- Help the children anwer the prepared questions in full sentences.

Shared text-level work
- The focus of the day's work is to observe carefully different pictures (particularly portraits) looking for similarities and differences.
- Explain to the children that you need help to devise some questions in order to learn all about paintings of different faces (or portraits) – whether they are in the classroom or the art gallery.
- Use a portrait poster to help the children think of some ideas. Suggest that they talk to their partner first.
- Hold up the poster and ask for the children's suggestions. What do they really want to know about this person?
- Compile a list, with the children helping you to scribe the words. Include questions such as:

> 1. What sort of person was this?
> 2. Where did he/she live?
> 3. What kind of clothes did he/she wear?
> 4. What clues are there in the picture?
> 5. How do you think he/she is feeling?

- Take the list of questions with you to the (class) art gallery.

Word-level work
- Take some digital photos of the gallery, the pictures (if permitted) and of the children interacting with the pictures for later use. Include pictures of the signs and labels that you see on the visit.
- During the visit (or while looking at the pictures in the class gallery), draw the children's attention to the signs, labels and captions all around them.
- Encourage them to read any high frequency words that appear on the captions and ask them to guess what the paintings might be called.

Focused group work
- Re-read together and try to answer (in the groups allocated for the visit) the list of questions you have prepared.
- Encourage the children to use clipboards to sketch their versions of the paintings.

Independent work
- If you are working in the classroom, follow the activities for the six Areas of Learning on page 113.

Plenary
- Later in the day, discuss the visit or the pictures observed. Ask the children if they saw a funny face, a scary face, an old face and so on. Write a list of all the types of faces observed on the flipchart.
- Look at the photographs taken (or if you did not go on a visit, talk about the pictures studied earlier) and ask the children to describe in detail what they can see.

Caption it!

Objectives

Early Learning Goals
● Communication p54-55.

Stepping Stone
● Use language for an increasing range of purposes.

NLS
T1: Through shared reading, to recognise printed and handwritten words in a variety of settings.
T12: Through guided and independent writing, to write labels or captions for pictures and drawings.
W6: To read on sight the 45 high frequency words to be taught by end of YR.

What you need

● Postcards and photographs from Day 1 (see page 114).
● photocopiable page 119, enlarged to A3-size
● sticky notes and pens
● a range of key words (such as was, in, the, at, look, saw, went, and so on) written on keys to form a display of 'key words'.

Shared text-level work

● Explain that you are going to write some labels for the photographs of the children and for the postcards that you bought. Talk about why we need labels and look at some other examples around the classroom.
● Explain that these photographs and the children's work will form a class art gallery and that they need to help organise the different pictures ready for the display.
● Talk about different types of faces such as *funny or sad; colourful or patterned faces* and look at examples.
● Now take one example and ask the children to talk to a partner about a suitable label for it.
● Scribe the label for the children, taking suggestions of how to spell it.
● Read the label together and repeat for several others, as time allows.

Shared word-level work

● Display some high frequency words and explain that it is important to know how to write these.
● Show the children the words, one at a time, and talk about distinctive features. Draw an outline around some words to help emphasise their distinctive shapes.
● As the children read the words with you, put them on display as 'key words' and encourage the children to use them when writing.
● Re-read the key words and put them into meaningful sentences, such as: *The picture was sad.* (Highlight the specific word.)

Focused group work

● Work with a small group of children and provide examples of photographs or pictures for the children to caption.
● Encourage paired and group discussion and then scribe an example for the children.
● Provide each child with sticky notes and photographs and encourage them all to 'have a go' at writing their own caption. Praise all attempts, particularly phonetically plausible spellings.

Independent work

● See the activities for the six Areas of Learning on page 113.

Plenary

● With the children gathered together at a convenient time during the day, talk about the caption you wrote earlier.
● Share one or two captions that the children have written in focused group work.
● Now explain that you have a pile of pictures and a pile of captions (use photocopiable page 119 or create your own) and that you need the children's help to match them.
● Hand out captions to different children and pictures to others.
● Ask the children to hold up the pictures and then read the examples of captions together. Ask the children to help you to match them.

Differentiation

Less able
● Scribe words for the children in focused group work, if necessary.

More able
● Encourage the children to write their own captions to go with the photographs and paintings.

Make a poster

Objectives

Early Learning Goals
- Writing p64-65.
- Thinking p56-59.
- Handwriting p66-67.

Stepping Stones
- Use writing as a means of recording and communicating.
- Use talk to connect ideas, explain what is happening and anticipate what might happen next.
- Begin to form recognisable letters.

NLS
T15: To use writing to communicate in a variety of ways.
S2: To use awareness of the grammar of a sentence to predict words.

What you need
- A3 paper
- a range of coloured pens and pencils
- examples of posters advertising events
- digital photographs or art postcards
- cassette recorder and body-action songs cassette (see PD, page 113).
- whiteboards.

Differentiation

Less able
- Provide support by scribing words for the children if necessary.

More able
- Encourage the children to write words for their posters.

Shared text-level work
- Remind the children of the art gallery or class version of a gallery. Show the children some examples of posters advertising forthcoming events.
- Read them with the children, emphasising the important information.
- Once you have decided what needs to be included in a poster for the class art gallery, draft the format (by drawing boxes and showing where words and pictures will go). Talk about this as a 'design'.
- Now model writing the poster, using different-sized lettering and plenty of colour, sticking on postcards and photographs if required. Emphasise the use of pictures to give information.
- Read the poster together and display prominently for other classes to see!

Shared sentence-level work
- Explain that you are going to practise handwriting to make sure the children's own posters look really attractive.
- Using the letters currently being learned, provide a prompt for letter formation, such as *top to bottom, lift and across* for the letter 't'.
- Ask the children to practise in different ways (in the air, on each other's backs) and finally on whiteboards.
- Monitor the children's work carefully with your usual adult support, emphasising the correct pencil grip.

Focused group work
- With a focused group of children, look again at the poster you prepared together. Talk about the need for more posters to put around the school.
- Ask the children to work in pairs to prepare posters, providing appropriate support for less able children. Remind them how to plan their designs before they begin.
- Provide pictures to be fixed to the poster and encourage them to include a range of drawings and writing.
- Read the children's work together.

Independent work
- See the activities for the six Areas of Learning on page 113.

Plenary
- With the children gathered together, refer to the body songs that some children have explored as part of Physical development (see page 113).
- Play one or two examples from a tape, such as 'Heads, Shoulders, Knees and Toes' or 'Looby Loo' and then sing the songs with the appropriate actions together.
- Emphasise how to point to the correct body parts. Have fun by asking the children to spot your deliberate mistakes, as you say *shoulders* and point to your knees and so on!

Invitations to the gallery

Objectives

Early Learning Goals
● Writing p64-65.

Stepping Stone
● Use writing as a means of recording and communicating.

NLS
T15: To use writing to communicate in a variety of ways, incorporating it into play and everyday classroom life.
S1: To expect written text to make sense and to check for sense if it does not.

What you need
● Examples of invitations
● a flipchart
● card
● pens
● Clip Art pictures
● blank invitations or cards
● silly sentences from photocopiable page 120, enlarged and cut into individual sentence.

Differentiation

Less able
● Show the children lots of examples of written invitations and talk about the words that are usually used in them such as *Dear* and *From.* Scribe the children's ideas for them, reminding them of the things that need to be included.

More able
● Encourage the children to have a go at writing their own invitations.

Shared text-level work
● Talk about whether the children have received invitations and discuss the inevitable number of party invitations they will have had, showing the children some examples.
● Explain that you are going to write an invitation to the headteacher, inviting them to come to the class art gallery for the special opening. Talk about what it is important to include on an invitation.
● With the children helping, write an invitation to the class art gallery for the following day. Write it on the flipchart to start with, before copying it out on to a smaller card.
● Read the invitation through together and choose a volunteer postperson to deliver it.

Shared sentence-level work
● Tell the children that you have some sentences that you think the computer has printed wrongly. Explain that you need their help to sort them out.
● Show the children examples of sentences from photocopiable page 120 and read them one at a time, with the children joining in.
● Talk about what they mean and discuss that they are nonsense. Ask the children to talk to a partner to correct each sentence.
● Write the correct versions on the flipchart with the children's help.
● Read a silly and a sensible sentence together and talk about how important it is to make sure that what you read makes sense.

Focused group work
● Working with a small group of children, look at the invitations modelled earlier.
● Explain that they are going to write some invitations to other people in the school. Give out the blank invitations that you have prepared and support the children to write their own, scribing the words, or parts of the words, if necessary.

Independent work
● See the activities for the six Areas of Learning on page 113.

Plenary
● With the children gathered together, talk about different types of faces and, sensitively, ask some children to stand and demonstrate different colours of hair, eyes, skin and so on.
● Explain that the way we look and the way we dress can vary from country to country. Show the children examples of faces from different times and cultures.
● Highlight for the children how important it is that we are all different and how boring (and confusing) it would be if we all looked the same! If possible talk about different cultures that the children have direct experience of commenting on jewellery, hairstyles, clothing and other traditions.

Listen!

Objectives

Early Learning Goals
● Linking sounds and letters p60-61.
● Communication p54-55.

Stepping Stones
● Hear and say the initial sound in words and know which letters represent some of the sounds.
● Use a widening range of words to express or elaborate ideas.

NLS
T14: To use experience of stories, poems and simple recounts as a basis for independent writing.
W2: Knowledge of grapheme/phoneme correspondences.

What you need
● Puppet
● tape recorder with recording facility
● blank tape
● personal stereo with tape of someone talking
● a list of CCVC words (or words relating to your current phonics focus).

Differentiation

Less able
● Help the children to rehearse speaking in full sentences before recording their ideas.

More able
● Encourage the children to use a range of vocabulary and suggest that they revise and improve the sentences they record as they go along.

Shared text-level work
● Show the class your personal stereo. Choose one or two children to listen to the stereo and tell the class what they heard (make sure it is speech).
● Tell the children that at some art galleries they have special tape recorders that tell you all about the pictures in the gallery.
● Explain that, although the class have already created a wonderful gallery of pictures and photographs with captions, it might be helpful to record some extra information so that visitors can look at the gallery even when the children are not available to show them around.
● Demonstrate a test recording on the tape recorder.
● Decide together what you could record about one of the pictures in the class art gallery.
● Give pairs of children the opportunity to talk about something suitable and take feedback.
● Now model recording a suggested sentence to match a picture and then play it back for the children. Ask the children for ideas to make the recording better and re-record.
● Explain that some children are going to help you record some more things on the tape for the class to hear later.

Shared word-level work
● Using a puppet, explain that the puppet can only speak in sounds (phonemes) and needs the children's help to say words.
● From the list of CCVC words (or the stage in phonics you are currently teaching) you have prepared, have the puppet say each word, saying each phoneme separately (c/l/a/p).
● Ask the children to tell the puppet the word each time. Make this a short, lively activity.

Focused group work
● In a guided group, continue the taping of a commentary on the class art gallery, encouraging a range of vocabulary. An example commentary could be: *Here is an example of a magical face. There is a strange pointed hat on the head, and the blue and red hair is very long and spiky.*
● Record some examples and then replay to check for sense.

Independent work
● See the activities for the six Areas of Learning on page 113.

Plenary
● Select a child to announce that the class art gallery is open and ready for visitors.
● With all the children watching, choose different children to show the visitor the pictures and say something about them. Provide adult support for this and encourage all attempts.
● Finally ask the visitor to listen to the commentary you have recorded.

Match the caption!

Magical face	Sad face	Silly face
Nasty face	KInd face	Scary face

TERM 2

Silly sentences

You can hear with your eyes.

The boy has a blue and pink face.

Ears are long and hairy.

A long spiky tongue looks pretty.

Fingers help you smell things.

The girl had tiny feet on top of her head.

Babies have grey beards.

UNIT 5

What made Tiddalik laugh?

This unit is based on a traditional tale from Australia. It comprises ten days' literacy activities and supports the National Literacy Strategy (Later Foundation Stage, Medium-term plan) focus on *Traditional stories*. The activities will help to develop the children's understanding of narrative. Linked activities are provided for all the six Areas of Learning with a strong emphasis on developing speaking and listening skills through drama, consideration in Personal, social and emotional development and developing literacy skills through story-telling and the study of traditional tales. The activities build towards Year 1 Term 1, Objective 4 of the *Speaking, Listening, Learning* guidance: to explore familiar themes and characters through improvisation and role-play.

WEEK 1

Day	Shared text-level work	Shared word-/ sentence-level work	Focused group work	Independent work	Plenary
1 Read about Tiddalik	Shared reading of 'What Made Tiddalik Laugh?'	Creating a word bank.	Guided retelling of traditional tale.	**PSED:** Looking after animals and pets.	Re-reading the story of 'What Made Tiddalik Laugh?'.
2 Retell the story	Retelling the story of Tiddalik with a storyhand.	Using context to read key words.	Guided retelling of traditional tale.	**CLL:** Role-play with animal masks.	Taking care of pets – preparation for a visitor.
3 Act it out!	Re-enacting the story of Tiddalik.	Creating jingles using initial letter sounds.	Guided retelling of traditional tale.	**MD:** Animal patterns.	Taking care of pets – questions for a visitor.
4 Change the problem	Adapting the story of Tiddalik (1).	Blending phonemes.	Guided retelling of traditional tale.	**KUW:** Contrasting hot and cold places.	Hot-seating – make Tiddalik laugh!
5 Change the ending	Adapting the story of Tiddalik (2).	Letter formation.	Guided retelling of traditional tale.	**PD:** Climbing like monkeys. **CD:** Clay models.	Reading an alternative tale – 'Diamonds and Toads'.

Key assessment opportunities
When working with children, look closely for:
● ability to discriminate initial letter sounds and generate words
● ability to retell a story
● asking questions coherently and in full sentences
● ability to use context cues for reading.
Record appropriately and ensure that this informs future planning.

Day	Shared text-level work	Shared word-/ sentence-level work	Focused group work	Independent work	Plenary
6 The story journey	Creating an alternative traditional tale.	Using the word bank – making sentences.	Guided writing of alternative stories.	**PSED:** Keeping cool.	Telling the story.
7 Part 1 of the story	Shared writing of alternative tale as wall story (part 1).	'Croaker' puppet, identifying final sounds.	Guided writing of alternative stories.	**CLL:** Using stories to create a story.	Keeping cool – animals and humans.
8 Part 2 of the story	Shared writing of alternative tale as wall story (part 2).	Alphabetical order.	Guided writing of alternative stories.	**MD:** Animal shapes.	Matching animal models and names.
9 Part 3 of the story	Shared writing of alternative tale as wall story (part 3).	Quick write – high frequency words.	Guided writing of alternative stories.	**KUW:** Investigating habitats using sand and water.	Reading individual stories.
10 Read our story!	Shared reading and editing of wall story.	Missing capital letters and full stops.	Guided writing of alternative stories.	**PD:** Animal dances. **CD:** Animal patterns.	Class production – story and dance.

Key assessment opportunities

When working with the children look closely for:
- ability to retell a story in sequence
- ability to match graphemes to phonemes
- ability to recall the alphabetical sequence
- ability to produce writing for a real purpose
- ability to spell high frequency words.

Record appropriately and ensure that this informs future planning.

CROSS-CURRICULAR ☐ **UNIT 5 WEEK 1** What made Tiddalik laugh?

TERM 1

Personal, social and emotional development

Taking care of animals
Early Learning Goal
Understand what is right, what is wrong, and why.
What you need
Pictures of different animals; corresponding pictures of items needed for each animal and objects (such as a water bowl for a dog, a bird feeder and so on); a real pet (if possible).
What to do
● Ask the children to explore the pictures and objects and talk about what each animal needs. Suggest that they match the animal pictures with the objects they need.
● Follow up with a whole class discussion during a plenary session.

Mathematical development

Make a pattern
Early Learning Goal
Talk about, recognise and recreate simple patterns.
What you need
Pictures of animals with clear patterns, such as a tiger, leopard, snake, giraffe and so on. Painting equipment and easels.
What to do
● Show the pictures of animal patterns and encourage the children to paint their own patterns through careful observation.
● At a convenient time, during a whole-class session, point out examples of repeating patterns.

Physical development

Climb like a monkey!
Early Learning Goal
Travel around, under, over and through balancing and climbing equipment.
What you need
Climbing frame and range of large apparatus.
What to do
● With a supporting adult, encourage the children to climb over, under and around the apparatus, pretending they are monkeys or other animals from the story.

Creative development

Mould an animal
Early Learning Goal
Explore colour, texture, shape, form and space in two or three dimensions.
What you need
Modelling materials such as clay, Plasticine or play dough; modelling tools and boards; plastic small-world animals.
What to do
● Encourage the children to look carefully at animals and select one.
● Ask the children to create their own model animal, providing some adult support if possible.

Communication, language and literacy

Act it out!
Early Learning Goal
Use language to imagine and recreate roles and experiences.
What you need
Pieces of card for masks; card strips for securing masks around heads; simple pictures of animals from the story to copy (see photocopiable page 139).
What to do
● Make the masks with the children.
● Encourage the children to re-enact the story, wearing their masks.
● If possible, provide adult support to help the children to remember the story; interact with each other; and think about the different characters of the animals.

Knowledge and understanding of the world

Where do I live?
Early Learning Goal
Observe, find out about and identify features in the place they live and the natural world.
What you need
Information books showing hot and cold places and animals, or a range of pictures or video extracts downloaded from the internet. Label all the pictures with the words *hot* or *cold*.
What to do
● Ask the children to look at the pictures of the places. Can they think what animals might live in each place.
● Provide the animal pictures and ask the children to match the animals to the places that they live in (the words will give them some clues).

TERM 1

CROSS-CURRICULAR ▢ **UNIT 5 WEEK 2** What made Tiddalik laugh?

Personal, social and emotional development

Keeping cool
Early Learning Goal
Dress and undress independently and manage their own personal hygiene.
What you need
Props for hot weather, such as sunhats, empty sun cream containers, cold drinks and so on; paper and pencils.
What to do
● Ask the children to write a list of the things we need when it is hot weather. Look at the props provided and encourage them to draw or write as appropriate.
● Follow-up with a whole class discussion during a plenary session.

Mathematical Development

Animal shapes
Early Learning Goal
Use language such as 'circle' or 'bigger' to describe the shape and size of solids and flat shapes.
What you need
Assorted shapes; animal pictures.
What to do
● Using pictures of animals as a guide, encourage the children to use the shapes to recreate different animals.
● If adult support is available, encourage the appropriate use of language, such as shape names and comparative vocabulary: *triangles, rectangles, a smaller square* and so on.

Physical development

Animal dances
Early Learning Goal
Show awareness of space, of themselves and of others.
What you need
Animal masks from Week 1 (see CLL, page 123); music, such as *The Carnival of the Animals* (Saint-Saens).
What to do
● With a supporting adult, play the music and encourage the children to imagine which animals might be represented by it.
● Let them respond differently to the different types of music, encouraging a range of movement and gestures.

Creative development

Animal patterns
Early Learning Goal
Explore colour, texture, shape, form and space in two or three dimensions.
What you need
Pictures of animals that clearly show their patterns; (see MD, page 123); potato halves pre-cut with animal patterns, such as spots and stripes; paper or plain white fabric; paint.
What to do
● Encourage the children to look carefully at the animal patterns. Show them the pre-cut potato printers and ask them to choose from the designs available.
● Ask the children to create their own design by dipping the cut potato into paint and then printing it on to paper or fabric.

Communication, language and literacy

Map the story
Early Learning Goal
Use language to imagine and recreate roles and experiences.
What you need
Story map created on Day 6 (page 130); A3 paper; pens and pencils; plastic animals.
What to do
● Provide the story map created on Day 6 (page 130) for the children to look at. Tell them that they need to make their own story map showing a story about the journey of the animals.
● Let them play with the plastic animals to help them to think up a story of their own.

Knowledge and understanding of the world

Animals in water and sand
Early Learning Goal
Observe, find out about and identify features in the place they live and the natural world.
What you need
Sand tray; water tray; range of plastic animals, some that live on land and some that live in water.
What to do
● Ask the children to sort the plastic animals into two groups: those that live on land and those that live in water.
● Suggest that they place the animals in the appropriate places (sand or water) depending on where they live naturally.
● Encourage a discussion of what different animals need to survive.

Read about Tiddalik

Objectives

Early Learning Goals
- Communication p50-53.
- Reading p62-63.

Stepping Stones
- Initiate a conversation, negotiate positions, pay attention to and take account of others' views.
- Begin to be aware of the way stories are structured.

NLS
T8: To locate and read significant parts of the text.
W10: New words from their reading and shared experiences.

What you need
- Pictures of Australia
- the story 'What Made Tiddalik Laugh?' from photocopiable pages 135-136, enlarged to at least A3 size.
- pictures of different animals in the story – in particular a platypus
- key vocabulary from the story printed in minimum 48 point font or handwritten on card: *Tiddalik, birds, animals, frog, wombat, kangaroo, parrot, snake, koala, monkey, platypus, thirsty, greedy*
- the traditional tale 'Diamonds and Toads', on photocopiable page 137.
- easel
- photocopiable page 138.

Differentiation

Less able
- Support the children to speak in complete sentences.

More able
- Encourage the children to use a range of descriptive vocabulary.

Shared text-level work
- Begin by talking about Australia and, if possible, show the children some pictures.
- Now introduce the story. Talk about who Tiddalik is and that this is a traditional story from Australia. Remind the children of other traditional tales you have read.
- Read the story to the children using a pointer.
- Read it a second time, encouraging the children to join in when you come to the repeated phrase *But Tiddalik did not laugh.*
- Talk about what sort of a character Tiddalik was (greedy) and how the other animals tried to trick him, or make him laugh.
- Ask the children to talk to their partner about what made Tiddalik laugh in the end.

Shared word-level work
- Show the children the prepared key words from the story. Read them one by one with the children and display them in a pocket chart, or on the wall.
- Ensure that the children understand the meaning of each word by reading the word individually (for example, *kangaroo*) and then saying the word in a sentence. For example, *A kangaroo hops on its back legs.*
- Ask for volunteers to point to words as you say them, assisted by the rest of the class.
- Continue in this way to help word recognition and to widen vocabulary.

Focused group work
- Read the story, 'Diamonds and Toads' from photocopiable page 137 to the children. When they are familiar with it ask them to help you to retell it.
- On an easel draw a 'storyhand', (see photocopiable page 138 for the format). With the children's help, fill in the storyhand for 'Diamonds and Toads'.
- Once you have created the storyhand together, help the children to retell the story by modelling parts for them and then encouraging them to try.
- Praise all the children's attempts at retelling the story.

Independent work
- See the activities for the six Areas of Learning on page 123.

Plenary
- With the children gathered together, talk about the story of Tiddalik and ask the children to tell their partner anything they can remember about it.
- Re-read the story using a pointer and encourage the children to join in.
- If time allows, discuss jokes and share one or two examples.

UNIT 5 DAY 2   What made Tiddalik laugh?

Retell the story

Objectives

Early Learning Goals
- Communication p50-53.
- Reading p62-63.

Stepping Stones
- Describe main story settings, events and principal characters.
- Begin to be aware of the way stories are structured.

NLS
T2: To use a variety of cues when reading: knowledge of the story and its context, and awareness of how it should make sense grammatically.
S2: To use awareness of the grammar of a sentence to predict words during shared reading and when re-reading familiar stories.

What you need
- The story 'What Made Tiddalik Laugh?' on photocopiable pages 135-136, enlarged.
- photocopiable page 138, enlarged
- sticky notes
- three or four sentences which include key words from the story (see Day 1, page 125) – printed in large font or written on card
- the story 'Diamonds and Toads' on photocopiable page 137.
- a flipchart
- pieces of card
- the storyhand made with the children on Day 1 (see page 125).

Differentiation

Less able
- Help the children to learn by heart some of the refrains from the story to give them confidence.

More able
- Challenge the children to think of three different ways to start the story.

Shared text-level work
- Remind the children of the story of Tiddalik. Explain that you are going to try and retell the story with the children's help, but first they need to remember the main parts.
- Show the children the storyhand from photocopiable page 138 and talk through the main events of the story.
- Encourage the children to talk to their partners about each part of the story.
Make sure the storyhand is clearly visible and tell the children that together, using the storyhand, you are going to retell the story of Tiddalik.
- Use story language to start the story, *Once long ago in a far off country there lived...* Point to the different sections of the storyhand to complete the tale, asking the children to help elaborate.

Shared sentence-level work
- Remind the children of the key words that they looked at on Day 1 (see page 125). Talk about how some words are quite difficult to read and what clues can help.
- Now refer to the context of the words as a good clue. Give an example, such as *funny,* and put it into a sentence: *He made a very funny face and everyone laughed.*
- Show the children a sentence you have prepared with the relevant word covered over with a sticky note. Talk about which word might fit and say it is one from the word wall.
- Reveal the word slowly, giving an additional clue with the initial letter(s). Repeat the activity with the other prepared sentences.

Focused group work
- Work with a new group of children as per Day 1 (page 125) using the story and storyhand from the previous day or choosing another familiar traditional tale.
- Invite the children to use the completed storyhand to retell the story.

Independent work
- See the activities for the six Areas of Learning on page 123.

Plenary
- With the children gathered together on the carpet, discuss the PSED activity about looking after animals and pets (see page 123) that some children have explored.
- Tell the children that a guest will be bringing their pet to show the class tomorrow. Explain that the children need to think of good questions to ask.
- Brainstorm some questions together, such as *What does he/she eat? Where does he/she sleep?* Write these on the flipchart as a reminder. Transfer the questions to cards with picture clues for the children to use the next day.

Act it out!

Objectives

Early Learning Goals
● Linking sounds and letters p60-61.
● Communication p50-53.
● Reading p62-63.

Stepping Stones
● Show awareness of rhyme and alliteration.
● Listen to stories with increasing attention and recall.
● Begin to be aware of the ways stories are structured.

NLS
T8: To locate and read significant parts of the text.
W2: Knowledge of grapheme/phoneme correspondences.

What you need

● The 'Tiddalik' story from photocopiable pages 135-136, enlarged
● the storyhand on photocopiable page 138
● cards with question prompts (see Day 2, page 126)
● a visitor with a pet
● the animal masks from the independent CLL activity (see page 123).

Differentiation

Less able
● Help the children to memorise one or two key phrases to give them confidence when acting out the story.

More able
● Encourage the children to tell you something about their chosen character before they act out the story.

Shared text-level work

● Remind the children of the story of Tiddalik and tell them that they are going to act out the story together. Remind the children of the characters in the story and give out the animal masks to some individual children.
● Explain that the rest of the class need to help you by joining in with key phrases and refrains and by making background noises (or sound effects)!
● Think of some background noises, such as the noise of the platypus emerging from his hole.
● Take the part of narrator and tell the story, encouraging the children to get into role and provide actions and appropriate noises.
● Invite the rest of the class to provide sounds as discussed, as well as telling jokes and singing silly songs on cue!
● Let the children build up to a terrible noise as they join in with the repeated refrain of *But Tiddalik did not laugh!*
● Ensure that you warn adjoining classes and have some fun!

Shared word-level work

● Gather together in a circle and follow on from the fun and jokes by talking about funny jingles, such as *Sally sips soup and sizzling sausages*.
● Talk about how each word in a jingle begins with the same sound.
● Ask the children to make up a jingle for Tiddalik, reminding them that each word must begin with the same sound.
● Choose other characters in the story or names of children in the class and ask the children to talk to partners to help them make up a jingle.
● Go round the circle, asking each child to have a go, making a note of those children that can or can't generate a jingle in this way. Provide adult support where necessary.

Focused group work

● Continue with the story retellings with a different group of children.
● As for Days 1 and 2, use the storyhand as a device to aid retelling, and encourage each child in the group to contribute a part of the chosen traditional story.

Independent work

● See the activities for the six Areas of Learning on page 123.

Plenary

● With the children gathered together, talk about looking after pets. If you have a class pet, remind the children of the ways that you all look after it.
● Introduce your visitor and their pet. Let the visitor talk briefly to the children before the children take turns to ask their prepared questions.
● Give the children the question cards made earlier and suggest that the children support each other in pairs as they ask their questions.

Change the problem

Objectives

Early Learning Goals
● Linking sounds and letters p60-61.
● Reading p62-63.

Stepping Stones
● Hear and say the initial sound in words and know which letters represent some of the sounds.
● Suggest how the story might end.

NLS
T7: To use knowledge of familiar texts to re-enact or re-tell to others recounting the main points in correct sequence.
W2: Knowledge of grapheme/phoneme correspondences.

What you need
● The story 'What Made Tiddalik Laugh?' on photocopiable pages 135-136, enlarged.
● the storyhand on photocopiable page 138
● a flipchart
● a puppet.

Differentiation

Less able
● Support the children to speak in complete sentences.

More able
● Ensure that the children are given plenty of opportunities to discuss possible problems and endings for the alternative Tiddalik story.

Shared text-level work
● Look briefly at the storyhand from the story of Tiddalik (photocopiable page 138) and then explain that the class is going to help you to adapt the story to create a new one.
● Refer again to the completed Tiddalik storyhand and start by saying that you are going to change the problem shown on the third finger (*that Tiddalik drank all the water*).
● Ask the children to talk to their partners about a different problem and discuss suggestions.
● Now draw a new storyhand on the flipchart and write the children's suggestion on to the third finger – they might, for example, want to make Tiddalik eat all the leaves on the trees instead.
● Ask the children to help you to write the beginning of the storyhand now that the 'problem' has been decided upon.
● Do the children think that the story will need a different ending? Agree on a possible solution together.
● Now with the class, and you as narrator, retell the different version of the story, encouraging plenty of whole-class participation.
● Explain that tomorrow you are going to look at other different endings to the story.

Shared word-level work
● Now or later, as appropriate, show the children a puppet and explain that this puppet can only speak in phonemes.
● Have the puppet tell the children a word which they have to identify. For example, h/o/t. Continue with a range of words, choosing those that are phonically regular (such as words with the same rime, for example, *lot, cot, dot, jot,* and so on).
● If time allows, ask the children to speak to the puppet in phonemes and prompt them as necessary.

Focused group work
● Continue as the previous three days (pages 125-127), retelling the story using the storyhand and encouraging the children to tell different parts of the story.

Independent work
● See the activities for the six Areas of Learning on page 123.

Plenary
● Explain that you are going to choose a child to take the part of Tiddalik and sit in the hot seat while the others have to make him or her laugh!
● Discuss different ways of making people laugh and refer to the story. Give the children time to talk to partners to think of some ideas.
● Now model the process by telling a joke or pulling a silly face!
● Ask for volunteers to make some more suggestions, ensuring that you keep the children on task.

Change the ending

Objectives

Early Learning Goals
- Handwriting p66-67.
- Communication p50-53.
- Reading p62-63.

Stepping Stones
- Begin to form recognisable letters.
- Use vocabulary and forms of speech that are increasingly influenced by experience of books.
- Suggest how the story might end.

NLS
T7: To use knowledge of familiar texts to re-enact or re-tell to others, recounting the main points in correct sequence.
W14: To write letters using the correct sequence of movements.

What you need
- The storyhand on photocopiable page 139 plus the storyhand made with the children on Day 4 (see page 128)
- whiteboards and pens for each child
- an enlarged or Big Book version of a traditional tale, such as 'Diamonds and Toads' on photocopiable page 137.

Differentiation

Less able
- Support the children to speak in complete sentences.

More able
- Ensure that the children are given plenty of opportunities to discuss possible problems and endings for the alternative Tiddalik story.

Shared text-level work
- Remind the class of the alternative version of the story created the previous day (see page 128) and quickly discuss what was changed. Then explain that the class are going to help you change it again.
- Say that this time you are going to change the resolution (how the problem is solved). In this version, Tiddalik drinks all the water but the others do not make him laugh. Ask the children to talk to their partners about a different solution and discuss suggestions.
- Explain that the children will need to change the fourth finger of the storyhand (the resolution). For example, this time the animals try to make Tiddalik cross, so that he opens his mouth to shout at them! Amend the storyhand as agreed.
- Now with the class, and you as narrator, retell the different version of the story encouraging plenty of whole-class participation.
- Talk about the different versions compared to the original story and find out which the class prefers. Alternative versions of the story can then either be recorded on tape or written for the children to re-read or listen to at a later date.

Shared word-level work
- Explain that you are going to practise handwriting.
- Using the letters currently being learned, provide a prompt for letter formation, such as *top to bottom, lift and across* for the letter 't'.
- Ask the children to practise in the air, on each other's backs and finally on whiteboards. Have fun telling them to rub it out and start again.
- Monitor all the children carefully with your usual adult support. Emphasise holding the pencil correctly.

Focused group work
- Continue as days 1 to 4 with a different group of children.
- Show the group some of the ideas that previous groups have had and encourage them to create their own storyhand to aid the retelling of one of their favourite traditional tales.

Independent work
- See the activities for the six Areas of Learning on page 123.

Plenary
- Talk about traditional tales together. Brainstorm a range of tales the children have read.
- Talk about all the traditional tales that the children have been working on in focused group work.
- Now read the story of 'Diamonds and Toads' (on photocopiable page 137) together with plenty of expression, encouraging the children to join in.
- Talk about any similarities with the story of Tiddalik, such as a happy ending.

The story journey

Objectives

Early Learning Goals
● Communication p54-55.
● Writing p64-65.

Stepping Stones
● Use a widening range of words to express or elaborate ideas.
● Use writing as a means of recording and communicing.

NLS
T12: Through guided and independent writing a) to experiment with writing in a variety of play, exploratory and role-play situations.
W10: New words from their reading and shared experiences.

What you need
● Flipchart/easel
● key words from Week 1 and corresponding sentences (see Days 1 and 2, pages 125-126)
● a range of different traditional tales
● a storybox (containing props to help develop a story, such as a toy animal, item of clothing, a picture of a jungle or other setting, coins, play people)
● one other storybox for guided group work, if possible.

Differentiation

Less able
● Help the children to sequence a story map correctly.

More able
● Encourage the children to include some words in their story maps.

Shared text-level work
● Begin by talking about the traditional tales read the previous week and talk about some of the main features of them.
● Explain that the children will be helping you to write a class traditional tale this week which will be displayed on the classroom wall (a wall story).
● Show the children the storybox and take out the items one by one, discussing their significance. For example, the toy animal could be the main character.
● Use the picture to decide as a class where the story takes place (the setting).
● Use the objects to decide what the problem and the solution will be (the plot).
● Explain that you are going to draw a map of the story.
● Model drawing a map, showing who is in the story at the start, where they go and the series of events.

Shared word-level work
● Remind the children of the key words from the previous week and quickly read the words together, asking one of the children to act as teacher and point to the words.
● Talk about new words from the story that they have just made up and write one or two to add to the word wall.
● Look at the distinctive features of the words, such as words within words, or particular letter strings to help to recognise the words in future.
● Ensure that the children understand the meanings of any new words by putting them into meaningful sentences. Write the sentence on the flipchart and read them together.

Focused group work
● Help the children to construct their own story maps. Spend some time brainstorming ideas first using a storybox (if possible have a different one).
● Help the children to work in pairs to draw their own story maps, adding as much detail as possible.
● Spend the majority of the time talking about their map as a vital prelude to writing.

Independent work
● See the activities for the six Areas of Learning on page 124.

Plenary
● Using the story map from the shared text-level work, explain that the class are going to help you to tell the story.
● Model using story language, following the map to tell the story, asking the children to help you and ensure that you do not miss anything out.

Part 1 of the story

Objectives

Early Learning Goals
- Communication p54-55.
- Writing p 64-65.

Stepping Stones
- Use a widening range of words to express or elaborate ideas
- Use writing as a means of recording and communicating.

NLS
T12: Through guided and independent writing to experiment with writing in a variety of play, exploratory and role-play situations.
W2: Knowledge of grapheme/phoneme correspondences.

What you need
- A flipchart or easel
- large sheets of paper for wall story (or interactive whiteboard)
- a puppet
- bag of assorted objects representing current sounds taught (initial or final)
- pictures of animals keeping cool.

Differentiation

Less able
- Help the children to develop story-sequencing skills during Focused group work.

More able
- Let confident children have a go at writing the words inside the speech bubbles.

Shared text-level work
- Using the story map from the previous day, remind the children of the story you have started to develop.
- Explain that you are going to write the first part of the story and that you would like the children to help you by adding speech bubbles.
- Using teacher demonstration, write the opening few sentences to the story, modelling saying sentences aloud as you write and asking for help with spacing, capital letters, appropriate spellings of common words and so on. If available, use an interactive whiteboard to write this.
- Re-read the sentences with the children. Talk about any possible speech bubbles you could add.
- Draw speech bubbles on the paper or board at appropriate places, asking the children to talk with a partner about possible things that the characters might say. These could just be short phrases or single words (for example, *Watch out!*; *Thief!* and so on).
- Re-read the first part of the story, encouraging the children to read the speech bubbles.

Shared word-level work
- Use the class puppet (in *Progression in Phonics* the puppet is called 'Croaker') to help the children to hear and say final sounds (adjust as appropriate to the children's current phonic level).
- With a bag of objects and the puppet, explain that the puppet has problems saying the final sounds. Model, by showing a brick to the puppet, for example – with the puppet saying *brill*.
- Ask the children to help by telling the puppet the correct pronunciation. Have fun with the puppet making mistakes, until the children help him get it right.
- Repeat the game with other objects.

Focused group work
- Continue to help the children to construct their own story maps as Day 6 (see page 130).

Independent work
- See the activities for the six Areas of Learning on page 124.

Plenary
- Discuss 'keeping cool' relating to the PSED independent activity on page 130.
- Talk about how humans keep cool and discuss the props from the activity. Warn the children about the dangers of too much sun and how it is important to cover up.
- Now look at the pictures of animals keeping cool (such as elephants dusting themselves; hippopotamuses wallowing in mud; dogs panting and so on) and talk about the similarities and differences between the animals.

Part 2 of the story

Objectives

Early Learning Goals
● Communication p54-55.
● Writing p64-65.

Stepping Stones
● Use a widening range of words to express or elaborate ideas.
● Ascribe meanings to marks.

NLS
T12: Through guided and independent writing, to experiment with writing in a variety of play, exploratory and role-play situations.
W3: Alphabetic and phonic knowledge through understanding alphabetical order.

What you need
● A flipchart or easel
● large sheets of paper for wall story (or interactive whiteboard)
● washing line across the classroom
● alphabet cards pegged in alphabetical order along the washing line with a sock hanging underneath each letter
● the children's name cards
● a range of plastic animals and corresponding names on card.

Differentiation

Less able
● Let the children place their own name card in the matching sock.

More able
● Ask the children to say whether they think the name card they are holding will go near the beginning of the alphabet, in the middle or near the end.

Shared text-level work
● Using the story begun the previous day (see Day 7, page 131), explain that you are going to write the next part. Reread the first part with the children.
● Refer back to the story map you created together on Day 6 (page 130) and orally rehearse the next sentence before writing it for the children, either on the flipchart or using the interactive whiteboard.
● Write several sentences in this way, with the children helping.
● Talk about any possible speech bubbles you could add and ask the children to talk with a partner about things that the characters could say. If time allows, write a speech bubble with the children's help.
● Re-read the second part of the story, encouraging the children to join in.

Shared word-level work
● Begin by singing an alphabet song (for example, the 'Alphabet chant' on photocopiable page 29).
● Now explain that you need the children's help to put their names in alphabetical order.
● Explain that you would like the children to put all the name cards in alphabetical order by placing them inside socks that are hanging underneath the letters of the alphabet on the washing line.
● Give out the name cards randomly to the children (but not to the child whose name it is, as this will be too easy for them!). Ask the children to take turns to find the corresponding letter of the alphabet and place it underneath in the sock.
● Ask the rest of the class to check each time.

Focused group work
● Continue as the previous day to help the children to construct their own story maps.
● Refer back to the class story map and share other examples of the children's work. Demonstrate again how to sequence the story.

Independent work
● See the activities for the six Areas of Learning on page 124.

Plenary
● Explain that you need some help with sorting animals and names.
● Show the children a box of animals and a pile of corresponding names. Give out the cards to individual children.
● Select one animal at a time and ask the child with the corresponding card to hold it up.
● Create a display in the classroom for later reference.
● Finish by playing a guessing game as children get ready to go home. Say for example, *I am thinking of an animal which is sometimes black and white and the word begins with 'c'.* Children who guess may whisper the answer as they leave.

Part 3 of the story

Objectives

Early Learning Goals
● Communication p54-55.
● Writing p64-65.

Stepping Stones
● Use a widening range of words to express or elaborate ideas.
● Ascribe meanings to marks.

NLS
T12: Through guided and independent writing to experiment with writing in a variety of play, exploratory and role-play situations.
W2: Knowledge of grapheme/phoneme correspondences.

What you need
● Story map from Day 6 (see page 130)
● the wall story from Days 7 and 8 (see pages 131-132)
● whiteboards and pens – one between two pupils.

Differentiation

Less able
● Help the children to put their ideas into complete sentences by elaborating on their suggestions and modelling the extended phrase.

More able
● Make some deliberate mistakes during shared writing and encourage the children to identify and correct them.

Shared text-level work
● Using the story from the previous two days (see pages 131-132), explain that you are going to write the next part.
● Re-read the story so far and refer to the original story map (see Day 6, page 130). Orally rehearse the next sentences and model writing them with the children's support.
● Talk about any further speech bubbles you could add and ask the children to talk with a partner about possible things the characters could say.
● Re-read the story, encouraging the children to join in.
● Discuss any similarities that your class story has with the Tiddalik story. Is it similar in any way to other traditional tales that the children are familiar with?

Shared word-level work
● Give out the whiteboards, one between two, and then say you are going to read a range of words which you want the children to write. Ask them to check with their partner first before writing.
● Read out a range of high frequency words, such as *as the, was, and, went* and so on.
● Ask the children to show you their words each time, so that you can check on their spellings.
● Sensitively use any errors as teaching points and ask the children to look carefully at mistakes (such as the reversal of *was/saw*).
● Reinforce the correct spellings.

Focused group work
● Continue as Days 6-8 (pages 130-132) to help the children to construct their own story maps.
● Encourage the children to orally rehearse their story map plan before they start to write or draw.

Independent work
● See the activities for the six Areas of Learning on page 124.

Plenary
● With the children together, ask some of the class to share their own story maps.
● Encourage the children to retell their stories using appropriate language.
● Talk about the similarities and differences between the children's stories. Are any of them similar to features that they noticed in Tiddalik or other traditional tales?
● Explain that tomorrow you are going to finish the work you have been doing on Tiddalik and other traditional tales by making a musical production of the children's class story.
● Decide on aspects of the production, choosing children to play different roles and planning sound effects.

Read our story!

Objectives

Early Learning Goals
● Communication p54-55.
● Writing p64-65.

Stepping Stones
● Use a widening range of words to express or elaborate ideas.
● Use writing as a means of recording and communicating.

NLS
T12: Through guided and independent writing to experiment with writing in a variety of play, exploratory and role-play situations.
S4: To use a capital letter for the start of own name.
W2: Knowledge of grapheme/phoneme correspondences.

What you need

● Story map from Day 6 (page 130)
● wall story from Days 7 and 8
● storyhand on photocopiable page 138
● lists of the children's names with some capital letters missing from first or second names (one between two children)
● musical instruments
● dressing-up clothes and animal masks (see page 124).

Differentiation

Less able
● Provide adult support for the children to help them find other names and make corrections.

More able
● Encourage the children to try to correct other children's names as well as their own.

Shared text-level work

● Refer to the story map and the story written over the past four days (see Days 6-9, pages 130-133).
● Re-read the class story with the children joining in, particularly with the speech bubbles.
● Explain that today the children are going to be editors and help you check the class story. First you need to check that all the main parts of the story are included, referring to a storyhand such as the one on photocopiable page 138 which shows the five main sections of a story (opening, build-up, problem, resolution, ending).
● Use the story map to check that all the sections are included. Does the story map give more information than a storyhand?
● Finally say that you need to check that all the sentences start with a capital letter and end with a full stop. Again, check this together.
● Explain that you are going to display the children's story so that they can go and read it any time. Tell them that you will be inviting them to paint and draw some pictures to add to the story.
● Ensure that you add the name of the class as the author and talk about who an author is.

Shared word-/sentence-level work

● Tell the children that you have received a list of the class names from the school office, but the computer has made some mistakes and forgotten to use capital letters for some of the names.
● Discuss the use of capital letters and show the children some different examples of capital letters around the classroom.
● Give out the lists, one between two, and ask the children to find their names and correct them for you.
● Ask the children to feedback some examples and discuss.

Focused group work

● Continue as per Days 6-9 (pages 130-133) helping the children to construct their own story maps.
● Remind the children of the importance of planning the whole story in order before writing or drawing.

Independent work

● See the activities for the six Areas of Learning on page 124.

Plenary

● Provide the children with props and dressing-up clothes and remind the children of their roles in the production.
● Act as narrator and read out the story slowly in order to allow the children to join in.
● Let more able children read out the text from the speech bubbles.
● Allow plenty of music and celebration, encouraging actions, gestures and musical instruments, as the children enjoy the fruits of their shared story!

What Made Tiddalik Laugh?

(A legend from Australia)

Once upon a time in a very hot country there lived a giant frog who was called Tiddalik.

One day it was even hotter than usual and Tiddalik was thirsty, so he went to the river for a drink. He took a long drink but he was still thirsty. He kept on drinking until there was no water left in the river and still he was thirsty. Next he went to a lake, and before long he drank all the water in the lake. He kept on drinking until every river, lake and stream in the whole country was dry. He grew bigger and bigger as he stored all the water in his huge tummy.

Tiddalik went to sleep but the next morning when the sun came up it was hotter than ever before and soon flowers, trees and grass started to die all over the land as there was no water to keep them alive.

Tiddalik slept on, but all the other birds and animals were thirsty and nowhere was there anything to drink. The animals looked at Tiddalik and knew he had drunk all the water.

'We must do something,' they said.

'What?' asked the birds.

'Make Tiddalik laugh,' said the Wise Wombat.

'Why?' asked the animals and birds.

'If we make him laugh, then all the water will spill out,' said the Wombat.

So the animals and birds decided to hold a 'Fun Day' with a joke competition, a dressing-up competition and a funny song competition. They all dressed up and looked very silly. But Tiddalik did not laugh.

What Made Tiddalik Laugh?

(Continued)

The kangaroos told jokes. But Tiddalik did not laugh.

The parrots sang very silly songs. But Tiddalik did not laugh.

The snakes hissed. But Tiddalik did not laugh.

The koalas made strange whooping noises. But Tiddalik did not laugh.

The monkeys screeched. But Tiddalik did not laugh.

What a terrible noise!

Deep in the earth a strange animal woke up and began to move out of his hole. It was a platypus. He had a huge beak and webbed feet like a duck, with fur like a mole and a long tail like a monkey.

The platypus looked cross. He did not like being woken up. He went up to the strange giant frog.

'Excuse me, do you mind not making such a lot of noise!' he said.

Tiddalik looked in surprise at the strange animal and, before he knew it, opened his mouth and started to laugh! As he laughed, huge amounts of water came out. It kept on coming and coming for hours and still Tiddalik could not stop laughing. In the end, the rivers filled up, the lakes filled up and the streams filled up.

Not long after that, the grass began to grow, the flowers started to come back and the trees became green again.

All the animals and birds were so happy and Tiddalik never drank so much again. Ever since then, frogs can store water in their bodies for days but are never as greedy as Tiddalik.

Diamonds and Toads

(A fairy tale from France)

Once upon a time there was a woman with two daughters.

The eldest daughter looked very much like her mother and, because of this, her mother loved her best. The two daughters were very different. The eldest was bad-tempered and nasty, and the youngest was kind and beautiful. The youngest daughter had to work much harder and clean the house.

One day, the youngest daughter was going to get water from the well, when she met a woman who asked for a drink. She gave her a cup of water straight away. The woman thanked her and said that she wanted to give her a special present for being so kind. The present was that, whenever the youngest daughter spoke, with every word a jewel or a flower would also come out of her mouth.

When the young daughter got home, her mother told her off for taking a long time. The daughter said 'Sorry', and at the same time a large diamond came out of her mouth. Her mother was amazed and asked her what had happened. Every time the daughter spoke, more diamonds came out of her mouth.

Her mother then greedily sent the other daughter to the well, but she grumbled all the way. When she got there, the same old lady, who was really a fairy, asked her for a drink. This time the eldest daughter was rude to the old lady, but finally gave her a drink. In response the woman said she would give her a present and, whenever she spoke, snakes and toads would come out of her mouth.

The daughter ran home and, as soon as she spoke to her mother, out came two snakes and two toads. The mother blamed the younger daughter for this and was so nasty that the young girl ran away into the forest.

Fortunately the king's son was coming that way from the palace and saw the pretty girl crying.

'What's the matter?' he asked.

She tried to explain and out of her mouth fell diamonds and pearls. When he finally understood the whole story, the prince fell in love with her. Soon they were married and lived happily ever after, surrounded by diamonds.

Tiddalik storyhand

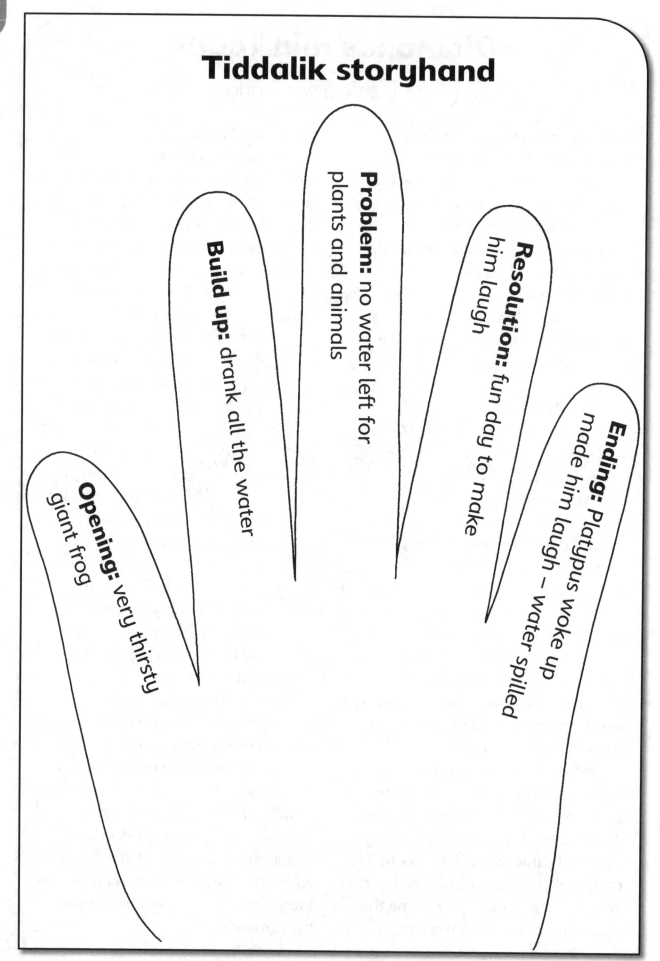

Opening: very thirsty giant frog

Build up: drank all the water

Problem: no water left for plants and animals

Resolution: fun day to make him laugh

Ending: Platypus woke up made him laugh – water spilled

Tiddalik masks

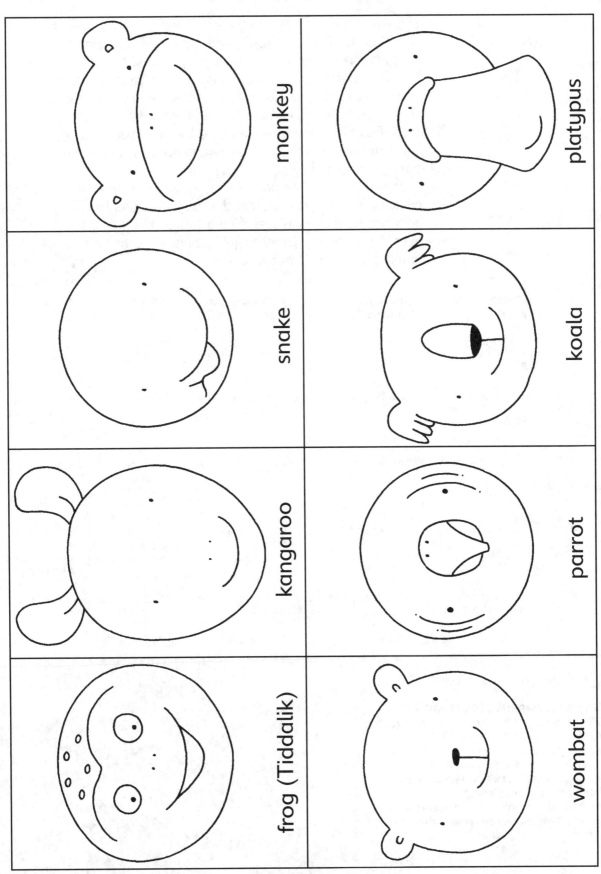

monkey

platypus

snake

koala

kangaroo

parrot

frog (Tiddalik)

wombat

UNIT 1

The picnic

This unit is based on the story *We're Going on a Picnic* by Pat Hutchins (Red Fox). It is a story about Rosie the hen with a vivid interplay between the words and pictures. It comprises five days' literacy activities and supports the National Literacy Strategy (Later Foundation Stage, medium-term plan) focus on *Narrative structure*. Linked activities are provided for all the six Areas of Learning with a strong emphasis on developing speaking and listening skills; promoting concern for others through sharing in Personal, social and emotional development; and developing literacy skills in the form of pictures and maps to represent the story structure. The activities build towards Year 1 Term 1, Objective 1 of the *Speaking, Listening, Learning* guidance: to describe incidents or tell stories from their own experience.

Day	Shared text-level work	Shared word-/ sentence-level work	Focused group work	Independent work	Plenary
1 Going on a picnic	Shared reading of *We're Going on a Picnic.*	Word wall.	Guided reading – sequencing the story.	**PSED:** Sharing pretend food.	Acting out the story in sequence.
2 Map it!	Drawing the story map of *We're Going on a Picnic.*	Handwriting practice.	Guided writing of story maps.	**CLL:** Writing lists.	Shared reading of *We're Going on a Bear Hunt.*
3 We're going on a bike ride!	Shared writing of 'We're Going on a Bike Ride'.	Phoneme count.	Guided writing of story maps.	**MD:** Sorting, counting and adding totals of fruit.	Retelling story maps.
4 What happened next?	Shared writing – story maps of 'We're going on a bike ride'.	Predicting words that fit.	Guided writing of story maps.	**KUW:** Using senses to investigate picnic objects.	Shared reading of the story *We're Going on a Lion Hunt.*
5 Comparing stories	Completing the shared story of 'We're going on a bike ride'.	High frequency word race.	Guided writing of story maps.	**PD:** Handling tools and malleable materials. **CD:** Painting fruit.	Creating a story in a circle.

Key assessment opportunities

When working with the children during guided reading and writing, look closely for:
● ability to recount a first-hand experience
● ability to speak clearly and audibly
● use of varied and interesting vocabulary when retelling experiences
● ability to recognise high-frequency words.
Record appropriately and ensure that this informs future planning.

Personal, social and emotional development

Sharing
Early Learning Goal
Work as part of a group or class, taking turns and sharing fairly.
What you need
Plastic plates; play fruit (if possible, fruit that breaks into segments such as from the Early Learning Centre, or alternatively use real fruit and have an adult cut it up).
What to do
● Ask the children to share the fruit out fairly.
● If an adult is available to work with the children, ask them to illustrate the point by not sharing fairly to start with and then discussing equal parts with the children.

Mathematical development

Adding fruit
Early Learning Goal
In practical activities and discussion begin to use the vocabulary involved in adding and subtracting.
What you need
Assorted play fruit; sorting rings; small whiteboards and pens.
What to do
● Ask the children to put the fruit into two sorting rings. Encourage them to sort the fruit by criteria, such as size and colour.
● Ask them to count how many pieces of fruit there are in each ring and then to represent this on their whiteboards. Encourage writing numerals or drawing a matching number of pieces of fruit, according to the children's ability level.
● Challenge the children to count how many pieces of fruit there are in total. More able children may be able to represent this as an addition sum.

Physical development

Making picnic food
Early Learning Goal
Handle tools, objects, construction and malleable materials safely and with increasing control.
What you need
Play dough; modelling tools and boards; real picnic items.
What to do
● Ask the children to make food for a picnic using play dough.
● Encourage them to look carefully at and copy real items.

Creative development

Painting fruit
Early Learning Goal
Explore colour, texture, shape, form and space in two or three dimensions.
What you need
Cut-up pieces of fruit, such as pomegranates or other fruits containing interesting seeds; easels and paints.
What to do
● Ask the children to look carefully at the fruits, in particular the seeds, and encourage careful observation of all the features.
● Ask the children to match the colours and paint their chosen fruit.

Communication, language and literacy

Writing lists
Early Learning Goal
Attempt writing for different purposes...
What you need
Pieces of paper for the children to write their lists onto (with the words: *On our picnic we will need ...* written at the top); a list of picnic foods with corresponding illustrations beside the words; pencils; the story, *We're Going on a Picnic* by Pat Hutchins (Red Fox).
What to do
● Encourage the children to look carefully at the illustrations in the story to help them to decide what is needed for the picnic.
● Give each child your prepared pieces of paper for writing lists on to. Let them refer to the prepared picnic food list and encourage all attempts at writing, drawing and so on.

Knowledge and understanding of the world

Feely bags
Early Learning Goal
Investigate objects and materials by using all of their senses as appropriate.
What you need
Drawstring cloth bag; assorted picnic objects.
What to do
● Place picnic objects inside the bag and ask the children to identify them by touching them.
● Encourage a wide range of vocabulary as the children describe what they can feel. Let them see the objects after they have guessed.

Going on a picnic

Objectives

Early Learning Goal
● Reading p62-63.

Stepping Stone
● Enjoy and increasing range of books.

NLS
T3: To re-read a text to provide context cues to help read unfamiliar words.
W5: To read on sight a range of familiar words.

What you need

● The story *We're Going on a Picnic* by Pat Hutchins (Red Fox)
● a Big Book version or several individual copies of *Rosie's Walk* by Pat Hutchins (Red Fox) or another book by the same author
● props for the story such as a basket, assorted fruit, pictures of a hen, a duck and a goose drawn on to large pieces of card
● key words from the story printed on card (*picnic, basket, berries, apples, pears, walked, hill, field, hen, goose, duck*)
● a flipchart.

Differentiation

Less able
● Support the children to read the story by reading through key words first and asking them to find the words in the text.

More able
● Provide a particular question for the children to find out from their reading.

Shared text-level work

● Introduce the story *We're Going on a Picnic* by first looking carefully at the cover and discussing the picture.
● Ask the children to predict what they think will happen in the story.
● Now read the story with plenty of expression using a pointer and encouraging the children to try and join in.
● Discuss what happened to the animals' picnic and look carefully at the illustrations, discussing how the pictures tell the full story. Talk about the importance of looking carefully at the pictures as we read to give us clues about what is happening.
● Re-read the story, with the children joining in, particularly with the repeated phrase *We're going on a picnic!*

Shared word-level work

● Show the children the prepared key words from the story. Read them one by one with the children and display them in a pocket chart or on the wall.
● Ensure that the children understand the meaning of each word by reading the word individually and then saying the word in a sentence.
● Ask for a volunteer (assisted by the rest of the class) to point to the correct word as you say it.
● Continue in this way, to help word recognition and to widen vocabulary. Revisit these words regularly during the week for a few minutes.

Focused group work

● Group children with similar reading needs for this activity (for example, those that need practice in guessing the word from the context of the sentence).
● Work with a group of children to read another story by Pat Hutchins (such as *Rosie's Walk*).
● Make some predictions about the story or, if it is familiar, talk about the characters and what happens. With *Rosie's Walk* talk about the similarities with *We're Going on a Picnic*.
● Now read the story together, modelling the use of a range of strategies to read unfamiliar words.
● Look carefully at the pictures to see how they add to the story.

Independent work

● See the activities for the six Areas of Learning on page 141.

Plenary

● Gather the children together and talk about all the characters in the story *We're Going on a Picnic*. List them on the flipchart and show the children the story props.
● Ask individuals to play the parts, using props.
● Explain that the children are going to act out the story while you retell it using the character pictures as prompts.

Map it!

Objectives

Early Learning Goal
● Writing p64-65.

Stepping Stone
● Ascribe meanings to marks.

NLS
T15: To use writing to communicate in a variety of ways, incorporating it into play and everyday classroom life.
W14: To write letters using the correct sequence of movements.

What you need

● The story *We're Going on a Picnic* by Pat Hutchins (Red Fox)
● a flipchart and pens
● small whiteboards and pens for every child
● a copy of *We're Going on a Bear Hunt* by Michael Rosen (Walker Books).

Shared text-level work

● Look at the story *We're Going on a Picnic* and examine the illustrations together very carefully.
● Talk about where the characters went (from their house across a field, up a hill, down a hill, down a path, around the lane and back to their house).
● Explain that this is rather like a circle, because the characters ended up at the same place they started from.
● Now say that you are going to draw a map of the characters' journey in the story. Model the process, starting by drawing a picture of their house and then making sketches of the different places they visited (the field, hill, path and lane). Draw a circular route with small sketches denoting the characters of duck, goose and hen.
● Using the story map, ask the class to retell the story while you point to the route.

Shared word-level work

● Explain that you are going to practise handwriting.
● Using letters currently being learned, provide a prompt for letter formation, such as: *top to bottom, lift and across* for the letter 't'.
● Ask the children to practise in different ways, such as in the air and on each other's backs and finally on whiteboards.
● Monitor carefully with adult support, emphasising the correct pencil grip.

Focused group work

● With a small group, look at the story map drawn during shared class work and then explain that the children will draw their own story maps.
● Remind the children of the places that the characters visited during the journey and then encourage the children to draw their own story maps.
● Help the children to write the names of the characters on their story maps and other key words. Encourage the use of the word wall to help them.

Independent work

● See the activities for the six Areas of Learning on page 141.

Plenary

● With the class gathered together on the carpet, explain that the title of this story is rather like another well-known story - *We're Going on a Bear Hunt* by Michael Rosen (Walker Books).
● Read the story to the children, encouraging plenty of actions to represent the different sounds and movements, such as *Splash, splosh!* to represent splashing through the river, and *Squelch, squerch!* to represent wading through the mud, and so on.
● Have fun with plenty of actions and encourage the children to join in with the repeated refrain of *We're going on a bear hunt*.

Differentiation

Less able
● Scribe some words for the children where necessary.

More able
● Encourage the children to write a range of words or phrases independently.

UNIT 1 DAY 3 ▢ The picnic

We're going on a bike ride!

Objectives

Early Learning Goal
● Writing p64-65

Stepping Stone
● Use writing as a means of recording and communicating.

NLS
T15: To use writing to communicate in a variety of ways, incorporating it into play and everyday classroom life.
W2: Knowledge of grapheme/phoneme correspondences through identifying and writing initial and dominant phonemes in spoken words.

What you need

● A flipchart
● individual whiteboards and pens (enough for one between two children)
● a class puppet
● the class story map made on Day 2 (see page 144).

Differentiation

Less able
● Scribe some words for the children where necessary.

More able
● Encourage the children to use the key words from the word wall to annotate their story maps.

Shared text-level work

● Remind the children of the story map of *We're Going on a Picnic* made the previous day (see page 143).
● Explain that together you are going to plan and write a class story based on going on a bike ride. Ask: *Who can ride a bike?* Tell the children that you are going to imagine that a group of people go for a bike ride.
● First decide together who will be in your story and write the names on the flipchart.
● Next ask the children to talk with their partners about where they could go on a bike ride. Take plenty of suggestions and then write the most popular ones on the flipchart.
● Remind the children of the story read yesterday and how the squirrel stole the different fruits. What could happen in their story?
● Together draw a story map of the class story using the ideas listed on the flipchart and explaining what is happening on the way.

Shared word-level work

● Give out the whiteboards and pens to pairs of children and then introduce the class puppet (who can only talk in phonemes).
● Say that the puppet is going to say a word in phonemes and they need to listen very carefully to count the number of phonemes the puppet is saying.
● Say a word in phonemes (such as p-i-c-n-i-c) and ask the children to talk to their partner and then write the number of phonemes on their whiteboards.
● Ask the children to show you their numbers and then repeat the word in phonemes to check the number, counting with the children. Ensure that you also say the whole word each time.
● Repeat with one or two words as time allows.

Focused group work

● Work with a small group of children to draw their story maps of going on a bike ride (or other experience such as going on a bus trip), using the class example as a basis.
● Ask the children to draw their own story maps, including places of their own choice.
● Help the children to write key words as well as the names of places and people on their story maps.
● Finish by asking each child to explain their story map.

Independent work

● See the activities for the six Areas of Learning on page 141.

Plenary

● Share some examples of the children's story maps. Encourage the children to explain to the class where they went and who was with them.
● Finish by telling the class all about a trip you have been on.

UNIT 1 DAY 4 ▢ The picnic

What happened next?

Objectives

Early Learning Goal
● Writing p64-65.

Stepping Stone
● Use writing as a means of recording and communicating.

NLS
T15: To use writing to communicate in a variety of ways, incorporating it into play and everyday classroom life.
S1: To expect written text to make sense and to check for sense if it does not.

What you need

● The story map from Day 3 (page 143).
● sentences from *We're Going on a Picnic* with a missing word in each one (either printed out in at least 48 point font or shown on an interactive whiteboard) (Permission granted).
● if possible a copy of *We're Going on a Lion Hunt* by David Axtel (Macmillan) or write an adaptation of the story *We're Going on a Bear Hunt* by Michael Rosen (Walker Books).

Differentiation

Less able
● Give younger children a choice of two words to fit in the sentence gaps.

More able
● Challenge older children to make up a missing word sentence for their partner to guess.

Shared text-level work

● Begin by looking at the story map of 'We're Going on a Bike Ride' drawn the previous day (page 144). Talk about the journey and what happened, jointly constructing a story.
● Explain that you are going to write some sentences to fit the story.
● Take suggestions from the children, orally rehearse a sentence and then write it on the flipchart.
● Encourage the children to suggest how to spell each word, emphasising the spacing between words and phonetically plausible spellings. Use words from the word wall to help.
● Continue in this way to write further sentences representing the story. Model re-reading each sentence to check it makes sense and orally rehearse each sentence before you write it.

Shared sentence-level work

● Show the children the sentences you have prepared with the missing words. Explain that they have come from the story *We're Going on a Picnic*. Emphasise that they need to read the whole sentence to decide what word could fit.
● Ask the children to talk to partners about possible words and take suggestions.
● Read the sentence again with the different suggestions and ask them which one they think is best.
● Write in the agreed word and explain that it is important to check for meaning as they read. Illustrate this by substituting a totally implausible word, such as *water* for *walk* and so on.
● Finish by re-reading the sentences together.

Focused group work

● Work with a different group as per the previous day (page 144) to draw story maps of going on a trip, using the class example as a basis.
● Talk about the children's ideas before they draw their maps.
● Encourage them to add place and people's names as well as some key words. Provide support as necessary.
● Finish by asking each child to explain their story map.

Independent work

● See the activities for the six Areas of Learning on page 141.

Plenary

● Talk about all the books that you have shared over the last few days. Discuss the similarities and the differences between the stories.
● Read the story *We're Going on a Lion Hunt* by David Axtel (Macmillan) if available. If not then adapt the story *We're going on a Bear Hunt*, changing the characters and setting. Tell your new version with plenty of expression.
● If time allows, retell the story, inviting the children to join in with the words and actions.

UNIT 1 DAY 5 🔲 The picnic

Comparing stories

Objectives

Early Learning Goal
● Writing p64-65

Stepping Stone
● Use writing as a means of recording and communicating.

NLS
T15: To use writing to communicate in a variety of ways, incorporating it into play and everyday classroom life...
W6: To read on sight the 45 high frequency words to be taught by the end of YR.

What you need

● The 'We're Going on a Bike Ride' story map and the beginning of the story written the previous day (see page 145)
● a range of six or seven high frequency words appropriate to the class printed in large font and laminated as individual words (two copies of each word).

Differentiation

Less able
● Use easier words in the word race.

More able
● Challenge the children to have a go at saying more difficult words in the word race.

Shared text-level work
● Look at the story map again together and re-read the beginning of the story written the previous day (page 145). Explain that you are now going to complete the story.
● Listen to the children's suggestions and orally rehearse sentences to complete the story of 'We're Going on a Bike Ride'.
● Scribe the children's sentences on the flipchart to complete the story. Emphasise reading for meaning and take phonetically plausible spellings.
● Reread the story when completed and then discuss how this compared with the original story of We're Going on a Picnic by Pat Hutchins (Red Fox).
● List the places visited in your own story and compare these with the places visited in the original story as well as the story We're Going on a Bear Hunt by Michael Rosen (Walker Books).

Shared word-level work
● Ask the children to make a circle. Explain that you are going to show them some words that will help them to read once they have learned how to recognise them straight away.
● Ask for two volunteers to try and read the words. Make two identical lines of words on the floor.
● Tell the children that they need to jump on each word and that, if they can read the word, they should say it aloud and then jump on to the next word. Make sure that the children understand that this is a word race.
● Say 'Ready, steady, go!' and ask the children to read the words while the rest of the class cheer them on.
● Ask several children to take turns at this, ensuring you support those who struggle.
● Provide the words for the children to read in the same way at other times in the day, possibly in your outdoor area.

Focused group work
● Work with a different group to draw their story maps of going on a trip as per the previous two days (see pages 144-145).
● Show some of the children's maps to give other children inspiration.

Independent work
● See the activities for the six Areas of Learning on page 142.

Plenary
● With the children sat in a circle, explain that you are going to create a different story of a journey. Agree together what this could be, basing it on the children's own experiences. Talk about the things that they did.
● Start the story off and then go round the circle asking each child to add a place they have visited. Include a repeated phrase such as We're going on a bus ride. What a sunny day!

UNIT 2

The travelling theatre

This unit is based on a recounted story of the visit of a travelling theatre company. It comprises five days' literacy activities and supports the National Literacy Strategy (Later Foundation Stage, Medium-term plan) focus on *Recounts* and *Shared experiences*. Linked activities are provided for all the six Areas of Learning with a strong emphasis on developing speaking and listening skills through the performance of a play; a focus on good listening in Personal, social and emotional development and the development of literacy skills in the form of writing recounts and captions to match photographs. The activities build towards Year 1 Term 1, Objective 2 of the *Speaking, Listening, Learning* guidance: to listen with sustained concentration.

Day	Shared text-level work	Shared word-/ sentence-level work	Focused group work	Independent work	Plenary
1 The travelling theatre	Shared reading of recount of 'The travelling theatre'.	Vocabulary extension – word wall.	Guided writing of recounts.	**PSED:** How to be a good listener.	Writing captions for photos.
2 The day the class ...	Shared writing of recount – sequencing with photographs.	Croaker puppet – blending sounds.	Guided writing of recounts.	**CLL:** Writing captions.	Good listening using cartoon characters.
3 Write about it!	Shared writing of recount – using a writing frame.	Muddled captions.	Guided writing of recounts.	**MD:** Sorting and describing shapes.	Creating a class puppet play.
4 The finished account	Completing shared writing of recount.	Spelling high frequency words.	Guided writing of recounts.	**KUW:** Using the digital camera.	Sharing children's recounts.
5 Everyday recounts.	Comparing recounts.	Find the missing word.	Guided writing of recounts.	**PD:** Making fairy peg dolls. **CD:** Acting out a story using puppets.	The class photo album.

Key assessment opportunities

When working with children during role-play look closely for:
- ability to sequence sentences correctly
- ability to use sequencing words appropriately
- ability to check for meaning when reading
- ability to blend phonemes correctly
- ability to spell a range of high frequency words
- ability to sustain effective listening.

Record appropriately and ensure that this informs future planning.

Personal, social and emotional development

How to be a good listener
Early Learning Goal
Maintain attention, concentrate and sit quietly when appropriate.
What you need
Paper; pens; adult assistance.
What to do
● Remind the children of the whole-class discussion of the features of a good listener (see Day 2, page 150).
● Ask the children to draw a cartoon showing a good listener (for example someone with huge ears!).

Physical development

Peg dolls
Early Learning Goal
Handle tools, objects, construction and malleable materials safely and with increasing control.
What you need
Wooden pegs; small pieces of felt; ribbon; lace; material scraps; wool; string; glue; scissors; pictures of fairies; completed peg dolls as examples.
What to do
● Show the children the finished peg dolls and fairy pictures and ask them to select their own materials to make a doll of their own.
● Encourage them to use a range of tools to cut and stick scraps of material on to the pegs.

Communication, language and literacy

Matching captions to photos
Early Learning Goal
Attempt writing for different purposes, using features of different forms such as lists, stories and instructions.
What you need
A range of digital photographs recording a class shared experience stuck on to A4 paper with spaces for the children to add captions; an example of a photo and caption on display; pencils.
What to do
● Provide a set of photographs in the class writing area.
● Ask the children to write a brief caption underneath each photograph.
● Invite the children to use the class word wall to help them with their writing and encourage them to make phonetically plausible attempts at a range of other words.

Mathematical development

Matching shapes
Early Learning Goal
Use language such as 'circle' or 'bigger' to describe the shape and size of solids and flat shapes.
What you need
A range of 2-D and 3-D shapes, including mathematical shapes and boxes from packaging; sorting rings; folded card with names of shapes written on.
What to do
● Ask the children to look carefully at the shapes and talk about what is special about each one.
● Place the card labels into sorting rings and read them with the children. Ask them to match the shapes to the labels in the rings.

Creative development

Puppet play
Early Learning Goal
Use their imagination in art and design, music, dance, imaginative and role-play and stories.
What you need
Range of puppets; a cardboard stage made from a box; pens; gummed paper shapes and so on.
What to do
● Explain that the children may use the puppets to act out a play (one they are familiar with).
● Ask the children to make an imaginary stage from the box, paper and pens.
● Encourage the children to have fun acting out a story with the puppets.

Knowledge and understanding of the world

Say cheese!
Early Learning Goal
Find out about and identify the uses of everyday technology and use information and communication technology and programmable toys to support their learning.
What you need
Digital camera (more than one if possible); range of photographs taken previously; photograph albums.
What to do
● With adult support, show the children how to use the digital camera.
● Encourage them to take photographs of activities in the classroom, focusing on what they particularly enjoy.

The travelling theatre

Objectives

Early Learning Goal
● Reading p62-63.

Stepping Stone
● Begin to be aware of the way stories are structured.

NLS
T7: To use knowledge of familiar texts to re-enact or re-tell to others, recounting the main points in correct sequence.
T14: To use experience of stories, poems and simple recounts as a basis for independent writing.
W10: New words from their reading and shared experiences.

What you need
● Photocopiable page 154 enlarged to at least A3 size
● a writing frame for each child
● key words from the text in at least 48 point font, printed on card or laminated (*first, next, then, after, finally, travelling, theatre, castle, costumes, fairy, princess, fireworks, prince*)
● a selection of photographs (either of activities in the classroom, or of a shared experience) printed and stuck on to A4 paper with spaces for captions.

Differentiation

Less able
● Provide a writing frame with only three boxes and encourage all attempts at phonetically plausible spellings.

More able
Encourage the children to work independently and complete all six boxes, using the word wall.

Shared text-level work
● Talk about any theatre groups that have ever visited the school and ask the children if they have any other experiences of theatre to share.
● Now explain that you are going to read an account of a travelling theatre visiting a school.
● Read the recount to the children, exploring the pictures at the same time. Have the children experienced anything similar? Perhaps some have seen a pantomime and can talk about the story, the singing, the funny jokes or tricks that went on.
● Reread the recount with the children joining in. Demonstrate how some words, such as *first, next, after that*, and *finally*, help us to sequence a series of events.

Shared word-level work
● Show the children the prepared key words from the story. Read them together and display them on the wall.
● Ensure that the children understand the meaning of each word by reading the word individually and then saying the word in a sentence.
● To help the children to learn sequencing words, ask individuals to stand in a line and choose another pupil to give out the cards in a sequence. Read the words together as each child holds up their card. Talk about the order (the last person should hold the word *finally*).

Focused group work
● Re-read the recount of 'The travelling theatre' with a group of children. Explain that they are going to write a recount using a similar format.
● Brainstorm together a shared experience that the children can recall and recount. Orally rehearse the order of each part.
● Now give each child a recount writing frame (see below) and ensure that they are clear about what to put in each box. Ask the children to draw a picture and write a sentence for each section.

One day	Then	Next
When	After that	Finally

Independent work
● See the activities for the six Areas of Learning on page 148.

Plenary
● Display the photographs of a shared experience and discuss what is happening in each picture. Write a short caption to fit each photo.

UNIT 2 DAY 2 ▢ **The travelling theatre**

The day the class...

Objectives

Early Learning Goal
● Writing p64-65.

Stepping Stone
● Use writing as a means of recording and communicating.

NLS
T14: To use experience of stories, poems and simple recounts as a basis for independent writing...
W2: Knowledge of grapheme/phoneme correspondences.

What you need
● Photographs of a shared class experience.
● a flipchart
● a puppet
● a range of objects corresponding to specific phonemes (such as initial consonant clusters)
● a bag.

Shared text-level work
● Display the photographs of a shared experience such as a school trip.
● Give the children the opportunity to discuss the experience, helping them to remember events and incidences.
● Ask the children to help you put the photographs in the correct order, sticking them to a piece of A3 paper. Write numbers underneath each one to denote the order.
● Now ask the children to look closely at the photographs and invite them to talk to their partner to suggest a sentence to put underneath the first one.
● Spend time listening to some of the children's ideas and together choose the sentence that is most appropriate.
● Write the first sentence with the children suggesting spellings. Ensure that you orally rehearse each sentence before you write it and that you read each sentence together when you complete it.
● Continue to write another sentence in this way, as time allows.

Shared word-level work
● Use the class puppet to help the children to hear and say initial consonant clusters (adjust as appropriate to the children's current phonic level).
● With a bag of objects and the puppet, explain that the puppet has problems saying the sounds. For example, show the puppet a scarf and have it say, *staff*. Ask the children to help by telling the puppet the correct pronunciation.
● Repeat with other objects and have fun with the puppet making mistakes until the children help him to get it right.

Focused group work
● Work with another group of children to write their own recounts of a shared experience as per the previous day (see page 149).
● Take time to rehearse the sentences that will go with each picture before the children write or you scribe them.

Independent work
● See the activities for the six Areas of Learning on page 148.

Differentiation

Less able
● Help the children to understand a basic sequence of beginning, middle and end.

More able
● Provide further blank writing frames for the children to experiment with during independent work.

Plenary
● Talk to the children about the importance of being a good listener. Ask an adult helper to role-play an example of bad listening with you. For example, ask them to fidget, avoid eye contact, talk across you and so on in an exaggerated manner.
● Now ask the children to think of the characteristics of a good listener and write down a few of the children's ideas on the flipchart.
● Share some of the children's cartoon drawings of a good listener (see PSED, page 148) or show the children one you have prepared.
● Use the cartoon(s) as a reminder to the children when reinforcing good listening.

Write about it!

Objectives

Early Learning Goal
● Writing p64-65.

Stepping Stone
● Use writing as a means of recording and communicating.

NLS
T14: To use experience of stories, poems and simple recounts as a basis for independent writing.
S1: To expect written text to make sense and to check for sense if it does not.

What you need

● A large writing frame (see page 149)
● muddled sentences adapted from the recount on photocopiable page 155 written or printed in a large font size
● the sequenced pictures and captions from Day 2 (page 150)
● a flipchart.

Differentiation

Less able
● Provide some more simple sentences for the children to put in the right order such as: *Then went they home.*

More able
● Challenge the children to take turns to be the teacher. Ask them to explain why the muddled sentences are wrong (see Shared sentence-level work).

Shared text-level work

● Look at the sequenced pictures and captions from the previous day.
● Now tell the children that you are going to write another recount.
● Display the recount writing frame and talk about the words that help us to get things in the right order.
● Now discuss a shared experience such as a walk to the park.
● Orally rehearse the sequence and ask the children what to put first, encouraging them to talk to partners before sharing answers with you.
● Invite the children who have written a recount in focused group work (see pages 149 and 150) to contribute ideas based on the work they have already done with you.
● Write one or two sentences in the correct sequence, emphasising the use of sequencing words such as *first*, *next*, and so on.

Shared sentence-level work

● Tell the children that you need some help because you have written an account but all the words have got muddled up.
● Read the following sentences to the children and talk about what is wrong with them:

> they First the stage together. Put
> they up. got Then dressed
> to the children Next sat all watch.
> acted out they the story. After that
> they and sang Finally danced.

● Take a sentence at a time and re-order the words by cutting up the sentences into individual words, or rewriting them on the flipchart. Ask the children to talk to partners to correct the sentence.
● Read the correct sentences together and talk about the importance of checking that what we read makes sense.

Focused group work

● Work with another group of children to write their own recounts of a personal experience.
● Ask the children to orally rehearse each sentence, using the sequencing words in the writing frame to structure their recount.
● Help them to write and draw one sentence at a time. Provide a frame with just three boxes for less able children to complete.

Independent work

See the activities for the six Areas of Learning on page 148.

Plenary

● Invite the children who have been exploring the puppets and stage to share this with the class (see CD, page 149).
● Ask the children to hold their puppets while the class creates a simple play for them, using the sequencing words.

The finished account

Objectives

Early Learning Goal
● Writing p64-65.

Stepping Stone
● Use writing as a means of recording and communicating.

NLS
T14: To use experience of stories, poems and simple recounts as a basis for independent writing.
S1: To expect written text to make sense and to check for sense if it does not.
W6: To read on sight the 45 high frequency words to be taught by the end of YR.

What you need
● The large writing frame from Day 3 (see page 151)
● individual whiteboards and pens (one between two pupils).

Differentiation

Less able
● Play a matching game to aid recognition of high frequency words. Provide two cards for each word and play games such as 'pairs' and 'snap'.

More able
● Ask the children to say a sentence that includes each of the high frequency words that they have been spelling (see shared word-level work).

Shared text-level work
● Share the recount that the children began on Day 3 (page 151) and re-read what has been written so far.
● Now ask the children to talk to partners about what is next and then take a range of suggestions, emphasising the correct sequence.
● Write the final sentences in this way, asking the children to suggest spellings and modelling orally rehearsing each sentence before you write.
● Re-read the whole recount with the children, checking for errors and that the sequence is correct.
● Ask the children if there is anything else that they would like to add. Where should it go in the sequence?

Shared word-level work
● Give out the whiteboards, one between two, and then say that you are going to read out a range of words for the children to write. Ask them to check with their partner first before writing.
● Read out a range of high frequency words, such as *they, and, like, was, went* and so on and then ask the children to write them.
● Ask the children to show you their words each time so that you can check on their spellings.
● Sensitively use any errors as teaching points and ask the children to look carefully at mistakes, reinforcing correct spelling.

Focused group work
● Continue as the previous day (page 151), with the children writing their own recounts based on personal experiences.
● Remind them of the sequencing words that will help them to structure their recounts and ensure that the children orally rehearse the order of their recount as they write and draw each section.
● Word with individual children to help them write and draw one sentence at a time.
● Provide a frame with just three boxes for any less-able children to complete.

Independent work
● See the activities for the six Areas of Learning on page 148.

Plenary
● With the class gathered together, ask some of the children who have been writing their own recounts to share them with the class.
● Read examples to the class and each time talk about the features of the recount and the sequence.
● Talk about the kinds of things that would make good recounts, such as outings, parties and so on. What were the most popular things that the children have written about?
● Praise the children's work and encourage all attempts at phonetically plausible spelling.

UNIT 2 DAY 5 📖 The travelling theatre

Everyday recounts

Objectives

Early Learning Goal
● Writing p64-65.

Stepping Stone
● Use writing as a means of recording and communicating.

NLS
T14: To use experience of stories, poems and simple recounts as a basis for independent writing.
S1: To expect written text to make sense and to check for sense if it does not.

What you need
● Recounts produced by the class
● two enlarged copies of photocopiable page 154
● recount words on card (*first, next, then, finally*)
● a highlighter pen
● sticky notes
● photographs and captions from independent work (see CLL, page 148)
● a large photograph album.
● a flipchart/easel.

Differentiation

Less able
● Choose simpler words to cover up for the children to work out.

More able
● Challenge the children with more difficult missing words in shared sentence-level work.

Shared text-level work
● Begin by re-reading the recount of 'The travelling theatre' from photocopiable page 154.
● Then with the children's help, read the different recount that you have written together (see pages 151-152).
● Ask the children to find out what is the same about these recounts and highlight them on the photocopy, using a highlighter pen.
● Now briefly outline a common event in the class (such as getting ready for lunch).
● Use the sequencing words and ask the children to help you to orally recount the sequence for your chosen everyday event.
● Hold the correct sequencing card up as you say each sentence. For example, ***First*** *you need to wash your hands.* ***Then*** *you line up in three lines.* ***Next*** *the dinner lady asks the children having a packed lunch to follow her.* And so on.

Shared sentence-level work
● Place your second enlarged copy of 'The travelling theatre' on your easel or flipchart and cover up a noun from each sentence with a sticky note.
● Ask the children to talk to their partners about the missing words.
● Take a range of suggestions for each sentence and write these on the flip chart or sticky note.
● Read the sentences with the different words and ask the children to say which ones make sense. Which word do they think fits best?
● Continue in this way to add all the missing words.

Focused group work
● Continue as the previous two days (page 151-152), with the children writing their own recounts based on personal experiences.
● Ask them to compare their ideas to the class and original recounts. What words have they used that are the same?

Independent work
● See the activities for the six Areas of Learning on page 148.

Plenary
● Take all the photographs and captions that have been written during the week (see CLL, page 148) and explain that you are going to put them in a class photograph album.
● Remind the children of the events that are captured in the sets of photographs (which have been stuck on to pieces of A4 paper with a caption underneath each photograph).
● Take a set at a time and remind the children of how important it was to get the photographs in the right order.
● Stick each set of photographs with accompanying captions in the album.
● Finally, together, re-read each set of captions.

📖 **153**

TERM 3

The travelling theatre

One day a travelling theatre came to school. There were actors and lots of boxes. It was very exciting.

We went into the school hall to watch the story of Sleeping Beauty. The princess was really beautiful.

First the actors unpacked and set up the stage. It looked like a real castle.

Finally there was a happy ending and Sleeping Beauty was woken up by the handsome prince.

Next they dressed up in lovely costumes. There was a fairy godmother and a wicked witch.

After that they sang songs and played lots of funny tricks. We all really enjoyed it.

ALL NEW 100 LITERACY HOURS · RECEPTION

◆SCHOLASTIC

UNIT 3

Playing with sounds and words

This unit comprises ten days' literacy activities and supports the National Literacy Strategy (Later Foundation Stage, Medium-term plan) focus on *Poems and chants*. The activities will help to develop phonological awareness and a range of phonic skills through playing with sounds and nonsense verse. The poems featured are ideal for beginning a collection of nonsense verse and will provide the children with ideas and inspiration for writing their own versions. Linked activities are provided for all the six Areas of Learning with an emphasis on developing speaking and listening skills and have strong links with Creative development. The activities build towards Year 1 Term 1, Objective 3 of the *Speaking, Listening, Learning* guidance: to ask and answer questions, make relevant contributions, offer suggestions and take turns.

WEEK 1

Day	Shared text-level work	Shared word-/ sentence-level work	Focused group work	Independent work	Plenary
1 Tickle a tiger	Shared reading of 'Don't Tickle Tigers'.	'Rhyming tennis' game.	Guided reading of nonsense verse.	**PSED:** Running the class library.	Invite a librarian to talk to the class.
2 Strange animals!	Shared reading of 'The Quangle Wangle's Hat'.	Blending nonsense words.	Guided reading of nonsense verse.	**CLL:** The class library.	Singing 'The Animal Fair'.
3 Hop like a kangaroo	Shared reading of 'Hopaloo Kangaroo'.	Using upper- and lower-case letters to play 'Snap!'	Guided reading of nonsense verse.	**MD:** Counting books.	Tongue twisters.
4 My favourite poem	Shared reading of nonsense verse.	High frequency word pairs game.	Guided reading of nonsense verse.	**KUW:** Classifying animals - same or different?	Finding books in the class library.
5 Animal alphabet	Class performance of favourite nonsense poem.	Animal alphabet.	Guided reading of nonsense verse.	**PD:** Hopaloo dance. **CD:** Painting of the 'Animal fair'.	Reading a selection of nonsense verses from the class library.

Key assessment opportunities
When working with children during role-play look closely for:
● ability to rhyme
● ability to blend nonsense words
● ability to blend phonemes
● ability to use a range of strategies to read unfamiliar words
● recognition of high frequency words.
Record appropriately and ensure that this informs future planning.

Day	Shared text-level work	Shared word-/ sentence-level work	Focused group work	Independent work	Plenary
6 Tiger tricks	Shared writing of adaptation of 'Don't tickle tigers'.	Phoneme frame.	Guided writing of nonsense poem.	**PSED:** Running the class library – taking turns.	Sharing examples of poems from guided writing.
7 Guess the animal	Shared writing of animal poetry.	Handwriting – letter formation.	Guided writing of nonsense poem.	**CLL:** Book making.	Sharing examples of poems from guided writing.
8 Kangaroo loo!	Shared writing of adaptation of 'Hopaloo Kangaroo'.	Writing nonsense words.	Guided writing of nonsense poem.	**MD:** Measuring the tiger!	Sharing examples of poems from guided writing.
9 Frolicking frogs	Shared reading of 'Frog frolics' and writing alternatives.	Reading for meaning.	Guided writing of nonsense poem.	**KUW:** Hot and cold - where do animals live?	Sharing examples of poems from guided reading.
10 Performing our poems	Performance of favourite nonsense poems.	Full circle – phonic game.	Guided writing of nonsense poem.	**PD:** Animals movements. **CD:** Creating a pet – junk modelling.	Performing in front of a visitor.

Key assessment opportunities

When working with children during guided writing look closely for:
● Ability to select a range of suitable words.
● Developing independence at writing for a purpose.
● Ability to blend phonemes.
● Beginning to form recognisable letters.
Record appropriately and ensure that this informs future planning.

Personal, social and emotional development

Playing together
Early Learning Goal
Work as part of a group or class, taking turns and sharing fairly.
What you need
The role-play area set up as a library (see CLL).
What to do
● As the children set up and role-play in the library emphasise the importance of taking turns to play the different roles and co-operating when setting up the area.
● Ask an adult to observe the children's behaviour.

Physical development

The Hopaloo dance
Early Learning Goal
Move with confidence, imagination and in safety.
What you need
Mats; space for the children to explore; suitable music with a mixture of tempos (try some traditional Aboriginal music, found in the 'world section' of good music stores).
What to do
● Encourage the children to hop like a kangaroo. Ask them to find out how far they can hop on one leg and then to change legs.
● Challenge the children to create a kangaroo dance – 'a hopaloo', listening to the music carefully and hopping quickly or slowly as appropriate.

Communication, language and literacy

The class library
Early Learning Goal
Use language to imagine and recreate roles and experiences.
What you need
A range of books - fiction, poetry and non-fiction; a book box/shelf; a librarian badge; library cards (small cards with space for the children to write their names with the words, for example, *Reception class library*); date stamp; labels; small pieces of card; a computer set up with a small database of book names; pens and pencils.
What to do
● Explain to the children that they need to set up a class library, with a section featuring the poetry books that you are looking at during shared reading. Ask an adult to support them.
● Ask the children to organise the books and then to check if they can find the corresponding books on the computer database.
● Encourage the children to play the roles of librarian and lenders.

Mathematical development

Taking stock!
Early Learning Goal
Use developing mathematical ideas and methods to solve practical problems.
What you need
Clipboards; a stock sheet denoting different types of books (hardback, paperback, Big Books); selection of books; pencils.
What to do
● Explain that you want the children to count up the class books (provide a box of books in a separate area from the class library).
● Encourage them, if possible, to make a tally chart using the stock sheet and then to write the corresponding numeral for each type of book.

Creative development

Animal painting
Early Learning Goal
Explore colour, texture, shape, form and space in two or three dimensions.
What you need
Painting materials and easels; pictures of different animals.
What to do
● Ask the children to paint one of the animals associated with the poems read. Show the animal pictures to provide inspiration.
● Create a display of the animals as an 'Animal Fair'!

Knowledge and understanding of the world

Same or different?
Early Learning Goal
Look closely at similarities, differences, patterns and change.
What you need
Small-world animals; sorting hoops; pieces of card; pens.
What to do
● Ask the children to sort the animals according to different criteria. For example, those with tails, long legs, big ears, stripes and so on.
● Encourage them to look carefully at what is the same about a range of animals.

Personal, social and emotional development

Choose a book
Early Learning Goals
Select and use activities and resources independently.
What you need
The class library set up as for Week 1 (see page 158).
What to do
● Encourage the children to use the class library as a resource for some real book lending. Once or twice a week let the children go into role as lenders in the library.
● Suggest that they choose a different kind of book each time and allow them to play imaginatively as they search for a book to share at home.

Physical development

Animal movements
Early Learning Goal
Move with control and co-ordination.
What you need
A large space (outdoors or indoors); a range of climbing equipment, mats, and so on; an adult helper.
What to do
● Ask the children to move around the equipment like an animal of their choice.
● Encourage suitable movements such as swinging like a monkey or slithering like a snake.

Communication, language and literacy

Bookmaking
Early Learning Goal
Attempt writing for different purposes using features of different forms such as lists, stories and instructions.
What you need
Book-making equipment to include blank zig-zag books, mini books and A4 sized sugar paper folded in half with two A4 sheets of white paper folded inside and stapled along the left hand margin; pencils and crayons; animal pictures.
What to do
● Provide a book for each child and ask them to draw an animal on each page, using the pictures as reference.
● Challenge the children to write their own nonsense words to describe the animal, such as the 'ringerly rhino' and so on.

Mathematical development

Measuring the tiger
Early Learning Goal
Use language such as 'greater', 'smaller', 'heavier' or 'lighter' to compare quantities.
What you need
Large pictures of a tiger; measuring tapes; rulers; pieces of string and wool; clipboard, paper and pencils.
What to do
● Ask the children to measure the tiger to find out how big it is.
● Ask an adult to encourage the children to use a range of non-standard and standard measures such as hands or rulers.
● Challenge the children to record the height and width of the animal.

Creative development

Creating a pet
Early Learning Goal
Express and communicate their ideas, thoughts and feelings by using a widening range of materials, suitable tools, imaginative and role-play.
What you need
Junk modelling materials; glue; sticky tape; painting equipment; toy animals.
What to do
● Ask the children to look at the toy animals and choose their favourite real or imaginary pet.
● Let them work in pairs to make a model of their favourite pet using the materials provided.
● Ask the children to paint their pets appropriately.

Knowledge and understanding of the world

Hot and cold animals
Early Learning Goal
Observe, find out about and identify features in the place they live and the natural world.
What you need
Small-world animals (including those that live in hot or cold places); pictures of hot and cold places; animal books.
What to do
● Ask the children to sort the animals into animals that live in cold places and animals that live in hot places by putting them on top of the corresponding pictures.
● If adult help is available, ask the children to discuss their ideas, referring to the books to find out more.

Tickle a tiger

Objectives

Early Learning Goals
● Communication p50–51.
● Linking sounds and letters p60–61.

Stepping Stone
● Enjoy rhyming and rhythmic activities.

NLS
T2: To use a variety of cues when reading.
W1: To understand and be able to rhyme through extending these patterns by analogy.

What you need
● Copy of the poem from photocopiable page 169, enlarged to at least A3 size
● a picture of a tiger
● a flipchart
● a set of poetry books with nonsense poems or alliterative rhymes
● a librarian (or school Literacy Co-ordinator) to talk to the children during the plenary session.

Differentiation

Less able
● Support the children by reading some lines, pausing at rhyming words for the children to fill in the missing words.

More able
● Provide a focused question for each poem, such as: *What colours are tigers?*

Shared text-level work
● Tell the children that over the week you are going to read a range of silly poems, many to do with animals and that today you are going to read one about a tiger. Ask the children to describe a tiger. Show them a picture of one.
● Read the poem to the children using a pointer and when you have finished, ask them what is funny about the poem. Talk about some of the words such as 'tangle' and 'lollop'. Write a list of them on the flipchart.
● Now re-read the poem with the children joining in. Underline all the words that alliterate on each line.
● Reread once more having fun with the words.

Shared word-level work
● With a child or other adult, model the game of 'rhyming tennis'. Take a simple CVC word (such as *den*) and explain that the partner has to think of another word that rhymes. This can be a nonsense or a proper word. Explain that this is called 'rhyming tennis' because we are bouncing words backwards and forwards with a partner. For example, *den, pen, ten.*
● Give the children time to have fun with rhyming words and then ask for volunteers to stand up and demonstrate.
● Use the children's examples and write the words on the board. Talk about whether they are real or nonsense words .
● If appropriate, use this as an opportunity to talk about the spelling of words such as *trick*. Explain how the phoneme /c/ is often written at the end of a word.

Focused group work
● Work with a group of children to read nonsense poems or rhymes.
● Ensure that you introduce each poem by talking about the subject and any unfamiliar words.
● Ask the children to read independently while you listen for any errors.
● Emphasise using a variety of cues to help read unfamiliar words and show how the predictable rhyme can help.
● Discuss the poems and particularly any nonsense words.

Independent work
● See the activities for the six Areas of Learning on page 157.

Plenary
● Explain that you have invited someone to come and talk to the children about setting up and using a library.
● Ask the visitor to explain how a library is organised; the importance of sorting books into sections; keeping records; time limits and so on.
● Ask the children who have been setting up the class library during independent activities (see page 157), to talk about what they have done.

Strange animals

Objectives

Early Learning Goal
● Linking sounds and letters p60-61.

Stepping Stone
● Enjoy rhyming and rhythmic activities.

NLS
T2: To use a variety of cues when reading.
W4: To link sound and spelling patterns by identifying alliteration in known and new and invented words.

What you need
● Copy of 'The Quangle Wangle's Hat' by Edward Lear
● a flipchart and pens
● your class puppet
● a set of poetry books with nonsense poems or alliterative rhymes.

Shared text-level work
● Remind the children of the poem read the previous day (see page 159). Talk about the type of poem it was and the kind of words used in it.
● Now say you are going to read another poem. This poem is called 'The Quangle Wangle's Hat'.
● Explain to the children that a 'Quangle Wangle' is a made up animal and that it is not a real animal, like the tiger is.
● Read slowly the first verse of the poem and talk through the various words – both real and made up.
● Read again, and display, the first four lines of the poem to the children and use lots of expression and enjoyment.
● Ask the children what they think the Quangle Wangle and the Crumpetty Tree might look like.
● Invite the children to help you draw a sketch on the flipchart of a Quangle Wangle sitting on top of the Crumpetty Tree. Encourage the children to be as imaginative as possible.

Shared word-level work
● Show the children your puppet and explain that it can only speak in phonemes.
● The puppet says the phonemes for each word and then the children have to blend the sounds to make a word.
● Choose CVC words such as *fin* and create other rhyming words such as *jin, lin, min* and so on. Encourage the children to suggest real and nonsense words.
● Write the suggested words on the flipchart with the children's assistance and then decide together which are real and which are nonsense words.
● Finish by asking individual children to say a nonsense word to the puppet in phonemes for the puppet to repeat.

Focused group work
● Continue as per the previous day (page 159) reading nonsense rhymes with a group of children.
● Encourage any confident children to recite a line of nonsense verse from memory.

Differentiation

Less able
● Support the children by reading the rhyme and asking them to provide missing rhyming words.

More able
● Encourage the children to read several poems independently.

Independent work
● See the activities for the six Areas of Learning on page 157.

Plenary
● With the children in a circle, ask them to join in with an animal rhyme or song such as 'The Animal Fair' found in Okki-Tokki-Unga (A&C Black).
● Have fun with the rhyme and talk about whether it is a nonsense poem.
● Discuss any similarities or differences with the other poems read over the last two days.

Hop like a kangaroo

Objectives

Early Learning Goal
● Linking sounds and letters p60-61.

Stepping Stone
● Enjoy rhyming and rhythmic activities.

NLS
T2: To use a variety of cues when reading.
S4: To use a capital letter for the start of own name.

What you need
● The poem, 'Hopaloo Kangaroo' from photocopiable page 170, enlarged to at least A3 size.
● a set of upper- and lower-case alphabet cards
● a set of poetry books with nonsense poems or alliterative rhymes
● a flipchart.

Shared text-level work
● Remind the children of the poems read over the last two days. Can anyone say what was special about them?
● Explain that you are going to read a poem about a kangaroo. Ask the children to talk to their partners about kangaroos.
● Invite volunteers to give feedback, summarising key facts.
● Now read the poem 'Hopaloo Kangaroo' on page 170 with plenty of expression.
● Talk about the poem and the nonsense words and how they change in each verse. For example, *jigaloo* in the first verse; *boogaloo* in the second and *hopaloo* in the third.
● Discuss the final verse of the poem and how this changes. Talk about the kangaroo's pouch and what the line *My baby in my pouch will be dancing too* refers to.
● Re-read the poem with a pointer, encouraging all the class to join in. Pause for the children to supply the next word.

Shared sentence-level work
● Demonstrate how names start with capital letters by writing some on a flipchart. Explain that sentences also start with capital letters.
● Now distribute alphabet cards to individual children (ensuring that you have some corresponding lower- and upper-case letters). Ask the children to stand up, one by one, if they have a capital letter. If a child has the corresponding lower-case letter, they stand up, point to the capital letter, and say, 'Snap!'.
● Reread the 'Hopaloo Kangaroo' poem with the text clearly visible. Use a pointer to read the poem and, as you read, ask a volunteer to tap the pointer each time you come to a capital letter.

Focused group work
● Continue as Day 1 (page 159) reading nonsense rhymes.
● Ask the children to vote for their favourite rhyme, explaining what they like about it.

Independent work
● See the activities for the six Areas of Learning on page 157.

Differentiation

Less able
● Help the children to recognise the capital letters at the start of their names.

More able
● Choose more able children to be the ones to tap on the pointer in shared sentence-level work.

Plenary
● With the children sitting in a circle, explain that you are going to think of some more nonsense rhyming words together.
● Say a word, such as *jog*, and pass it round the circle inviting each person to try and change it (*bog, cog, fog*). Explain that it helps to go through the alphabet, putting a different letter at the beginning of each word.
● Finish by telling the children that tongue twisters are sentences that are difficult to say because they use words that all start with the same sounds. Tell the children a tongue twister, such as *She sells sea shells by the sea shore.* Ask them to repeat it quickly. Did they find it difficult?

My favourite poem

Objectives

Early Learning Goal
● Communication p54-55.

Stepping Stone
● Use a widening range of words to express of elaborate ideas.

NLS
T2: To use a variety of cues when reading.
W6: To read on sight the 45 high frequency words to by taught by the end of YR.

What you need
● A simple nonsense or rhyming poem of your choice
● duplicate copies of various high frequency words on card
● a Big Book of poems, preferably containing some nonsense poems or action rhymes
● a set of poetry books with nonsense poems or alliterative rhymes
● a flipchart.

Differentiation

Less able
● Emphasise different reading strategies to support the children in their reading of the nonsense rhymes.

More able
● Encourage the children to learn a nonsense rhyme by heart to share with the rest of the class in a plenary session.

Shared text-level work
● Remind the children of the other poems read during the week and then say that you are going to read them a different poem.
● Explain to the children that everyone has poems and stories that they particularly like and that this is a poem that you like so you want to share it with the children.
● Show the children your chosen book and read the poem with lots of expression and enjoyment.
● Tell the children briefly what it is you like about the poem (the nonsense or rhyming words, the use of alliteration and so on).
● Read the poem again. Ask if there is anything the children like about the poem. Is there anything they dislike about it?
● Invite the children to tell you of any poems or rhymes they particularly like. Can they explain why they like them? Perhaps they have actions or are funny.
● Finally, reiterate that everyone likes different poems and stories and that is why the library is so useful. It means that everyone can choose something they want to look at and read.

Shared word-level work
● Ask the children to sit in a circle and place the high frequency word cards in the centre, face down.
● Choose a child to turn a card over, say the word and then replace it, face down.
● Continue in this way (as for a 'pairs' game) and if a child turns a card over that corresponds to a previous one, they must try to remember where it is. If they locate the matching card, they may keep both cards.
● Continue until all the cards are turned over and matched.

Focused group work
● Continue as per Day 1 (see page 159) reading nonsense rhymes with small groups of children.
● Can the children find the nonsense-rhyme books in the class library?

Independent work
● See the activities for the six Areas of Learning on page 157.

Plenary
● Ask the children if any of them can remember the name of a nonsense poem from the ones they have been reading during the week. Write the name of it on the flipchart.
● Now talk about the class library that the children have been creating and working in during independent work (see page 157).
● Where might the children find the nonsense rhyme books in the class library. Are they information books? Decide together where they should look. Ask a volunteer to go and find them.
● Finish by reading a nonsense rhyme together. Ask the children if there is anything they like or dislike about the poem.

UNIT 3 DAY 5 ☐ Playing with sounds and words

Animal alphabet

Objectives

Early Learning Goal
● Linking sounds and letters p60-61.

Stepping Stone
● Listen with enjoyment, respond to stories, songs and other music, rhymes and poems, and make up their own stories, songs, rhymes and poems.
● Show awareness of rhyme and alliteration.

NLS
T2: To use a variety of cues when reading.
W3: Alphabetic and phonic knowledge through understanding alphabetical order through alphabet books, rhymes and songs.

What you need

● The poems from pages 169 and 170 enlarged to at least A3 size
● two enlarged copies of the 'Animal alphabet' from photocopiable page 171, one cut up into individual cards
● a set of poem books with nonsense poems or alliterative rhymes.

Differentiation

Less able
● Provide adult support as necessary during shared word-level work.

More able
● Encourage the children to think of more than one animal with the same first letter.

Shared text-level work

● Re-read the selection of nonsense poems read during the week.
● Ask the children to talk to their partners about their favourite poem and have a class vote on the favourite. Discuss what they particularly like about the chosen poems.
● Re-read the favourite poem with all the children joining in and having plenty of fun. Apportion parts of the poem or a chorus to different groups.
● Practise the poem several times and perform, if possible, for an audience (another class or teacher).
● Talk about how to alter the poem and change some of the nonsense words. For example, in 'Hopaloo Kangaroo' change the word *jigaloo* to *wigaloo* and so on. Substitute alternative words and reread the poem.
● Explain that next week the children will be writing their own nonsense poems.

Shared word-level work

● Now show the children the 'Animal alphabet' from photocopiable page 171. Look at other examples of alphabets, such as a classroom frieze, and remind the children of the 'Alphabet chant' from Term 1 (see photocopiable page 29).
● Read the 'Animal alphabet' together and ask the children to think of any other animals to go with some of the letters.
● Distribute the individual animal cards to the children in the class, asking them to pair up if you have more than 26 pupils, or giving some children duplicates if you have less than 26 pupils.
● Say the alphabet together and ask the children to hold up their animal cards at the appropriate time.
● Finally ask the children to line up in the correct order of the alphabet, using a classroom frieze or enlarged copy of the complete 'Animal alphabet' to help them.

Focused group work

● Continue as Day 1 reading nonsense rhymes with small groups of children.

Independent work

● See the activities for the six Areas of Learning on page 157.

Plenary

● Ask the children who have been organising the class library to show you the poems they have chosen to include.
● Read one or two of them together and then ensure that their favourite rhymes are displayed prominently in the class library.
● Finish by reciting the 'Animal alphabet' together with other alphabet songs such as the 'Alphabet chant' on photocopiable page 29.
● Ask the children to think of favourite animals for next week when they will be writing their own nonsense poems.

Tiger tricks

Objectives

Early Learning Goal
● Writing p64-65.

Stepping Stone
● Begin to break the flow of speech into words.

NLS
T14: To use experience of stories, poems and simple recounts as a basis for independent writing, eg. re-telling, substitution, extension, and through shared composition with adults.
W2: Knowledge of grapheme/phoneme correspondences through identifying and writing initial and dominant phonemes in spoken words.

What you need
● The poem 'Don't Tickle Tigers' from photocopiable page 169, enlarged to at least A3 size or displayed using an interactive whiteboard (Permission granted)
● a flipchart and pens
● individual whiteboards for pairs of pupils and sufficient whiteboard pens.

Differentiation

More able
● Encourage the children to work independently, substituting words.

Less able
● Let the children orally suggest suitable words for you to scribe during group work.

Shared text-level work
● Remind the children of the poem, 'Don't Tickle Tigers'. Re-read it, with the children joining in.
● Now explain that the children are going to help you to write a different version of the poem.
● Leave the first line as it is and then ask the children for an alternative to the word *tangle* in the second line and trick in the *third*. Work through various possibilities such as *mangle* or *kick*.
● If you are using an interactive whiteboard, then amend the poem in pen on the whiteboard, if not, then write alternative lines on the flipchart. Ask the children for suggested spellings as you write.
● Continue in the same way, writing alternative words in the remaining lines.
● Reread the alternative poem with the children and talk about which version they prefer.

Shared word-level work
● Give out whiteboards and pens to pairs of children and ask them to draw two vertical lines to divide the frame into three, or use phoneme frames if available. (If the children are working at Step 5 or above, blending consonant clusters - see *Progression in Phonics* (DfES) - then divide the boards into four.)
● Read out a CVC word and ask one child from each pair to write the corresponding letters in the separate sections, with their partner helping and checking.
● Invite the children to hold up their boards and look carefully for correct versions, sensitively using any errors as teaching points.
● Repeat, with the other child in the pair writing the word.

Focused group work
● Work with a group of children to write a nonsense poem. This could be based on any nonsense poem, such as 'The Ning, Nang, Nong' by Spike Milligan, but ensure that the children are familiar with it.
● Model first using a writing frame (the chosen poem written out with key words missing and blank spaces for substituting rhyming words).
● Provide the children with writing frames and encourage them to write their own poems.

Independent work
● See the activities for the six Areas of Learning on page 158.

Plenary
● Encourage the children that have written their own nonsense poems to read them to the class.
● Discuss some of the nonsense words and then ask the children to suggest further rhyming words.
● Invite a volunteer to be the teacher and write some of the words on the flipchart.

Guess the animal

Objectives
● Linking sounds and letters p60-61.

Stepping stone
● Enjoy rhyming and rhythmic activities.

NLS
T14: To use experience of stories, poems and simple recounts as a basis for independent writing eg re-telling, substitution, extension, and through shared composition with adults.
W14: To write letters using the correct sequence of movements.

What you need
● A small selection of animal cards from photocopiable page 171, including *cat*.
● the following words on card, enlarged and split into three lines to make a poem: *A cat with claws can cause catastrophe*
● sticky notes
● a flipchart and pens
● individual whiteboards and pens for all pupils.

Differentiation
Less able
● Draw the children's attention to all the words that begin with the blend 'pl'.

More able
● In shared text-level work ask the children to devise a strategy for altering the words, such as changing one of the vowels.

Shared text-level work
● Show the children a small selection of animal cards from photocopiable page 171, for example: *cat, dog, frog* and *hen*.
● Underline the first letter of each word (*c, d, f, h*).
● Ask the children to say together the name of each animal as you point to it.
● Tell the children that you written 'a little poem' about one of these animals, but you have missed out the word that tells them which animal it is.
● Display your pre-prepared 'poem' with the relevant word covered up with a sticky note and read it to the children, pointing to each word in turn (missing out the name of the animal).
● Read again with the children the choice of animals from the cards and ask them to guess which is the right animal for the poem.
● Read the poem, inserting any of the children's suggestions to see if it is the correct answer.
● When the children have agreed on the right animal, remove the sticky note to reveal the word.
● Ask the children to read the poem with you as you say it together.

Shared word-level work
● Explain that you are going to practise handwriting.
● Remind the children of your usual prompts for letter formation, such as *top to bottom, lift and across* for the letter *t* and practise letters making CVC combinations (such as *cat*).
● Ask the children to practise each letter in different ways, such as in the air or on each other's backs.
● Have fun asking the children to 'rub out' their attempts before having another go.
● After practising in this way, the children should write the letters on individual whiteboards.
● Monitor carefully with adult support, emphasising the correct way to hold a pencil.

Focused group work
● Continue as the previous day (page 164) working with a group of children to write their own nonsense poems using a writing frame.

Independent work
● See the activities for the six Areas of Learning on page 158.

Plenary
● With the children gathered together, talk about the poems that some children have been writing.
● Share the poems with the class, encouraging those children who have written them to read them to the class.
● Discuss some of the nonsense words as per the previous day (page 164) and ask volunteers to write some of the words on the flipchart.

Kangaroo loo!

Objectives

Early Learning Goal
● Linking sounds and letters p60-61.

Stepping Stone
● Continue a rhyming string.

NLS
T14: To use experience of stories, poems and simple recounts as a basis for independent writing, eg re-telling, substitution, extension, and through shared composition with adults.
W4: To link sound and spelling patterns by discriminating 'onsets' from 'rimes' in speech and spelling.

What you need
● The poem, 'Hopaloo Kangaroo' from photocopiable page 170, enlarged to at least A3 size
● a flipchart and pens
● magnetic letters and board.

Shared text-level work
● Remind the children of the 'Hopaloo Kangaroo' poem and re-read it together.
● Explain that today you are going to write an alternative version of the whole poem (not just changing a few words as on Day 7, page 165).
● Start by underlining all the nonsense words in the original poem and talk about these. Say you are going to think of some different words.
● Say that you are going to call it 'Kangaroo Loo' and devise four lines together that can be played with to make a nonsense verse (see below).
● Have lots of fun, ensuring that you brainstorm a list of nonsense rhyming words before putting them into a short poem.
● Read the class poem together with lots of expression.

> Kangaroo Loo!
> Kangaroo Loo goes .... (bittity boo)
> He jumps so high and shouts............... (hoppity hoo!)
> .... (Bittity, boppity, hoppity, hoo!)
> That's the way, hops Kangaroo Loo!

Shared word-level work
● Using magnetic letters and a magnetic board (if not available then write words on the flipchart), demonstrate that many words share the same ending. Provide some examples such as *jump, bump* and *lump.*
● Talk about the terms *onset* and *rime* and write the onset in one colour and the rime in another.
● Provide a rime and choose a child to add an onset. Now ask another child to change the onset to make another word (by using magnetic letters or by writing the word on to the flipchart). Ensure that the children realise that the rime stays the same.
● Make a list of words in this way. Explain that the children may use the words on the list to help make up their own nonsense rhymes.

Focused group work
● Continue as Day 6 (page 164), working with a group of children to write their own nonsense poems using the writing frames.
● Try and encourage the children to be creative and explore different possible rhymes as in the shared text-level work.

Independent work
See the activities for the six Areas of Learning on page 164.

Plenary
● With the children gathered together, talk about the poems the children have been writing today.
● Share the poems with the class, encouraging those children who have written them to read them to the class.
● Finish by re-reading the class poem 'Kangaroo Loo'.

Differentiation

Less able
● Encourage the children to orally suggest suitable words for you to scribe during focused group work.

More able
● Challenge the children to work independently during group work, substituting words.

Frolicking frogs

Objectives

Early Learning Goals
● Linking sounds and letters p60-61.

Stepping stone
● Recognise rhythm in spoken words.

NLS
T14: To use experience of stories, poems and simple recounts as a basis for independent writing, eg re-telling, substitution, extension, and through shared composition with adults.
S2: To use awareness of the grammar of a sentence to predict words during shared reading and when re-reading familiar stories.

What you need

● The poem 'Frog frolics' from photocopiable page 170, enlarged to at least A3 size
● a flipchart and pens.

Differentiation

Less able
● Encourage the children to talk about their favourite animals.

More able
● Talk about the difference between nonsense words that are made-up words and real words that have been put in the wrong place (that is, they are ungrammatical).

Shared text-level work

● Start by talking about frogs and what they look like.
● Read the poem 'Frog frolics' to the children and talk about some of the words, particularly the verbs: *flop, hop,* and *stop.*
● Ensure that the children know what the words mean. If there is space and the children can move around safely, ask them to demonstrate these actions.
● Compare the poem with other poems read during the past two weeks. Does this poem use nonsense words? Talk about the use of words that begin with the same sound.
● With the children, explore some alternative words for the verbs. For example, you could replace *flop* with *flip* and *hop* with *skip.*
● Write a list of alternative verbs and if you are using an interactive whiteboard, write these above the corresponding verbs.
● Reread the poem, using alternative verbs and have fun with absurd versions.

Shared sentence-level work

● Look again at the poem 'Frog frolics' and the highlighted verbs that you have substituted during shared text-level work (above).
● Discuss how we need to check that things make sense when we read them, and that this can help us to read words that we don't know.
● Provide a couple of examples from the poem, substituting a word that does not make sense (such as a noun or adjective instead of a verb – for example, *green* for *flop*).
● Have fun reading some nonsense versions and ask the children to talk to a partner to think of a more sensible word that would fit.

Focused group work

● Continue as Day 6 (page 164), working with a group of children to write their own nonsense poems using the writing frames.
● Read through some of the previous groups' work and discuss it with the children.

Independent work

● See the activities for the six Areas of Learning on page 158.

Plenary

● With the children gathered together, talk about the poems the children have been writing today.
● Share the poems with the class, encouraging those children who have written them to read them to the class.
● Look at the range of poems read and discuss what they have in common (all about animals).
● Finish by saying, or singing an animal rhyme such as 'The Animal Fair' from *Okki-Tokki-Unga* (A&C Black).
● Explain that tomorrow the class will be performing all the animal poems with plenty of noise and actions!

Performing our poems

Shared text-level work

● Begin by quickly re-reading the poems used over the last two weeks.
● Tell the children that you are going to practise performing the poems and that you would like everyone to join in. Help the children to practise varying the level of expression and the volume of their voices appropriately. Say that you are going to invite someone to watch a performance of the poems later in the day.
● Choose different children to take the parts of the animals and, as you read each poem, encourage them to carry out all the actions. Remind the children of the independent work they did on animal movements (see PD, page 158) and ask them to show you any moves they developed during this work.
● If time and space allow, re-read one or two favourite poems, inviting the whole class to move appropriately and join in with the chorus.

Shared word-level work

● Explain that you are going to play the 'Full circle' game (from *Progression in Phonics*, page 29).
● Give out the A4 letters to individual children.
● Tell them the first word and ask the children who have the letters that make up that word to come out to the front of the class.
● Write the word on the flipchart.
● Now change the word (for example from *bat* to *cat*) and ask the children to say which child needs to sit down (the child holding the letter 'b') and which child should now come to the front (the child holding the letter 'c').
● Continue in this way, with as many words as possible, until you come back to the original word again.

Focused group work

● Continue as Day 6 (page 164) working with a group of children to write their own nonsense poems using the writing frames provided.
● Support their work by playing games such as substituting ungrammatical words for the children to spot.
● Demonstrate changing the onset of a word to create another new nonsense word.

Independent work

● See the activities for the six Areas of Learning on page 158.

Plenary

● Explain that you are going to perform the rehearsed poems with movements for an audience or guest. Ask a child to escort the guest(s) to the classroom and when all the children are ready, perform!
● If possible, ask an adult to take some digital photos of the children to display later in the classroom.
● Encourage the guest to ask the children what they like about their favourite poems.

Funny poems 1

Don't Tickle Tigers

Don't try and tickle a tiger,
Don't go and tangle his tail,
Don't try and trick him
Or tumble and trip him:
Your game will most certainly fail.

Don't even look at a lion,
Don't go and lie in his den,
Don't lollop after him,
Lick him or laugh at him:
That way your life's at an end.

Tigers and lions are dangerous,
So keep right away from their lairs,
And while we are talking Precautions:
The same goes for hippos and bears!

Celia Warren

TERM 3

Funny poems 2

Hopaloo Kangaroo

(extract)

If you can jigaloo
jigaloo
I can do
the jigaloo too
for I'm the jiggiest
jigaloo kangaroo

If you can boogaloo
boogaloo
I can do
the boogaloo too
for I'm the boogiest
boogaloo kangaroo

But bet you can't hopaloo
hopaloo
like I can do
for I'm the hoppiest
hopaloo kangaroo

Gonna show you steps
you never knew.
And guess what, guys?
My baby in my pouch
will be dancing too.
John Agard

Frog Frolics

Slipperty slopperty,
flipperty flop.
A cute little froggy
is learning to hop.

She comes to the water,
so now will she stop?
Hipperty hopperty,
in with a PLOP!
Tony Mitton

◖SCHOLASTIC

Animal alphabet

ape	**hen**	**ostrich**	**vulture**
bat	**insect**	**penguin**	**whale**
cat	**jaguar**	**queen bee**	**fox**
dog	**kitten**	**rat**	**yak**
elephant	**lion**	**snake**	**zebra**
frog	**mouse**	**tiger**	
giraffe	**nanny goat**	**unicorn**	

UNIT 4

Rapunzel

This unit is based on the fairy story 'Rapunzel' and an alternative version of the tale. It comprises five days' literacy activities and supports the National Literacy Strategy (Later Foundation Stage, Medium-term plan) focus on *Narrative: language features*. It will promote understanding of the features of fairy stories and gives a focus for writing an alternative version. Linked activities are provided for all the six Areas of Learning with a strong emphasis on developing speaking and listening skills through oral retelling, examining consequences of actions in Personal, social and emotional development and developing literacy skills in the form of producing a class wall story. The activities build towards Year 1 Term 1, Objective 8 of the *Speaking, Listening, Learning* guidance: to act out own and well-known stories, using different voices for characters.

Day	Shared text-level work	Shared word-/ sentence-level work	Focused group work	Independent work	Plenary
1 Rapunzel	Shared reading of the traditional story, 'Rapunzel'.	Word wall – vocabulary extension.	Guided retelling of a fairy story.	**PSED:** Right or wrong? Consequences of actions.	Reading a well-known fairy story.
2 Rosanna	Shared reading of the alternative fairy story, 'Rosanna', looking at language features.	High frequency word 'Bingo'.	Guided retelling of a fairy story.	**CLL:** Writing captions.	Singing, 'There Was a Princess Long Ago'.
3 Create a fairy story	Shared writing of a fairy story – planning (using cards, objects and a spinner).	Reading for meaning – mixed up sentences.	Guided retelling of a fairy story.	**MD:** Comparing different lengths of hair.	Acting out and sequencing a fairy story.
4 Writing a fairy story	Shared writing of a fairy story – beginning.	Using sound buttons to represent phonemes.	Guided retelling of a fairy story.	**KUW:** Reviewing types of buildings.	Story circle game.
5 Our fairy story	Shared writing of a fairy story – middle.	Checking full stops and capital letters.	Guided writing of the fairy story – ending.	**PD:** Dressing up as characters in the story. **CD:** Creating towers using blocks and boxes.	Reading and acting out the class fairy story.

Key assessment opportunities

When working with children during guided reading and writing look closely for:
- ability to use correct story language
- ability to retell a story in the correct sequence
- use of a range of descriptive words
- ability to match phonemes to graphemes
- recognition of high frequency words
- ability to use capital letters and full stops appropriately.

Record appropriately and ensure that this informs future planning.

CROSS-CURRICULAR ☐ UNIT 4 Rapunzel

Personal, social and emotional development

Right or wrong?
Early Learning Goal
Consider the consequences of their words and actions for themselves and others.
What you need
The story 'Rapunzel' on photocopiable pages 179-180; pens; pencils and crayons.
What to do
● Ask an adult to work with a group to discuss some of the actions of the characters in the story.
● Invite the children to draw one of the following: the shoemaker climbing over the wall to take the witch's apples; the witch taking Rapunzel to the tower; or the witch cutting off Rapunzel's hair.
● Ensure that the children are given the chance to discuss the consequences of these actions.
● Make links to this in plenary sessions during the week.

Mathematical development

Short and long!
Early Learning Goal
Use language such as 'greater', 'smaller', 'heavier' or 'lighter' to compare quantities.
What you need
Assorted lengths of 'plaits' (approximately ten), made from plaited wool; a tower.
What to do
● Ask the children to compare the different plaits, and to find the shortest and the longest.
● Provide a tower (such as the one the children are making in Creative development (below) or one made from bricks) and ask the children to see if one of the plaits would be long enough to reach the bottom.

Physical development

Dressing up!
Early Learning Goal
Use a range of small and large equipment.
What you need
Dressing-up clothes and appropriate props to go with the story (such as a princess, prince, wicked witch and so on).
What to do
● Ask the children to dress up as different characters.
● Encourage independence in dressing and undressing.
● Challenge the children to take on different roles and be creative.

Creative development

Make a tower!
Early Learning Goal
Use their imagination in art and design, music, dance, imaginative and role-play and stories.
What you need
Large building blocks; cardboard boxes; corrugated cardboard.
What to do
● Talk about the tower that Rapunzel was kept in. Now challenge the children to use their imagination to create a tower just like it.
● Provide assorted boxes and blocks and encourage the children to experiment with shapes and arrangements, working together as a team.

Communication, language and literacy

Writing captions
Early Learning Goal
Use their phonic knowledge to write simple regular words and make phonetically plausible attempts at more complex words.
What you need
Pictures of scenes from the story (such as a princess in a tower) - these can be drawn or created from Clip Art.
What to do
● Give each child a picture from the story and ask them to write an accompanying caption underneath.
● Encourage them to start with a capital letter and end with a full stop, making phonetically plausible attempts at spelling.

Knowledge and understanding of the world

Buildings
Early Learning Goal
Observe, find out about and identify features in the place they live and the natural world.
What you need
A range of books or a CD-Rom containing pictures of different types of buildings (such as castles, houses, schools and so on).
What to do
● Ask the children to find out what they can about different buildings.
● Set them specific tasks, such as finding tall buildings, small buildings and so on.

Rapunzel

Objectives

Early Learning Goal
● Reading p62-63.

Stepping Stone
● Listen to an join in with stories and poems, one-to-one and also in small groups.

NLS
T5: To understand how story book language works and to use some formal elements when re-telling stories.
W10: New words from their reading and shared experiences.

What you need

● Photocopiable pages 179-80 enlarged to at least A3 size, or scanned on to a computer and displayed on an interactive whiteboard
● a range of other fairy story books
● props for a fairy story (such as a long plait, a picture of castle or tower. and so on)
● a simple fairy story for guided reading, preferably as a Big Book
● several words from the story printed in minimum 48 point font or handwritten on card (such as *shoemaker, lettuce, witch, tower, prince, climb, window*)
● a flipchart and pens.

Differentiation

Less able
● Support the children in group work by prompting with questions and reminders of key events.
● Model speaking in full sentences by elaborating on the children's responses.

More able
● Ask the children to retell the next part of the story independently.

Shared text-level work

● Talk about fairy stories with the children. Show them some book covers and talk about some of the titles, asking the children if they have heard of them before.
● Explain that you are going to read a fairy story to them called 'Rapunzel' and ask if anyone knows the story. Discuss any recollections.
● Read the story and when you have finished, talk about what is the same in all fairy stories (happy endings, magical events and so on).
● Re-read the version of 'Rapunzel' on photocopiable pages 179-180, this time, pointing to the phrases *Once upon a time* and *they lived happily ever after.* Explain to the children that these phrases are very often found in fairy stories.
● Discuss other common features of fairy stories such as how there is often a wicked witch and a prince and princess.
● Finally re-read the story with the text displayed, encouraging the children to join in, particularly with the repeated refrain.

Shared word-level work

● Show the children the prepared key words from the story. Read them, one by one, with the children and display them in a pocket chart or on the wall.
● Ensure that the children understand the meaning of each word by reading the word individually and then saying the word in a sentence.
● Say a word and invite a child to point to the matching word on the wall as you say it.
● Continue in this way to help word recognition and to widen vocabulary. Try and revisit these words together during the week.

Focused group work

● Work with a group of children to retell a fairy story. Use a simple text of a familiar tale with accompanying pictures to help the retelling.
● Encourage all the children to participate and first brainstorm together everything they know about the tale.
● Now sequence the story together and verbally rehearse what happens at the beginning, middle and end of the story – make small sketches or write key words on the flipchart to aid memory.
● Encourage the children to use language such as *Once upon a time* as you retell the story together.

Independent work

● See the activities for the six Areas of Learning on page 173.

Plenary

● Read a different fairy story to the children using a variety of suitable props. Remind them of the words that a fairy story might begin and end with.
● If time allows, retell the story together, with different children acting out the parts.

UNIT 4 DAY 2 🔲 Rapunzel

Rosanna

Objectives

Early Learning Goal
● Reading p62-63.

Stepping Stone
● Begin to be aware of the way stories are structured.

NLS
T5: To understand how story book language works and to use some formal elements when re-telling stories.
W6: To read on sight the 45 high frequency words to be taught by end of YR.

What you need
● Photocopiable page 181 enlarged to at least A3 size
● 'Bingo' game cards (see photocopiable page 19), adapted as necessary, to cover the words currently being taught
● the corresponding high frequency words on card
● a simple fairy story for guided reading, preferably as a Big Book
● the action song/rhyme 'There Was a Princess Long Ago' found in *This Little Puffin* compiled by Elizabeth Matterson (Puffin).

Differentiation

Less able
● Provide adult support for the children during the 'Bingo' game. Make some extra 'Bingo' cards with words to meet their specific needs.

More able
● Let the children work in small groups to play the 'Bingo' game again, this time taking turns to be the caller.

Shared text-level work
● Remind the children of the story of 'Rapunzel' and tell them that you are going to read a different version to them.
● Ask the children what sort of beginning and ending they would expect to hear if it is a fairy story.
● Read the story of 'Rosanna' to the children (photocopiable page 181). Ask them to talk about what is different and what is the same about this story compared to the story of 'Rapunzel'. Which story do they prefer and why?
● Focus on the happy ending for everyone in this version and talk about what happened to the wicked witch.
● Re-read the story together, using a pointer to point to the text as you read. Encourage the children to join in, especially with the repeated refrain.
● Explain that tomorrow they will be writing a whole-class fairy story.

Shared word-level work
● Tell the children that you are going to play 'Bingo', giving one of the three 'Bingo' cards to each pair of children
● Read out the words from your word cards and ask the children to listen out carefully for the words that are on their Bingo cards.
● Explain that if they have a word that matches the one you have called out they must cross it out on their card.
● When all their words have been crossed out, they need to shout out 'Bingo'!
● Play the game once or twice as time allows.

Focused group work
● Work with a different group of children and continue as Day 1 (page 174) to retell a fairy story. Brainstorm together everything the children can remember about a familiar tale and then sequence the story together.
● Encourage the children to use the correct language features, such as, *Once upon a time*, as you retell the story together.

Independent work
● See the activities for the six Areas of Learning on page 173.

Plenary
● Now tell the children that you are going to learn a song about a princess in a tower and read through each verse of 'There Was a Princess Long Ago'. Ask the children to repeat each verse after you.
● Clear some space in the classroom and sing the song through with the children carrying out some suitable actions.
● Have some fun with the song and then ask the children to come and sit down with you. Encourage them to talk about what they think are the similarities between the song and the two stories they have heard over the last two days.

Create a fairy story

Objectives

Early Learning Goal
● Reading p62-63.

Stepping Stone
● Begin to be aware of the way stories are structured.

NLS
T14: To use experience of stories, poems and simple recounts as a basis for independent writing.
S1: To expect written text to make sense and to check for sense if it does not.

What you need
● A story spinner made from card
● the cards on photocopiable page 182 enlarged, copied on to card and cut out
● two or three sentences from the story of 'Rapunzel', written or printed in a large size onto card; cut the sentences up into individual words and put Blu-Tack on to the back of each word, stick them on to the flipchart in a random (but not the correct) order
● dressing-up clothes and props from independent work (see page 174)
● a simple fairy story for guided reading, preferably as a Big Book
● a flipchart.

Differentiation

Less able
● Model speaking in full sentences during group work, by taking the children's responses and elaborating upon them.

More able
● Ask the children to retell the next part of the story independently.

Shared text-level work
● Explain that you are going to make up a fairy story together.
● Show the children the story spinner and the cards and ensure that the children know what each picture represents. (To make the spinner, cut out a circle of card and pierce it in the middle. Divide it into four sections with the words: *events, characters, objects, settings*. Add a pencil to the centre and it is ready to spin!)
● Ask the children to form a circle. Put the story spinner in the middle with the cards in three piles.
● Ask individual children to take turns to spin the spinner and then pick an appropriate card. Read the cards together and discuss them.
● When you have a good selection of cards, use some of them to create a story together.
● Encourage the children to help you to make up a complete story with a happy ending.
● Rehearse the story together and ensure that the class can recall the main details. Make some notes on the flipchart under the headings *beginning, middle* and *ending*.

Shared sentence-level work
● Tell the children that you have some sentences from the story of 'Rapunzel' that have become muddled up. Show the children the sentences you have created earlier.
● Read the sentences and ask the children what is wrong with them.
● Explain that it is important to make sure that we check for meaning when we read.
● Ask volunteers to change the word order and, each time, read the sentence with the class to check if it is correct.
● Do this with as many sentences as you have prepared or as time allows.

Focused group work
● Continue as Day 1 (page 174) to retell a fairy story. Brainstorm together everything the children can remember about a familiar tale and then sequence the story together.
● Encourage the children to use phrases, such as *A long time ago*, as you retell the story together.

Independent work
● See the activities for the six Areas of Learning on page 173.

Plenary
● Talk about the independent work (see PD, page 173) that the children have been doing – dressing up as fairy-story characters.
● Ask for volunteers to take the parts of chosen characters in a fairy story and dress up accordingly.
● Use the story spinner and cards to have fun acting out a fairy story together!

Writing a fairy story

Objectives

Early Learning Goal
● Reading p62-63.

Stepping Stone
● Begin to be aware of the way stories are structured.

NLS
T14: To use experience of stories, poems and simple recounts as a basis for independent writing.
W2: Knowledge of grapheme/phoneme correspondences through reading letters that represent the sounds.

What you need
● The story plan from Day 3
● a flipchart and pens or interactive whiteboard
● story game cards from photocopiable page 182
● a simple fairy story for guided reading, preferably as a Big Book.

Differentiation

Less able
● Use additional adult support to encourage the children to participate in the story game during the plenary session.

More able
● In shared word-level work, invite the children to write a word of their choice on the flipchart with the corresponding number of sound buttons underneath.

Shared text-level work
● Go through the story plan with the children, ensuring that everyone is quite familiar with the main events.
● Now explain that you are going to write some of the story on large paper (or use the interactive whiteboard) in order to create a 'wall story' for the children to read.
● Ask the children how to begin and then write the first few sentences of the class fairy story created the previous day. As you write, take the children's suggestions of suitable spellings. Use a mixture of teacher demonstration and teacher scribing.
● Read through each sentence as you write and explain to the children how it is important to check for mistakes or to see if something has been missed out.
● Display the beginning of the story on the classroom wall and illustrate it to create a *Once upon a time...* display.

Shared word-level work
● Write a word on the flipchart.
● Draw sound buttons underneath the word (large dots) to represent each phoneme.
● Ask the children to come out and say each phoneme as they press the 'buttons', then challenge them to say the whole word.
● Repeat, asking all the class to say the phonemes and then the whole word.
● Continue with other words as time allows.

Focused group work
● Continue as Day 1 (page 175) to retell a fairy story. Brainstorm together everything the children can remember about a familiar tale and then sequence the story together.
● Encourage the children to use story language and phrases as you work together.

Independent work
See the activities for the six Areas of Learning on page 173.

Plenary
● Ask the children to sit in a circle and explain that you are going to play a story circle game.
● Put the story game cards (from photocopiable page 182) in the centre of the circle, this time mixed in one pile.
● Model the activity, by taking a card and starting the story: *Once upon a time there was a beautiful princess.*
● Explain that the next person has to take a card and carry on the story with help from the rest of the class.
● Support the children as much as necessary as they say their sentences and praise all attempts at telling the fairy story.
● Continue in this way to have fun creating a unique tale!

UNIT 4 DAY 5 ▢ Rapunzel

Our fairy story

Objectives

Early Learning Goal
● Reading p62-63.

Stepping Stone
● Suggest how the story might end.

NLS
T14: To use experience of stories, poems and simple recounts as a basis for independent writing...
S4: To use a capital letter for the start of own name.

What you need
● The story plan from Day 3 (see page 176) and the first part of the story from Day 4 (page 177).
● two sentences from a fairy story (these could be from 'Rapunzel') printed on the computer with full stops and capital letters missing – either displayed on an interactive whiteboard or printed in a large font
● large pen.

Differentiation

Less able
● Provide plenty of support to the children as they correct sentences in the shared sentence-level work.

More able
● Encourage the children to speak some of the lines as they act out the class fairy story.

Shared text-level work
● Remind the children of the story written the previous day and read this together.
● Now explain that you are going to write the next part of the story.
● Ask the children to talk to their partners to decide on the next sentence.
● Take a range of suggestions and then write one on the board. Read this through and ensure that everyone is happy with it.
● Continue to write several sentences in this way and explain that you will work with a group of children later to write the ending.

Shared sentence-level work
● Show the children the sentences from Rapunzel and explain that there is something wrong with them.
● Ask the children to talk to their partners to see if they can find out what is wrong.
● Listen to the children's suggestions and then invite pairs of children to use a large pen and correct the sentences on the flipchart or on the interactive whiteboard.
● Read the sentences through together and talk about why we need full stops at the end of sentences and capital letters at the beginning.
● Remind the children to check when they are writing to remember to put them in.

Focused group work
● Invite a group of children to help you to finish the class story.
● Read the story so far through together.
● Check the children's ideas against the original story plan and ask them to think of the next sentence. Write sentences as the children suggest them and re-read constantly to check they make sense.
● Point out to the children the use of capital letters at the beginning of sentences and full stops at the end.
● Near the end of the story, ask the children if there is anything else they wish to add and, if so, which section of the story it should go.
● Ensure that you finish with the phrase, *They lived happily ever after.*

Independent work
● See the activities for the six Areas of Learning on page 173.

Plenary
● Gather the children together and explain that you have now finished the class fairy story. Show the children the finished version.
● Read it to the children with plenty of expression and then re-read the story together, encouraging everyone to join in.
● Now or later, reread the story again, with some children acting out the different parts using dressing-up clothes and props.
● Display the finished result for the children in your story corner and encourage the children to read it in their own time.

Rapunzel

Once upon a time there lived a poor shoemaker and his wife who had no children. Next to their cottage lived a witch who had a beautiful garden. The shoemaker's wife asked her husband to go and pick some apples from the witch's garden as they looked so delicious.

One night the shoemaker climbed into the garden and was just about to pick some apples when the witch caught him. He was terrified.

'Do not fear,' said the witch. 'You can have as many apples as you like, but when your first child is born you must give the child to me.'

The man was so surprised, he said, 'Yes, of course.' Then he ran home as fast as he could.

Soon afterwards the shoemaker and his wife had a beautiful baby daughter. To their horror, the witch came and took the baby away, saying that the shoemaker had agreed to it. The witch called the baby 'Rapunzel' and took her to live in a lonely tower in the middle of a wood. The tower had no doors and the only way in was through a window high up in the

wall. When the witch came to see her, she would call out:

Rapunzel, Rapunzel,
Let down your hair
That I may climb
As if by a stair.

The girl would let down her long golden hair and the witch would climb up, holding on to the hair, to the window to see her.

One day, a handsome prince came riding through the wood and heard a voice singing. He looked around and saw, to his amazement, a tall tower with a beautiful girl at a window. He kept a close watch and, once more to his amazement, he saw a wicked witch call out and then climb up the girl's hair. He waited until the witch had gone and later called out himself:

Rapunzel, Rapunzel,
Let down your hair
That I may climb
As if by a stair.

Down came the golden hair. As quick as he could, he climbed up to the window and into the tower. The girl was frightened, but she soon

Rapunzel

(continued)

realised that he was kind.

The prince came to see her every day and they fell in love. One day, the prince said, 'Will you come away with me and be my wife?'

Rapunzel replied that she would, as he seemed so kind and gentle, but said sadly, 'How can I leave this tower?'

Then Rapunzel had an idea. She decided to make a ladder from silken thread. The prince agreed to bring her some thread each day and she worked hard so that eventually the ladder grew longer and longer.

One day, Rapunzel was so excited that the witch guessed that something was going on. 'Oh no, I will not let you escape,' she cried.

The witch cut off all Rapunzel's hair, and then took her away to a dark, lonely place in the woods. The witch then waited for the prince to arrive and fastened Rapunzel's long plaits to a hook in the window. The prince climbed straight up and was horrified to find a witch and not the lovely Rapunzel.

'Aha!' cried the witch, 'Your dear sweetheart has been carried away by wild animals and you will never see her again because those wild animals will scratch your eyes out!'

The prince was so upset he jumped out of the window and fell in a bush of spiky thorns. When he pulled himself out, he found that he was blind. He wandered for weeks eating only berries and crying for his lovely Rapunzel. But one morning, he heard the sound of beautiful singing and he realised it was her. He ran towards the sound and, when Rapunzel saw him, she rushed to him crying with happiness. As she hugged him, some of her tears fell on the prince and to his amazement he found he could see again!

The prince called his horse and then took Rapunzel off to live in his kingdom. There they lived happily ever after

THE END

Rosanna

Once upon a time there was a beautiful girl called Rosanna. She had long golden hair and could sing like a bird. When Rosanna was a child, a wicked witch had taken her from her parents. The witch kept Rosanna in a big, tall tower with one small window at the top and no entrance below. Each morning Rosanna opened the window to sing and each morning the witch came with some bread and milk. Each time the witch called out:

Rosanna, Rosanna! Let down your hair!

Then Rosanna uncoiled her long hair and the witch climbed up it.

The years went by, and one day a prince was riding through the forest and heard Rosanna singing. He was enchanted by her voice and kept going back to the tower to listen. One morning, while the prince was hiding in the bushes near by, the witch arrived and he heard her call out to Rosanna:

Rosanna, Rosanna! Let down your hair!

He watched in amazement as the witch climbed up Rosanna's long hair. The very next day he decided to try the chant himself:

Rosanna, Rosanna! Let down your hair!

He copied the witch's gruff voice and so Rosanna let down her hair. In a few seconds the prince had climbed up. At first Rosanna was afraid. She had never seen a prince before. But he was gentle, kind and very handsome. After that he visited her every evening and soon Rosanna loved him as much as he loved her. But one morning Rosanna said to the witch, 'Why are you so rough when you climb up my hair? The prince never hurts me.'

Immediately, the witch knew that Rosanna had been tricking her. When she knew this, she took Rosanna back to her parents.

The prince found Rosanna and took her and her family to safety. He took the wicked witch to his palace. The prince asked a magician to make a potion to heal the witch from her nastiness. When the witch was cured the magician fell in love with her and they were married at once. The prince brought Rosanna and her parents safely to the palace where the prince and Rosanna were also married. They had two children of their own and everyone lived happily ever after!

THE END

Story game cards

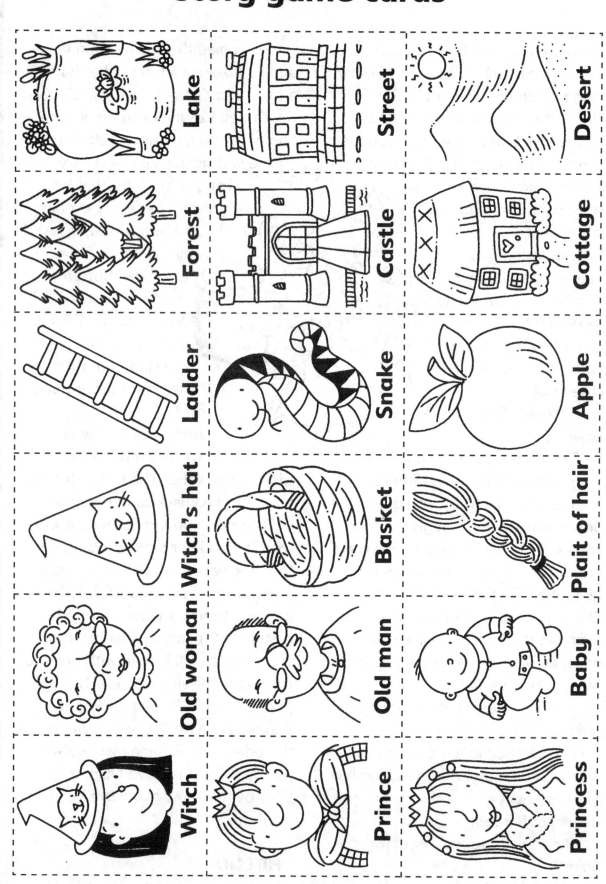

Lake

Street

Desert

Forest

Castle

Cottage

Ladder

Snake

Apple

Witch's hat

Basket

Plait of hair

Old woman

Old man

Baby

Witch

Prince

Princess

UNIT 5

Where do animals live?

This unit is based on a non-fiction text and comprises five days' literacy activities. It supports the National Literacy Strategy (Later Foundation Stage, Medium-term plan) focus on *Information texts (questions and answers)*. It will help the children's ability to form suitable questions and find answers in information texts. Linked activities are provided for all the six Areas of Learning with a strong emphasis on developing speaking and listening skills through devising questions and answers, understanding diversity in Personal, social and emotional development and developing literacy skills through reading non-fiction texts and shared writing of leaflets. The activities build towards Year 1 Term 1, Objective 3 of the *Speaking, Listening, Learning* guidance: to ask and answer questions, make relevant contributions, offer suggestions and take turns.

Day	Shared text-level work	Shared word-/ sentence-level work	Focused group work	Independent work	Plenary
1 Where do animals live?	Shared reading of information text.	Using context to read words.	Guided reading of information texts using KWL grids.	**PSED:** Similarities and differences.	Fiction or non-fiction?
2 Asking questions	Writing questions for information texts.	Word wall.	Guided reading of information texts using KWL grids.	**CLL:** Matching animals – questions and answers.	Match the answer to the question.
3 Finding answers	Finding answers from information texts.	Spelling practice.	Guided reading of information texts using KWL grids.	**MD:** Estimating and counting.	Circle game – 'Just like me!'
4 Write a leaflet	Writing information leaflets.	Alternative sounds and spellings.	Guided reading of information texts using KWL grids.	**KUW:** Investigating how objects and materials feel.	Guess the animal.
5 Information leaflets	Completing information leaflets.	Nonsense sentences.	Guided reading of information texts using KWL grids.	**PD:** Animal hides. **CD:** Musical animals.	Who lives here?

Key assessment opportunities
When working with children look closely for:
● ability to discriminate between fiction and non-fiction texts
● ability to devise suitable questions
● ability to ask and answer questions coherently and in full sentences
● ability to read for meaning.

Personal, social and emotional development

We are all different!
Early Learning Goal
Understand that people have different needs, views, cultures and beliefs, that need to be treated with respect.
What you need
A computer; a range of downloaded pictures of homes and people from different countries around the world.
What to do
● Ask the children to examine the pictures and to find different ways of grouping them. For example, those living in wooden homes, those living in tents and so on.
● Celebrate the differences in shared class work.

Physical development

Animal hides
Early Learning Goal
Show awareness of space, of themselves and of others.
What you need
A digital camera; a range of objects to construct hides, such as blankets, plastic frames, large blocks and cardboard boxes.
What to do
● Ask the children to use the range of materials provided to make an animal hide.
● Encourage the children to cooperate with each other as they work.
● Ask an adult to take pictures with a digital camera.

Communication, language and literacy

Questions and answers
Early Learning Goal
Speak clearly and audibly, with confidence and control and show awareness of the listener.
What you need
Questions and answers related to different animals, such as: *Which animal lives in a kennel and likes to go for walks? (A dog.)* Put the questions and answers on separate cards for the children to match. Place the cards in separate piles.
What to do
● Ask an adult to support the children as they work with a partner to take turns to turn over a card. Can they match the correct question and answer? If they succeed in matching, they may keep the cards.
● The child with the most pairs wins.

Mathematical development

Guess how many!
Early Learning Goal
Use developing mathematical ideas and methods to solve practical problems.
What you need
Pictures of frogspawn or termites in a mound; buttons or other small objects; individual whiteboards and pens.
What to do
● Ask the children to look at the pictures of frogspawn or termites and estimate the number.
● Now let the children estimate the number of buttons (or similar) in a pile.
● Ask the children to check by counting and encourage them to work together to ensure that they only count each object once.

Creative development

Make the sound
Early Learning Goal
Recognise and explore how sounds can be changed.
What you need
A range of musical instruments; a recording of assorted sounds (animal sounds if possible).
What to do
● Ask the children to listen to sounds on tape and then reproduce them with the musical instruments.
● Encourage careful listening to reproduce the sounds as closely as possible.

Knowledge and understanding of the world

Feel it
Early Learning Goal
Investigate objects and materials by using all of their senses as appropriate.
What you need
A feely bag; a range of differently textured objects, such as furry material.
What to do
● Ask the children to take turns to guess the objects in the bag.
● Encourage them to feel and listen carefully to any sounds that the objects make as they touch them.
● Ask the children to talk about which material would keep them warm in winter and link this to their work on animals.

Where do animals live?

Objectives

Early Learning Goal
● Reading p62-63.

Stepping Stone
● Know information can be relayed in the form of print.

NLS
T6: To re-read frequently a variety of familiar texts.
S2: To use awareness of the grammar of a sentence to predict words during shared reading and when re-reading familiar stories.

What you need

● Photocopiable pages 190 and 191 enlarged to at least A3 size or scanned on to a computer and displayed on an interactive whiteboard
● pictures of animals from books, posters or copyright-free images downloaded from the internet
● a range of prepared questions relating to the texts, printed in large font or written on to card, such as: *Why do some animals like to live in ponds?*
● multiple copies of a non-fiction book suitable for guided reading
● a box of mixed fiction and non-fiction books.
● sticky notes
● a flipchart.

Differentiation

● When conducting guided reading, try to group the children according to any particular strategies they need to reinforce and provide a focus for each session accordingly.

Shared text-level work

● Show the children the pictures of animals and talk about where the animals live.
● Now show the children photocopiable pages 190 and 191. Look at the pictures together before reading each extract.
● Read the extracts to the children and say you have some questions you want them to answer. Read the prepared questions, one by one, with the children.
● Now re-read the relevant extract and ask the children to talk to a partner to see if they can find the answer.

Shared sentence-level work

● Look again at the extracts with the children, this time covering some of the key words with sticky notes.
● Talk to the children about which words might fit. Have fun by suggesting some nonsensical words or substituting verbs for nouns.
● Take a range of suggestions from the children and discuss that it is important to read for sense.
● Give extra clues by peeling back part of the note and using the initial letter(s) to help you.

Focused group work

● Give out multiple copies of an information book and work with a small group of children to predict what they will find out from it.
● Look carefully together at the cover, including title, picture and blurb and ask the children to talk about what they would like to find out from the book.
● Now write a KWL grid on the flipchart with three columns saying: *What do we **know**? What do we **want** to find out? What did we **learn**?*
● Fill in what the children know already about the book and what they would like to find out.
● Rehearse with the children any strategies they can use to read words they don't know, such as sounding out and reading on and guessing.
● Ask the children to read the text independently and listen to each child as they do this, supporting them where necessary.
● Now go back to the chart and fill in what the children have learned from their reading.

Independent work

● See the activities for the six Areas of Learning on page 184.

Plenary

● Ask the children to help you to sort out some muddled-up books into piles of story books (fiction) and information books (non-fiction).
● What clues will they look for to tell the difference between the two types of book? Model the process with one or two books.
● Now ask individuals to come and choose a book, look for clues and then suggest which pile to put it in.

UNIT 5 DAY 2 🔲 Where do animals live?

Asking questions

Objectives

Early Learning Goal
● Reading p62-63.

Stepping Stone
● Know information can be relayed in the form of print.

NLS
T6: To re-read frequently a variety of familiar texts.
T11: Through shared writing to understand that writing can be used for a range of purposes.
W5: To read on sight a range of familiar words.

What you need

● Photocopiable pages 190 and 191, enlarged as previous day
● key words from the text printed on card or laminated: *pond, tadpole, colony, mound, termite, tunnel, sledges, underground, marmots, mountains, burrows, huddle*
● the questions and answers from Day 1 (see page 185)
● multiple copies of a non-fiction text suitable for guided reading
● a flipchart and Blu-Tack.

Differentiation

Less able
● During guided reading support the children by reading less familiar words together and by looking for the words in the text.

More able
● Provide a range of questions for the children to answer from selected extracts of a non-fiction text.

Shared text-level work

● Show the children the extracts from photocopiable pages 190 and 191. Ask them to talk to their partners about the sort of animals that live in ponds, colonies, the snow and underground.
● Show the children an example of a question from the previous day (see page 185) and talk about how non-fiction books help us to answer questions.
● Now explain that you want the children to think of a good question about animals that live in ponds. Remind them of the examples from Day 1 and then ask them to talk to their partners to think of some more questions.
● Invite the children to share their questions with the rest of the class and write one or two of their questions on the flipchart with the children's help.
● Read through examples of questions with the children and explain that tomorrow you will be finding and writing good answers.

Shared word-level work

● Show the children the prepared key words from the text. Read them, one by one, with the children and display them in a pocket chart, or on the wall.
● Ensure that the children understand the meaning of each word by reading the word individually and then saying the word in a sentence.
● Say a word, such as *pond*, and ask for a volunteer to come and point to it on the wall, assisted by the rest of the class where appropriate.
● Continue in this way to help word recognition and to widen vocabulary. Revisit these words regularly during the week for a few minutes.

Focused group work

● Continue as Day 1 (see page 185), working with a different group of children.

Independent work

● See the activities for the six Areas of Learning on page 184.

Plenary

● Stick the questions and answers up on the flip chart in a random order. Show them to the children and explain that you need the children's help to match the questions and answers.
● Read a question at random using a pointer, encouraging the children to join in.
● Now read out the different answers and ask the children to talk to their partner to see if they can find the correct one.
● Listen to the children's suggestions and gradually match the questions and answers with their help.
● Encourage all the children to participate in this matching activity, praising their attempts.

UNIT 5 DAY 3 Where do animals live?

Finding answers

Early Learning Goal
● Reading p62-63.

Stepping Stone
● Know information can be relayed in the form of print.

NLS
T6: To re-read frequently a variety of familiar texts.
T11: Through shared writing to understand that writing can be used for a range of purposes.
W9: To recognise the critical features of words, eg shape, length, and common spelling patterns.

What you need
● Photocopiable pages 190 and 191 enlarged
● questions from Day 2 (page 186)
● individual whiteboards and pens (one between two children).

Differentiation

Less able
● Support the children to answer questions in full sentences by repeating and elaborating upon their responses.

More able
● Invite one or two children to help fill out the KWL grid during focused group work.

Shared text-level work
● Begin by reading the questions written the previous day.
● Explain that you want to write some answers, but that first you will need to check the information in the extract.
● Read one question at a time and ask the children where they might look for the answer. For example, is it about animals in the snow or animals underground?
● Allow time for the children to talk to partners and then choose a child to point to where the answer can be found.
● Now ask the children to say the answer in a full sentence.
● Listen to the children's suggestions and write the answers on the flipchart.
● Continue in this way to write answers to several questions.

Shared word-level work
● Give out the whiteboards, one between two, and say that you are going to read a range of words that you want the children to write. Ask them to check with their partner first, before writing.
● Read out a range of high frequency words, such as *they, make, and, like, come, there* and so on, and ask the children to write them down.
● Ask the children to show you their words each time so that you can check their spellings.
● Sensitively use any errors as teaching points and ask the children to look carefully at any mistakes (such as *thay*). Reinforce correct spellings.

Focused group work
● Continue as Day 1 (see page 185), working with a different group of children.
● Show the children the grids from the previous two days and work with a different set of books if possible.

Independent work
● See the activities for the six Areas of Learning on page 184.

Plenary
● Ask the children to sit in a circle and explain that, just as animals are all different, so are people. Make links to the children's independent work on similarities and differences and the different places that people live in around the world (see PSED page 184).
● Now say that you are going to play a game called 'Just like me!'. Start by choosing an item of clothing, such as black shoes and say: *Everyone wearing black shoes, stand up!* All those wearing black shoes must stand and say, *Just like me!*
● Go on to choose other items in this way.
● Extend the game to where people live. For example, *Everyone living in a flat/bungalow* and so on.
● Finish by celebrating the fact that we are all different, but that it is much more interesting this way.

Write a leaflet

Objectives

Early Learning Goal
● Reading p62-63.

Stepping Stone
● Know information can be relayed in the form of print.

NLS
T11: Through shared writing to understand that writing can be used for a range of purposes.
W4: To link sound and spelling patterns.

What you need
● Four pictures of familiar animals from magazines, posters or copyright-free images downloaded from the internet
● scissors
● glue
● information leaflets
● A3 paper
● a flipchart and pens
● a feely bag and a range of soft toy animals.

Differentiation

Less able
● During shared work, help the children to talk in complete sentences by repeating their phrases and adding extra details to make full sentences.

More able
● Encourage the children to make their own individual leaflets.

Shared text-level work

● Explain to the children that you are going to write a class information leaflet about animals. Show the children some published leaflets.
● Take an A3 sheet and fold it in half, explaining that this will be the leaflet.
● Show the children the range of pictures you have collected (preferably ones that can be cut out to stick to the leaflet).
● Explain that you are going to write some information about the pictures.
● Now ask the children to look at the pictures and think of a way that they are all the same (for example, all pets). Think of a good title for the leaflet.
● Write the title and stick a different picture to each page of the leaflet.
● Look at a picture at a time and ask the children to talk to their partners to think of a good sentence to match the picture.
● Discuss the children's suggestions and select one to write together.
● Write one or two sentences to match each picture, reading the sentences back every time.

Shared word-level work

● Take some words that have been suggested during shared text-level work and talk about alternative spellings.
● Work through one or two examples of words (such as hutch and cage) and their possible spellings. Ask the children to segment each word as you spell it together. They might suggest, for example, that *cage* is spelled *c/a/j*.
● Use this as an opportunity to reinforce that we have recognised spellings for words even though sounds can be represented in different ways.

Focused group work

● Continue to find out about animals through guided reading. Help the children to fill out KWL grids as per Day 1 (see page 185).

Independent work

● See the activities for the six Areas of Learning on page 184.

Plenary

● Gather the children together and tell them that you have a bag containing a toy animal and that you want a child to feel the toy (without looking) and describe it for everyone to guess.
● Model an example first, emphasising good description of the features of the toy, such as *It has a long tail, pointy ears* and so on.
● Now choose a child to have a go and have fun guessing the animal.
● Substitute different toy animals and invite other children to take a turn.
● Finish by talking about where each animal lives.

Information leaflets

Objectives

Early Learning Goal
● Reading p62-63.

Stepping Stone
● Know information can be relayed in the form of print.

NLS
T6: To re-read frequently a variety of familiar texts.
T11: Through shared writing to understand that writing can be used for a range of purposes.
S1: To expect written text to make sense and to check for sense if it does not.

What you need
● The children's information leaflet started on Day 4 (page 188)
● pictures of animals as per the previous day
● nonsense sentences about animals printed in a large font, written on card or typed and displayed on an interactive whiteboard (for example: *Horses and cows run in cages./ Hamsters and gerbils hunt in jungles.*
● pictures of animals on card or in non-fiction books.

Differentiation

Less able
● Use slightly simpler sentences in shared sentence-level work.

More able
● Encourage the children to make up a nonsense sentence for their partner to correct.

Shared text-level work
● Show the children the leaflet begun the previous day and read through what you have written together. Explain that you need to finish the leaflet.
● Look carefully at the remaining pictures and take suggestions from the children about what they could write about them. Ensure that you allow time for 'partner talk' to encourage maximum participation.
● Scribe the children's suggestions, encouraging phonetically plausible attempts at spelling but using the opportunity to discuss how the word is spelled.
● Read through the sentences together.
● Finish by re-reading the entire leaflet and explain that this will go in the class book corner for the children to re-read independently.

Shared sentence-level work
● Tell the children that you have been writing some sentences about animals, but that there is something wrong with them. Ask the children if they will help you to put them right (if you have an interactive whiteboard, this would be an excellent opportunity to display the sentences on it and then to amend them with the children's help).
● Read the sentences, one at a time, and ask the children to talk to partners about what is wrong with them. Listen to the children's suggestions and then orally rehearse an agreed sentence.
● Write the correct sentence on the flipchart or on the interactive whiteboard, emphasising that we must always read for meaning and check that what we read or write makes sense.

Focused group work
● Work with a different group of children to fill out a KWL grid (see Day 1, page 185) based on shared reading of a non-fiction text.
● Make a display of all the KWL grids completed over the course of the week and read them together, looking for similarities and differences.

Independent work
● See the activities for the six Areas of Learning on page 184.

Plenary
● With the children on the carpet, explain that you are going to play a guessing game.
● Describe an animal and where it lives and ask the children to guess which animal it is. For example: *I am big and furry with stripes. I live in the jungle and hunt other animals.*
● Now ask for volunteers to take a turn. Show the volunteer the picture of an animal (whispering some details if necessary).
● Ask the child to describe the animal and where it lives for the rest of the class to guess.
● Continue in this way, with one or two other animals, encouraging the children to listen carefully.

TERM 3

Where do animals live? 1

In a pond

Many animals live in ponds. They find good places to hide and lots to eat.

Frogs and toads live in ponds. They lay their eggs and these turn into tadpoles that swim around and wriggle their tails.

Different kinds of fish live in ponds.

Sticklebacks make nests to lay their eggs on.

In a colony

Most ants live in huge groups called colonies. They help each other to build big nests for their young.

Some ants carry leaves to their nests. They keep them in special places like gardens and then fungus grows on them, providing good things to eat.

Termites build giant mounds of earth with tunnels. These have places for food as well as special places for the young.

Photographs 1 © Ingram Publishing 2 © Corel 3 © Photodisc, Inc

◀SCHOLASTIC